If You Knew Suzy

If You Knew Suzy

A Mother, a Daughter,
a Reporter's Notebook

Katherine Rosman

HARPER

An Imprint of HarperCollins*Publishers*
www.harpercollins.com

The names and identifying characteristics of some of the individuals featured throughout this book have been changed to protect their privacy.

HarperCollins books may be purchased for educational, business, or sales promotional use. For information, please write: Special Markets Department, HarperCollins Publishers, 10 East 53rd Street, New York, NY 10022.

FIRST EDITION

                    Library of Congress Cataloging-in-Publication Data
Rosman, Katherine
    If you knew Suzy : a mother, a daughter, a reporter's notebook / by Katherine Rosman—1st ed.
        p. cm.
    Summary: "Wall Street Journal culture reporter Katherine Rosman reconnects with her late mother by reporting on the life she led outside of her roles as mom and wife"—Provided by publisher.
    ISBN 978-0-06-173523-3
    1. Motherhood. 2. Mothers. I. Title.
    HQ759.R658   2010
    306.874'30973—dc22

                                                        2009049966

10 11 12 13 14   ID/RRD   10 9 8 7 6 5 4 3 2 1

To my mother's grandchildren,
so they may know her

Contents

CONTENTS

If You Knew Suzy

Chapter One

PMS (Postmortem Shopping)

Technically, you can't call it grave robbing if the person hasn't been buried yet.

What is the right and proper thing to do on the day your mom dies? For two and a half years, she battles an illness that ultimately comes to define your life. You schedule your every activity—which stories to pitch to your editors, when to have let's-get-pregnant sex with your husband—around your mom's appointments with oncologists and radiologists, her PET scans, her mood swings. In every way but the physical, you have cancer too. For two and a half years. And then one day, just like that, she dies. So what do you do?

My sister Lizzie and I dug into Mom's wallet, harvested her credit cards, and went shopping.

"It's what Mom would want," Lizzie told me with all the authority of a big sister.

I believed her. I still do. We were mom's girls. So even though we were adults and married to men who preferred that our mom not buy us clothes and household trinkets and makeup, she would. She didn't go over the top, spending vast sums of money on items for which we'd have no use. But when she saw something she thought we would love, she went for it. She was our mom. We were her girls. Inevitabilities like adulthood and marriage didn't change that.

Certainly, Mom's illness did not weaken her penchant for shopping. At a time when fate forced her to rely on her children in ways no parent wants, scouring online sites and making purchases on our behalf became Mom's way of asserting that she was still the mama lion who could nurture her cubs. And so the packages from Shopbop.com—cardboard boxes and plastic pouches marked by a large, round orange sticker—regularly greeted me when I returned to my New York City apartment after work.

Internet access in heaven, though, is presumably unreliable. So on the day that Mom died, we decided to do for her what she couldn't do for herself: take her Visa out for a last spin. We guessed, rightly, that our stepfather Bob would receive Mom's final credit card bill and pay it without giving us any hassle. He had been married to Mom for thirty-one years and understood our dynamic well. He would see the charges from June 24, 2005, and he would know that Lizzie and I were grasping for an escape from a world that was shockingly, horrifyingly post-Mom.

IT BEGAN IN Tucson, Arizona, at about one a.m., when the overnight nurses woke us from an hour's slumber to tell us that Mom had died. We called the hospice nurse. She showed up and headed back into Mom and Bob's bedroom. Lizzie, Bob, and I sat in the den in a silence that was finally interrupted by the sound of squeaky wheels. I craned my neck to identify the source and saw a guy from the mortuary wheeling a gurney into the house. When he left, the squeaking sounded different—I guess because the gurney was bearing weight, a body, my mom's body. We had kissed her around midnight—just about an hour before—and told her we were going to lie down for a bit. And then she was gone.

When the nurse left, we went back into Mom and Bob's bedroom. Without speaking, the three of us climbed into their bed. Bob was on his side. Lizzie was on Mom's. I was in the middle. We held hands. We didn't talk. I kept my eyes open. I tipped my head to lean it on Lizzie's shoulder and caught sight of the hospital bed that had been set up a few days earlier next to their king-size bed. The sheets were ruffled—evidence of Mom's recent presence. But she wasn't in it anymore. And I knew she wasn't in the bathroom or the kitchen or anywhere in the house. She was just gone. One minute you're devoting your life to caring for your sick parent— looking at everything in the world through the lens of her condition. And then, *poof.* For years, my mom had been suffering from stage-four cancer. I knew what "terminal" meant; I understood statistical realities. Yet I was stunned when she actually died.

We lay in Mom's bed for, maybe, forty-five minutes. At about three a.m., when it was about six in Detroit—where Lizzie and I were raised, and where Mom would be buried—we made some calls. The funeral home. Our stepbrother Jimmy. Lizzie and I called our dad in Detroit. I called my husband, Joe, in New York. Lizzie called hers, Mitchell, in L.A. We waited a few more hours. Then we called Mom's brother Eddie, who lives a few miles from Mom in Tucson. He said he would drive over to Grandma Charlotte's to tell her in person.

Later that morning, Lizzie and I headed to Grandma's to try to console her. And we brought with us the green envelope-style leather wallet—still filled with credit cards, still smelling sweetly of Mom.

THROUGHOUT THE LONG siege of Mom's illness, I got my nails done every week.

Or more often. Once, near the very end, I told my mom I was running out for a manicure. In a weak and creaky voice, she managed to say, "I've never heard of anyone getting more manicures than you." I paused, cocked my head in thought, and realized it would be my third that week.

Though at the end of Mom's life I was abandoning my job, my husband, and New York City to spend about half my time at her Tucson home, I would yearn to leave her house almost instantly upon arriving. When Mom lost the ability to get out of bed and when ever-larger doses of Oxycodone limited her awake time, I'd create lists of errands that required attention. But those trips to the grocery or medical supply store provided only geographical escape. Scanning the aisles for nutrients that Mom might be able to get and keep down (yogurt, Cream of Wheat) and products that would ease the indignities of her decline hardly had the desired effect.

Manicures became my thing. This surprised me at first, because I was never one to take precious care of my nails—I bit them well into my twenties. But as my mom got sicker, I became more attached to the rituals of grooming. Philip Roth wrote that a shave in the barber's chair Friday afternoons freed his grandfather from the "dour exigencies that had trapped him." Paying attention to grooming in ways I never had before allowed me to feel pulled together when I wasn't. Somehow, two coats of Vanity Fairest or Limo-Scene became my best defense against cancer's injustices.

As the pious have known for centuries, rituals amid uncertainty can bring unexpected comfort. I found this to be true when sitting across a table from an anonymous woman who would clean, clip, and file my nails and cuticles. We'd barely utter a word but for this exchange:

Her: "Quick dry? A dollar more."

Me: "Yes."

I had become superstitious about nail polish top coats that purport to dry wet nails quickly. They didn't always seem to work as magically as I wished they would. But that didn't stop me from paying one dollar more every single time I sank into the pink vinyl. Your nails will dry instantly! The chemo might work! It was not a time to turn away from hope.

And in the end, I'd walk out of the shop with pretty nails and hands that looked nurtured, even carefree—totally unlike those of someone whose mother was dying of lung cancer.

AT THE CLOSEST major intersection to Mom's house in the Santa Catalina foothills, there were nail shops in strip malls at three of the four corners. First, Lizzie and I went to the nicest of the salons. It's not the type of place that can generally accommodate walk-ins, and on this day, it couldn't. We popped back in Mom's car and headed across the street to a no-frills competitor— nondescript and virtually indistinguishable from thousands of nail places across the country that have opened their doors to the chipped masses in recent years.

Some man filling in the acrylic on the talons of a customer pulled a hospital mask from over his mouth and grumbled, "Thirty to forty minutes." Then he replaced the mask and went back to work.

I was *furious*—like seriously, irrationally livid. How dare he ask us to wait on the very day that our sixty-year-old mother died?

That first thought was followed by a potent wave of anger: How is it that these other women woke up in the morning and thought, "Hmm, it's Friday, June 24 . . . nothing special about this day . . . I think I'll get my nails done," when I woke up on June 24 at about one a.m. to be told that my mom was dead? How could this be a normal day for them—for anyone?

Rat-tat-tat, that sense of indignation was deflated and replaced by *this* panicked realization: I was getting a pre-shopping-spree manicure on that very same day. On June 24. On a day that—in my very own life, in fact—was very, very extraordinary. On the day my mom died. *How could I?*

I remember a friend from my high school and college days telling me about a powerful memory from the day of her mother's funeral. Michelle had just completed her freshman year in high school when her mom died of cancer at thirty-nine. As Michelle, her father, and her three little brothers drove to the funeral home, they passed by a trendy aerobics studio in suburban Detroit into which leotard-clad women were rushing. She thought, *"My mom just died.* How can they be going to work out?"

That story always stuck with me, long before it would have

personal resonance. And yet there I was, searching the racks for the right shade of polish.

I turned to Lizzie. "Is it really okay that we're doing this?"

"Mom's finally not suffering anymore," Lizzie said, taking my hand. "If she could celebrate that with us, she'd be standing here now."

There can't be a prescribed etiquette for the day the suffering ends for someone you love. It's a horrible day, *and* it's filled with joy. Your mom is gone for good, but she is never again going to fight for breath, that look of terror etched on her gaunt face. You get your own life back, no longer fearing a middle-of-the-night phone call, but you know that your mom will never call you again. It's a day of agonizing and exhilarating contradictions.

I laced my fingers into my sister's. She was right. If Mom could join us on the day she died for a little mani and shopping, she most certainly would.

"It's been forever since I've been able to spend a day out with my girls," she'd say, jutting her proud chin forward for emphasis. "My treat!"

NONE OF THIS is to say that Lizzie and I enjoyed an easy-breezy outing at the mall. We didn't. Neither of us could muster the enthusiasm to try on any clothes—an unwillingness that can really take the *whee!* out of spree. But as we drove toward La Encantada (my mom's favorite mall in Tucson because it has both a great market for organic apples and an Apple store), the mission took on a feeling of importance, like we had to do it, like Mom was depending on us, like if we didn't go shopping, then the terrorists (and cancer) had won.

We went into a small store that sold cheap summer accessories, mostly flip-flops, sunglasses, and hats. I bought two pairs of twenty-dollar flip-flops—one of which I have since lost, one of which I wear now as I type. We went on to a shoe store that offered comfortable flats at sensible prices. There, Mom splurged on me. I (she) spent about $200 on three pairs—purple ballet flats that never fit right, comfy black loafers that are devoid of any chic quotient, and black velvet flats emblazoned with diamond-esque rhinestones. I call them my "party shoes," and they are the focus of attention and compliments any time I wear them. They were the perfect trinity for this schizophrenic day: One pair evokes nothingness with its joyless aesthetic. Another pair is celebratory. And a third causes my feet to ache.

ON OUR WAY back to Mom and Bob's house after our postmortem shopping excursion, we stopped at a cool little boutique that sells makeup, moisturizer, and such.

Back in the pre-illness days, when I tried to heed my husband's call to cease my familial freeloading, I made exceptions for things like jars of Kiehl's moisturizer. Fine, it might be inappropriate for a married woman to let her mommy buy her pretty dresses, but who's going to get hurt by a few ounces of antiaging eye cream? No one.

So this is where I truly lost control. I snagged six two-ounce jars of Kiehl's moisturizer at about $30 a pop. I don't remember what went into the calculation that led me to go for six—instead of, say, four or eight. Perhaps I thought that the time it would take to work my way through six jars was ample to cushion the sadness, or that the amount of cream was sufficient to reverse the aging that Mom's cancer had wreaked upon my once strain-free face.

Either way—it can now be acknowledged—Kiehl's moisturizer isn't meant to be bought in bulk like scratchy toilet paper. I used the cream so sparingly that the consistency of the two last jars got chunky before I even opened them. The overstocking was evidence that the reality of the day was wearing on me.

As we were about to pay for our loot, Lizzie looked at me and said, "Your eyebrows are awful." (Thanks!)

As long as I was there, I said to the woman at the register, could they fit me in for a quick brow appointment?

I remember very little about the woman who led me into the waxing room. But what I do remember is this: When she greeted me with the pleasantry, "How is your day going?" I answered truthfully.

"My mom died today," I heard myself say.

Her eyes widened, absorbing my inappropriate disclosure. "Wow," she said, never looking up from the bowl full of wax she was stirring. "I'm sorry."

I couldn't be stopped. I went into overshare overdrive, telling her about the cancer, how young and healthy Mom had been, how badly she suffered, how Bob, Lizzie, and I had never left her alone throughout the ordeal despite the fact that Lizzie and I lived in other cities.

The waxer then told me about her son. They were completely out of touch. She had him when she was very young, and now she didn't even know where he was living. She spoke of the estrangement matter-of-factly.

For a moment, my mind raced back to a conversation I had

about a year before with a glamorous woman in New York. We were at a swank party in the backyard of a gorgeous Greenwich Village brownstone. I told her I had been traveling nonstop for nearly a year and a half to care for my ailing mother. She looked at me, her brow furrowed and perplexed. "I would never do that for my mother," she said.

Her comment enraged me—as so much enraged me during that time: How could she be so blasé? How could she take her mother for granted as mine was dying?

My thoughts were jolted back to the present by the ripping of congealed wax from my skin. (Happens.) I looked at the waxer. I thought of the woman in New York. And on the day that my young and beautiful mother was so brutally taken from the world, I felt sadness neither for Mom, nor for myself, nor for Lizzie—nor for the way our unique family closeness had been cut short by cancer.

Instead, I felt a visceral pity for all those who had no basis for understanding the joy derived from such bonds, and the pain experienced at their severing.

I paid the bill and walked out of the store, hand in hand with Lizzie. Momentarily, I was awash with the sense of our own good fortune.

Chapter Two

The Curses (and Occasional Blessings) of Being a Mother to Daughters

In July of 2003, Lizzie was nine months pregnant with her second child, and Mom and I were in Los Angeles in anticipation of the birth. It was a crazy time: not only was Lizzie on the precipice of labor—and not only was Mom scheduled to have a dangerous operation on her lung in the coming weeks—but in a fluke, I somehow contracted the meningitis virus and ended up in a hospital across town from where Lizzie was set to deliver.

Against the backdrop of this tension, Mom and Lizzie, inevitably, got into a huge fight. As they stood in Lizzie's driveway darting barbs at each other, the rhetoric intensified. My mom began to storm off, and then she stopped, turned back, looked Lizzie dead in the eye, and said, "I hope you have a daughter." I don't think she meant it in a nice way.

MOTHER-DAUGHTER RELATIONSHIPS ARE complex. In our family it was particularly so because we weren't just dealing with two people.

In confronting the outside world, Mom, Lizzie, and I were solid, impenetrable, a trio united in love and loyalty. Internally, we were a vortex of shifting alliances and manipulations. It was me and Lizzie and Mom; Lizzie, me, and Mom, them and me; us and her; the three of us bobbling about in a lotto bin, tumbling out in various combinations. We were the (West) Bloomfield (Michigan) Triangle.

Once, when I was sixteen, I got caught smoking a cigarette. My mom was out running errands, and I sneaked onto our back porch and lit up. It was summer. Lizzie was home from college and was out on the lake we lived upon, sailing on a beat-up two-seater with a friend. I was trying to spot them on the water, which meant I wasn't paying attention to what was going on in the house. Which meant, unbeknownst to me, Mom got home and saw me smoking.

In our family, smoking was verboten. Though Mom had smoked in college and after, she quit in the 1970s and instantly grew intolerant of smoke. The subsequent death of her father, my grandpa Leo, from lung cancer (many years after he had quit) cemented her visceral hatred of cigarettes. Mom thought that anyone who smoked despite having an intellectual grasp of the health implications was weak-willed. Bob, who didn't quit until years after Mom did, was cast outside—even in the dead of the Michigan winter—any time he wanted to indulge his habit.

Upon seeing her young daughter smoking, well, I think Mom would have been happier to find me injecting heroin. She ran out onto the porch, and in a voice shrill and powerful, she screamed, "How could you do this to me?" (I decided this was, perhaps, not the right time to point out the narcissism of her reaction.)

Apparently her scream reverberated over the water; Lizzie heard it from across Pine Lake and began heading toward shore. After she docked, she raced up the lawn to our house. I had been too scared to go inside, so I stood frozen in place on the porch. We walked into the house together. Mom was standing in the kitchen. I could see she was shaking. "Get to your room," she said, spitting each word out, staccato.

I did as told. A few hours later, I came downstairs for dinner as usual: I set the table and poured my glass of milk. (Young enough to crave milk; old enough to crave cigarettes.) Throughout the meal, Mom didn't talk to or look at me. I'd never seen her so angry.

I went to bed early, and when I woke in the morning, I expected the storm to have passed. It hadn't. Mom still was giving me the silent treatment. As she and Lizzie were hanging out in the kitchen, I approached her and started crying.

"I'm really, really sorry, Mom," I said.

She forcefully ignored me and instead locked her eyes on Lizzie. "I think I'm going to take you shopping today, sweetheart," she said. (She played dirty.)

And here is where the triangulating, the shifting of alliances, came into play: Lizzie no longer felt she could stand on the sideline. So she committed the second-most-forbidden sin.

"Shut up, Mom," she said. (Oh yes, she did!)

"C'mon, Katie," Lizzie said, as Mom and I stared in disbelief. "Let's go."

I looked at Lizzie, with wide eyes that said *Really?*

She answered my glance: *Yes, really. Come on.*

We walked toward the front door. Mom stood frozen with

shock in the kitchen for a moment. Then she charged after us, buzzing with rage. "You girls!" she sputtered—an accusation. Mom was never articulate when she was really furious and I could sense her struggling to come up with words to hurl at us. "I—I—I—*I rue the day you were born*!"

By now Lizzie and I had stepped across the threshold of the front door. Lizzie pivoted to face Mom.

"Whatever, *Shakespeare*," she said with a smirk.

Mom slammed the door in our faces.

My heart was pounding out of my chest. I may have stopped breathing. I looked at Lizzie. She appeared a bit stunned, as if she couldn't believe the way she had just talked back to Mom. Then we both started laughing hysterically.

By that evening, when Lizzie and I returned (after aimlessly driving around in her car, listening to music and smoking cigarettes), the temperature in the house had nearly normalized. Mom stopped storming about; the sulking subsided. Soon, we were all hanging out together in the kitchen. It was as if the whole thing hadn't happened.

Lizzie had protected me, her baby sister, from Mom's wrath. She knew Mom couldn't stand to be at odds with both of us simultaneously. It left her feeling too alone.

ONE DAY IN August of 1987, I told my mom I'd be sleeping over at the house of a new friend, Karen. I had chosen Karen purposely because Karen had a taste for mischief and gave the impression that she'd be the type of girl to watch your back when you were hatching an elaborate scheme in which you lie to your mother about where you will be spending the night.

I had a serious boyfriend. We were in love in that desperate, breathless, teenage way. Mike was seventeen, and I was fifteen. We were inseparable, much to the annoyance of both of our parents. Especially to his parents, who just so happened to be out of town the night I was allegedly planning to sleep at Karen's. For days, Mike and I had been staying on the phone late into the night, whispering about our scheme. I would have Mom drop me off at Karen's, and Mike would then pick me up right after.

Notwithstanding the descriptions in this book of my smoking, drinking, and lying, I was actually a fairly good kid. My mom trusted me, and as far as she knew, I was worthy. I was a very conscientious student who got good grades. I rejected peer pressure in terms of drinking and driving and taking drugs. No weird pierces, no tattoos. I didn't have a strict curfew, but I never stayed out very late. And I was a virgin (though Mike explicitly hoped that my spending the night at his house sans parents might rid me of that condition).

I think my mom believed that you can't stop a teenager from being a teenager; you can only hope that your children will exercise good judgment when it really matters. I wasn't reckless, and I knew that my mom knew that.

So though I would have to leave my mom the number to Karen's house before the big "sleepover," I assured my accomplice that my mom would never check up on me there. "She like so would never suspect a thing," I told Karen in the pidgin English invariably I spoke.

Except, of course, that my mom did. She suspected something, all right. Because I was with Mike every Saturday night, and why would I suddenly be making plans to sleep at the house of some girl I hadn't much hung out with before? Because she probably heard me whispering on the phone all the time, and knew something was afoot. Because she wasn't an idiot. Because I was.

Mom dropped me off at Karen's, and Mike picked me up as planned. Mike and I went to the movies, as planned. We drove back to his house, and as he pulled his car into his driveway, we could see that my mom's car was parked in his driveway and she was standing there waiting for us. Not planned.

Mom had called Karen's house, and, as it turns out, she wasn't as deft a liar as I had hoped.

"Get in the car," Mom barked at me. As if I were a child! Mike stood on the pavement in silence, stunned that sex had slipped out of his grasp. (He was thisclose!) I said nothing and did as I was told, because I was a child.

During the five-minute drive home, neither Mom nor I spoke. Once we arrived at our house, I walked straight up to my room, climbed into bed, reached for the phone, called Mike, and whispered, "I think I'm in big trouble." When I heard my mom walking up the stairs toward my bedroom, I hung up.

She knocked in that parental way—*I'm not asking for permission to come in, I'm letting you know I'm about to come into your room*—then opened the door and walked toward me. I was sitting up in bed, legs covered by a quilt. I looked at Mom with a mixture of shame and fear.

She could be very tough. When Lizzie and I were growing up, we knew our mom to assert her displeasure—and to assert it loudly. Oh, there was yelling. And a slammed door was not unheard of. Yet I knew my latest transgression—lying—transcended all of that. I anticipated a withering look: a squinty-eyed, daggers-in-the-pupils stare (lips pursed, eyebrows unified) that telegraphed anger and disappointment without voice-raising; that reminded me that lying was unacceptable; that confirmed I was grounded forever.

But Mom's eyebrows stayed in place. She climbed in bed next to me. She linked her arm through mine. She said, "I know that growing up and being in love can be really painful and confusing." Like an overwrought pressure valve, I burst into tears.

I didn't tell her I had been considering having sex; I didn't have to. She shared her overarching, philosophical opinions about sex in a manner more calm and free of judgment than I could have reasonably wished. She said she understood that I probably didn't think I'd be in love many more times in my life, but that I would. She said that sex was a very special thing, and the more people you share it with, the less special it can become. She said that a woman and man can feel close without sex, and that it shouldn't be considered a tool employed to prove love or commitment. She said she knew Mike and I were in love and that he fundamentally was a good person. But, she said, seventeen-year-old guys are motivated by hormones, and their arguments for why having sex is a really good idea should be treated with skepticism. She said that when two people were mutually ready for sex, neither would feel any hesitation, fear, or stress. Left unsaid was her presumable belief that when the time was right for sex to be had, one of the participants would not be her fifteen-year-old daughter. "What's the hurry?" she said. "If you two are meant to be together, there will be plenty of time."

This was the first time I had ever really considered the fact that my mom wasn't just a mom. She was a woman too, someone who had suffered through her own growing pains, someone who had learned a thing or two from experiences that went beyond driving Hebrew school carpool and fixing my breakfast.

All these years later, I remember how lucky I felt in that moment: to have a mother who was wise, and who would and could talk to me in an honest and compassionate manner. She treated me like an adult, even though I hadn't behaved like one. She didn't try to dictate the way I should act, even though I knew she had a pretty firm opinion on the matter. She was gentle in approach and sensitive in verbiage. She showed no disapproval or disappointment. She turned a situation in which I should have been in serious trouble into an opportunity to tell me that she believed me deserving of her trust. What a good mom. That night I slept like a baby.

The next day I lost my virginity.

I ALWAYS HAVE been sensitive, perhaps overly so, a searcher who feels pain (my own and others') deeply. My adolescence and young adult years—the years when you figure out who you are as an individual and what you want to do with your life—were full of angst. Much of it was self-imagined melodrama, but some of it was legitimate. I shared it all with my mom, and she listened, aching as a mother does when she knows her kid is in turmoil. When Mom offered advice, I listened but mostly I ignored it—I wasn't looking for advice. Mostly, I needed to get it out, to say the words aloud: I'm scared, I'm sad, I'm embarrassed, I'm insecure. What I sought from her was comfort and acceptance. She gave me both.

Lizzie is different from me. She doesn't process things as

openly as I do, and I don't just mean that she doesn't write books about her feelings. When we were growing up, she was more able to ignore family politics and to let nasty comments from bitchy teenage girls roll off her back. She was happy-go-lucky, or so it seemed to me, her little sister who socially wasn't quite as at ease.

Of course, we've both matured since then. As an adult, Lizzie will share her aggravations and disappointments with me, and presumably with others. But she still can be introverted about the deeper issues. While I tend to dive into the middle of emotionally charged situations (whether it's appropriate for me to do so or not), Lizzie gets involved only when necessary and then tries to extricate herself quickly. Lizzie is not afraid to make waves where the waters might otherwise be calm. But for the most part, she likes her life to be as nonconfrontational as possible (though this leads to some passive-aggressive behavior).

Mom and Lizzie had a less complicated relationship than Mom and I did. Though Lizzie was no angel—as her younger sister, I saw it all—she wasn't nearly as motivated to act in purposeful opposition to Mom as I was. As a kid, she didn't have a chip on her shoulder about Mom not having a traditional career. As an adult, she didn't need to make different choices just to make different choices. Lizzie and Mom connected over things they both loved, among them: making things beautiful in their homes and making delicious things in their kitchens. Even today, I think Lizzie feels closest to Mom when she is in the kitchen, cooking for her family. In some ways, Lizzie knew Mom better than I did, or at least she understood her more. So when Lizzie says that Mom would love knowing that we went shopping on her dime the day she died, I believe that Lizzie knows what she's talking about.

While Lizzie understood Mom better than I did, Mom understood me better than Lizzie does. Or at the very least, Mom was more forgiving and less judgmental of my philosophical musings. Just before I married Joe, I had this epiphany that I was shifting from "my family of origin" to "my family of choice." I thought about this a lot, and to me, recognizing this transition represented a significant rite of passage. I would tell Mom and Lizzie about all these revelations. While Lizzie found the terms I used to be mere psychobabble, and the sentiment offensive, Mom recognized and totally accepted that I need to wander off onto these introspective, self-analytical jags. "That's a really interesting way to look at it, sweetheart," she probably said.

When we were growing up, Lizzie had a lot of control over my life. She always mothered me, and I adored the attention. A young girl could not have looked up to her big sister more. I thought she and her friends were the coolest, and I emulated them whenever possible.

Today Lizzie and I live very different lives: situated on different coasts, married to different types of men. But we talk at least twice a day. It's not unheard of for us to bicker; it's more eye-rolling than actual disagreements. Whereas Mom came to understand that I was going to do things my own way—even when I was doing so to spite her—Lizzie still holds out hope that one day I might come to accept that her approach (to everything) is best.

True, I can be a bit of an organizational mess. Though my clothes are usually clean and folded, it's anyone's guess in which drawer any given item might be. I have been known to have bare cupboards and refrigerators dominated by condiments. On my kitchen counter, there usually is a neat(ish) stack of mail, coupons, and scrawled-upon pieces of notepaper that I really do intend to deal with one day. I get overwhelmed. I lose my keys and sunglasses a lot. I often forget to pay my cell phone bill, and getting out of the house on time is a daily, chaotic struggle.

When I complain to Lizzie about how exasperated I get by these matters—things that Lizzie manages effortlessly—she has a lot of suggestions: special key hooks, simple recipes, items that I should always keep in the pantry. Did you know all you really need to make a brisket is Lipton onion soup mix and a bottle of chili sauce? It irks Lizzie that I noncommittally say, "Oh, interesting idea," when she tells me such things. I'm not disagreeing. It does sound simple, and for her, it probably is. But even after all this time, she doesn't get that I could pick up the soup mix and chili sauce, but I'd never remember to buy the brisket.

Mom didn't quite know how I held together my busy, disheveled life. I'm sure she and Lizzie talked about what a mess I was. "That's Katie," I can hear her saying with a sigh. It hurt my feelings, sometimes, that when Mom and Lizzie looked at my life, what they saw was the mess. But more fully than Lizzie, Mom came to see past it, to see that my life, was in fact, pulled together. She came to agree that I was a highly functional member of society despite the fact that I washed my whites with my colors and often left my cell phone on the subway. When I complained to her about how harried I was, she listened to me vent, often biting her lip, resisting the urge to tell me that things would be a lot easier if I paid my bills on time and made a to-do list. She understood that, however stubborn or self-defeating it might be, I was going to do things my way.

Even though Lizzie and I don't see eye to eye on so many

things—sometimes being different is what sisterhood is about, for better or worse—she and I are very, very close. And however dissimilar we were once and are now, when Mom was sick, we were a team.

We each had our roles, and we, with Bob, covered the gamut of Mom's needs. I tape-recorded doctor's appointments; I made charts so the aides could maintain logs of what medication Mom took when; Joe and I were her round-the-clock, drop-everything computer technicians, who made sure Mom could log on to eBay whenever she wanted, something she did a lot as her physical strength diminished. I got in the shower with her and shaved her legs when she couldn't do it herself. I got a manicurist to come to the house to give her a pedicure in bed. I probed Mom to talk about things. Often, Mom didn't appreciate this, but sometimes she confided her fears to me, and I think that comforted her.

Lizzie ran Mom's household in Tucson, even when she was in Los Angeles trying to run her own. She cooked chicken, soups, and casseroles exactly the way Mom would like them. She made sure there was plenty of food in the refrigerator and freezer for Mom and Bob. Lizzie brought her kids with her to Tucson on some of her visits because she knew that giving Mom the opportunity to be a grandmother was the best medicine she could provide. And during these visits, she managed to balance the needs of her kids with those of her mother—never letting their play get too chaotic for Mom; never letting her sons know they were in a sick house. Once, Lizzie drove Mom around Tucson for two hours, looking for wildflowers that Mom would be able to glimpse from the car window.

Even as Mom grew sicker and more homebound, Lizzie made sure she had the organic cookies she liked in the pantry, the fruit was washed, the extra crates of Arizona Iced Tea were stacked, the beds were made with the proper linens, and the duvets were correctly folded at the end of the beds, so that when you climbed in, the comforter unfolded from the foot of the bed to the head, accordion-style.

These were not matters of keeping up appearances. Lizzie was working very hard to help Mom preserve her dignity as she was losing the ability to perform the personal rituals that were important to her.

SUZANNE GOLDBERG (she had no middle name) was born to Charlotte and Leo Goldberg in Pontiac, Michigan, in 1944. Uncle David came along a little more than a year later. Uncle Eddie was born six years after that.

Grandma Charlotte grew up in the Depression in Pontiac, and was a graduate of Eastern Michigan University. During the Depression, it was considered a frivolity to send girls to college, and Grandma was always proud to be raised by parents who thought her education just as important as her brothers'. Grandpa Leo grew up poor in New Bedford, Massachusetts, and attended Harvard University on scholarship. Leo got his doctorate in astronomy from Harvard and worked as a professor at the University of Michigan for much of Mom's youth.

It was a happy, active life for the Goldberg family in Ann Arbor in the 1950s. Even though they were one of only a few Jewish families, there was little anti-Semitism. They were well-liked members of the university community. Mom was pretty and popular. At school, she was a cheerleader and on the field hockey team. With her siblings, she spent a lot of time ice-skating on the frozen surface of Base Lake in Dexter, Michigan, outside Ann Arbor. The whole family, including, sometimes, my mom's cousins, Steve and Leslie, often spent their weekends there. They also were members of the Ann Arbor Figure Skating Club. Mom trained hard and became accomplished. Eventually she got her parents involved, teaching her dad to skate. (Charlotte was an incredible athlete and didn't need much help.)

Each year, the Goldbergs performed in the club's annual ice show. Leo and Charlotte would dress as cowboy/girl with Eddie and David, in mouse costumes. Not surprisingly, Mom made sure she was in the most dramatic, attention-getting getup: once she dressed as a showgirl, in all black and glittery gold. Eddie and David preferred ice hockey—David went on to play college hockey at the University of Massachusetts. But whether they wanted to take part in the ice shows was not relevant; Leo made participation mandatory. "Dad was the Joe Jackson of the Skating Goldbergs," Eddie told me, likening this world-renowned astronomer to Michael Jackson's dad.

Leo frequently spoke at conferences and presented research at universities around the world, so he and Charlotte traveled frequently. Seven years older than Eddie, Mom took to mothering him. In the summer of 1958, for instance, Charlotte and Leo flew to Moscow, where Leo addressed the International Astronomical Union. Mom, thirteen, spent much of the time at Camp Michigama holding her baby brother's hand. But she was mischievous too. At the World's Fair in New York, she dragged Eddie along with her as she cut the long lines by approaching old ladies who had dutifully been waiting for hours and saying, "Oh, there you are, Grandma!"

In 1960, when Mom was entering the eleventh grade, the Goldbergs moved to the Boston area when Leo became a professor of astronomy at Harvard University. (Five years later, he became director of the astronomy and astrophysics department.) The move marked the continued ascendance of Leo as one of the great scientists of his day. But Boston, Cambridge, and Harvard were stuffier, and more status conscious, than Ann Arbor and the University of Michigan. Grandma—an athlete and career woman who wasn't motivated by the social hierarchy of university wives—didn't love it there.

Mom was of two minds. She liked the sophistication of the East Coast. This was something of a bond between her and Leo. He was a serious academic, but he had an ego and liked to see himself climbing up through the social ranks that must have seemed completely out of reach to him as a poor Jewish boy growing up in a tenement. But Charlotte was very much a child of the Depression. She was (is) practical and thrifty. She didn't share Mom's and Leo's interest in being fashionable. A few years after moving to Boston, the family had plans to visit New York. Leo asked my mom to make the arrangements. When the family arrived in Manhattan, Mom divulged that she had booked them into the Waldorf-Astoria. My grandma Charlotte was disgusted. (Eddie loved exploring the luxuries of the Waldorf: "I thought the bidet was a drinking fountain.")

Yet, overall, the transition to the Northeast was difficult for Mom. When she and Uncle David first went to a figure-skating club in Boston to sign up, they were told, "With a last name like

Goldberg, you can't skate here." The cheerleading squad at her prestigious private school wasn't that welcoming to Jews either. As soon as Mom could, she returned to Ann Arbor, this time as a student at U of M in the fall of 1962.

On her first day of school, Mom met Nanci Josephson Rands, who became a lifelong friend. Nanci was sitting alone in the cafeteria of their dormitory, Mary Markely Hall. Mom breezed in. She was wearing a short skating skirt and a matching sweater set. Her ice skates were slung casually over her shoulder. "She was absolutely beautiful. She was the coolest. She was Suzy Co-ed," Nanci told me.

Mom walked over to the table where Nanci was sitting. She slid into the seat next to Nanci and said, "Can I join you?" During lunch, Nanci asked Mom about her skates. Mom said she was teaching skating to kids with disabilities. Nanci went a few times to watch Mom. "She was magic on the ice," she said.

In progressive Ann Arbor, Mom was back in her element. Among the first Jews to pledge Kappa Kappa Gamma, she could be seen bopping in and out of the stately sorority house on the corner of Church and Hill streets, her dark blond Jackie Kennedy bob framing her face. Sometimes she would tell her friends that she felt like an outsider, being the only Jew. But she didn't hide her roots. In December, she would teach people how to play dreidel. And she would take her best friends (some of whom had never known a Jewish girl before) with her across the street to the Alpha Epsilon Phi house—a Jewish sorority—to sample bagels and lox.

Her social life was active. She and her roommates in the Kappa house used to have dating competitions. Though her roommate Diane Menendez Nilstoft won the Date Arranged Furthest in

Advance (Diane was asked in June to be someone's New Year's Eve date), Mom swept the Most Dates in a Weekend category. In one weekend, she had six different dates (to which she wore six different outfits, naturally): Friday-night happy hour parties, Friday-night regular parties, the football game at Michigan Stadium on Saturday afternoon, Saturday-night dinner and parties, Sunday studying, and Sunday dinner. If Mom or Diane had a date set up for a Saturday night, but then got asked out for that night by a cuter guy, they would bump the original Saturday-night guy to Sunday studying or Sunday dinner. "We were pretty horrible," Diane said.

At the time there was a local adage that claimed, "Nine out of ten girls in the Big Ten are beautiful, and the tenth one goes to Michigan"—the idea being that the coeds at the University of Michigan were brainy and therefore ugly. In response, a book was published in Ann Arbor each year, aimed at showing off the school's attractive women. It was called *And the Tenth One Goes to Michigan*. Her senior year, Mom was featured in it, posing in her crewneck sweater, plaid kilt, knee socks, and penny loafers.

MOM SPOKE FRENCH fluently, and she spent much of her junior year in France, attending classes at the Sorbonne. At first, she lived with a French family in Paris before moving into a residential hotel for young women. In one of the dozens of letters written on tissue-thin blue airmail paper in perfect penmanship that she mailed home to her parents, Mom wrote:

> We've had some real excitement around here since yesterday. Julie and I decided to leave this mad house. We got along

*fine with Madame until last weekend, in spite of all her pe-
culiarities. But, last weekend, we discovered that Christian
has been deceiving us and lying to us. And, Julie had friends
here last weekend and because of a pack of lies, Christian
ruined all of her plans. And, while I was in bed with a fever,
Mme. just let me sit in my room without even giving me a
cup of tea all day long. To [hell, crossed out] heck with this
family jazz!*

Mon Dieu! The drama!

Back in Ann Arbor for her senior year at Michigan, she
met my dad, Robert Rosman. He was a dashing, charismatic
third-year law student—the focus of much female attention.
Mom initially played it cool, feigning indifference. Her strategy worked. Several months after graduating, she and Dad were
married in Boston. They moved to New York for a year, but by
1969 they had settled back in Detroit, where my dad was raised.
Lizzie was born that June. I came along in March of 1972. Then
things came apart for Mom. My dad fell in love with another
woman and left a few months after I was born. In just a few
years, she had gone from Six-Date-a-Week Suzy to a castoff. She
was twenty-seven. In a city where she had no family and, suddenly, no husband, Mom focused her energy on her two young
daughters.

But she wasn't alone for long. She was set up on a blind date
with a successful local businessman, eleven years her senior. Bob
Rosin instantly launched into a full-court press. When Mom
said she didn't feel comfortable accepting expensive gifts from
him, Bob would show up at our apartment each night with arm-

loads of groceries, a few books for Lizzie and me, a tube of lipstick for Mom. They were married in April of 1974, when I was two years old.

Though we loved Bob, and Bob loved us, the situation was complicated. Bob had three children from his first marriage—Natalie, Tommy, and Jimmy—who were caught in the undertow that often snags children of divorce: protectively loyal to their mom and confused about their place in the life of their dad, who was now living with two young stepdaughters. Added to this mix was Bob's mother, Grandma Mollie—a matriarch who seemed more fond of Bob's ex-wife than of Mom. On several occasions, Grandma Mollie reminded Mom, Lizzie, and me that "blood is thicker than water."

"You're not *real* Rosins," she would say.

That we were not Rosins was a point also frequently made by our dad, Bob Rosman. (For those of you keeping score: yep, Mom first married a man named Bob Rosman; next she married a man named Bob Rosin.) In first grade, when I registered at school as "Katie Rosin" because I wanted to have the same last name as my mom, my dad exploded.

"Your last name is Rosman," I remember him roaring at me, as we sat in a park one weekend afternoon.

Yet our place in his family was also ill defined: Dad had married Dessa, the woman he had fallen for while married to Mom. They bore two daughters—my sisters Amanda and Emily. Lizzie and I slept over most weekend nights at Dad and Dessa's. We played with our sisters, read to them, helped potty-train them, gave them spelling tests on swear words, cuddled them, fought over toys . . . we became sisters in more than name. But though

I think Dessa and Dad intended to include Lizzie and me in the family they were building, we didn't feel a part of it. Dessa often rolled her eyes when I (as little girls are wont to do) explained that my mom did things differently than she did. And more than once we overheard Dad and Dessa talking about their "family" when they were only referring to themselves and Amanda and Emily. Those are little things, but they are just the sort of signals children pick up on, and it was painful for Lizzie and me. And it's my opinion that we became (and remain) close to Amanda and Emily despite Dad and Dessa (who subsequently divorced), not necessarily because of them.

So Mom was rejected by a husband who chose to leave her for another wife. And then she married a man who loved us all but who never insisted otherwise when his relatives told us we were the B team.

These are the threads that, braided together, created the dynamics between my mom, my sister, and me. It was a relationship that would—and in many ways still does—dominate our lives.

Chapter Three

To Do:
Promise Mom on Her Deathbed
I Won't Write About Her Death,
Write About Her Death

On a cold winter evening in 2005, I stood on a subway platform at Rector Street in Manhattan waiting for an uptown train. In my mind, I was elsewhere: Southfield, Michigan, at the podium of the Ira Kaufman Chapel, where I knew Mom's funeral would one day take place. I was delivering a eulogy that even in my daydream seemed smartly conceived and well organized.

Instinctively, I found myself reaching into my purse to grab a notepad. When the time actually came to write Mom's eulogy, maybe I would crib from the structure of this speech-in-my-head. But before I made one mark on my pad, I stopped myself.

It wasn't the first time I had given serious thought to Mom's funeral—and what I would say to the community of her Detroit friends and family who would gather upon the occasion of her death. I am a writer. Written or spoken, words are my mechanism, my only tools for processing emotion. For months I had considered how important it was to me that I take the necessary time to craft a meaningful postscript to my mom's life—a remembrance of her spirit, her complexities, and the emotional turmoil that we had all waded through since her diagnosis in late February of 2003.

But each time I hit upon a worthy theme, turn of phrase, or organizing principle, I restrained myself from taking note. Mom had forbidden me. "I can't bear the thought of you imagining me dead," she said one day as I sat in bed next to her. "You've got to promise me that you'll never write a eulogy about me. I need to know you won't give my eulogy."

Certainly I never discussed my thoughts about delivering her eulogy with her. But I had, in fact, grown morbidly obsessed, as people like my husband Joe well knew. Each day, I would read not just the obituaries printed in the *New York Times* but the paid death notices too. That wasn't all. Regularly, I furtively checked the Web site for Ira Kaufman. Since it was the funeral home most often used by people in the suburban Detroit Jewish community I grew up in, I would scan its e-death notices just to see who had passed away, if I knew their grandchildren, and—when the recently departed were not in their late seventies or eighties—if I could discern the cause of their demises from the charities to which the families requested honorariums to be sent. Joe would sometimes walk up behind me while I was reading the obits and catch me unaware. "Anyone good die today?" he would ask, wryly.

* * *

FROM THE MOMENT of her diagnosis, my mom was steely in her determination to beat the disease. If she considered death a possibility—and I assume that in private moments she did—she never acknowledged it until the very, very end. She was positive, spiritual, and determined. Open-minded, she embraced the dictates of what she had long referred to, disparagingly, as "Western medicine." She submitted to three surgeries and countless rounds of chemo and radiation. But she held tighter to her long-held beliefs in the healing powers of exercise, meditation, and organic diet. If pure will were enough, she certainly would be alive today.

But will wasn't enough, and when we learned a few months after her diagnosis that her disease was more complicated than we originally thought, Mom's optimism crossed into denial. She never did things in half measures, and her denial was potent. As I saw it, it was as poisonous to her emotional health as the tumors in her lungs were to her physical well-being. It prevented her from discussing the realities that cancer presents. It prevented Mom and me (and Mom and Lizzie) from engaging in the honest discourse that defined our adult relationships with her. It prevented me from asking questions about choices she had made in her life, about regrets and triumphs, about mortality's impact on spirituality.

Once Lizzie pulled out an old photo album and brought it to Mom as she lay on the couch. Mom refused to look at it with Lizzie, and darted her an annoyed look.

It was verboten to discuss any outcome but full recovery. Mom took any comment indicating that you had considered the remote possibility of her not overcoming the disease as a betrayal. Nostalgic questions were met with angry silence. Attempted State of the Union conversations—acknowledgments of our appreciation for the wisdom she had shared and the sacrifices she had made—were one-sided. Examinations of spiritual beliefs relating to after-death philosophies were unthinkable.

I'm a journalist who has been trained to be skeptical. And I'm a person who has never been very good at keeping my feelings locked inside or my opinions to myself. So I struggled to comply with Mom's wishes. Lizzie and I would have discussions about how Mom deserved to choose the way she faced her own death. But when a doctor talked about a drug's 10 percent rate of effectiveness, I found it very, very difficult to ignore—like some giant cancer-ridden elephant in a room—the other 90 percent. More often than I would have thought possible, I controlled myself as Mom spoke excitedly of the certain success she expected from a treatment. But often I couldn't, or at least I didn't, control my reaction. And my insistence on pointing out the other side of the coin led to epic fights that sometimes ended with Mom slamming the phone down after spitting out ferocious words like, "I know things would be much easier for you if I were dead." Such arguments left me incapacitated by rage and guilt.

And so, that evening on the subway platform, I reacted to my elegiac inspiration by letting the idea disappear into my mental mush. But as an approaching train whooshed by me, sending dank air into my face, I was struck with a thought that didn't seem nearly as obvious as perhaps it should have: Mom was processing her death her way, but I had the right to process the resulting grief my way. Lizzie had once said to me: "The living have rights, too." I decided I would let go of all funereal thoughts until after Mom died. Then, I'd write my memorial to her.

Stepping on the train, I felt freed from guilt, which, in retrospect, surprises me. The decision to ignore my mom's deathbed wishes was, I now recognize, the greatest acknowledgment of her mortality.

Dear Mom:

I remember the way you used to wake me up for school by planting a million soft kisses on my forehead and cheeks. I remember when, at Quarton Elementary, some kids were teasing me and you gave me permission to swear at them and give them the finger. The swear words you taught me were "go jump in a lake" and "go suck an egg" and the finger to flip them, or so you told me, was the ring finger. (No wonder they teased me.) I remember Joe telling me that when he called to ask your permission to propose to me, you were driving and started screaming so loud and crying so hard, he begged you to pull over to the side of the road. I remember that every single morning before school, you made me peanut butter toast and that you packed me a lunch in a brown paper bag every single day, and that you mixed chopped-up apples in my tuna pitas. And I remember that most days, once at school, I tossed that lunch in favor of Twinkies and chocolate milk. I remember how you said that when you went from Rosman to Rosin you didn't even need to get new stationery or luggage. I remember that you told me, when I was in the depths of adolescent misery, that my life was going to flourish, that my brain was going to take me places I couldn't even fathom. I remember that when you were mad, no one could scream louder than you. Or slam doors harder. Or hang up phones with more ferocity. I remember you playing records by Donna Summer and Duran Duran and Gloria Gaynor. I remember you, Lizzie, and me dancing around the island in the kitchen as we did the dishes. I remember that you made dinner every single night, and that you made Lizzie and me drink a glass of milk no matter what. I remember the letters you wrote to me at camp—every one of them saying the same thing: that you and Bob had played golf and then had dinner with friends at the club. And I remember wondering even then whose enjoyment was the primary motivator when sending Lizzie and me off to the north woods of Minnesota for eight weeks every summer. I remember all of the clothes you wore when I was a little girl—your leather zip-to-the-knee high-heeled boots, your leotards, your Sonia Rykiel purses that had the "SR" logos, which you said stood for Suzy Rosin. I remember watching Dynasty in your bed on Wednesday nights. I remember having parties every single time you went out of town and lying to you about them. I remember our talks about sex and intimacy. I remember every moment of the speech you gave at my wedding, and at Lizzie's wedding. I remember the dance you choreographed and performed at your fiftieth birthday party. I remember your bakery and the bags of crushed Heath bars I drew handfuls from. I remember your golf outfits and how cute you looked on the course and how you lost to Julie Korotkin in the *finals every time. I remember how you made us trade in our Halloween candy for trail mix and stationery. I remember how you always used to tell me my skin was like strawberries and cream, and Lizzie's was like peaches and cream. I remember how you misused swear words and danced like you belonged in an MTV video. I remember when you told me that when people need to wear everything on their back— money and happiness—it might just mean they don't have much of either. I remember the stories you told me about growing up in Ann Arbor and Boston, about field hockey and cheerleading, about being the only Jewish kid. About U of M and Kappa Kappa Gamma. About snagging Dad, about picking up the pieces, about falling in love with Bob. About the log you kept of every date you went on in college that tracked each guy by fraternity affiliation. I remember what you told me about loyalty, about the importance and benefits of sticking through the rocky moments in marriage. I remember distinctly how unattached to material items you were when the house burned down. I remember doing the puzzle together over the phone. I remember how you would fill in wrong answers and come up with other words to make your wrong answers fit.*

I remember how you saw all my faults and still genuinely believed I was perfect, how addicted you were to e-mail and eBay, how a day that you couldn't manage to get online coincided with a slowdown of the U.S. economy. I remember how much power you took from your Hebrew name, Ariella Chaya, and how the roar of Ariella became your battle cry. I remember your smell, your stunning beauty, your perfect nose, how you asked Dr. Brooks if you could still get Botox when on chemo. I remember how you dragged yourself with a walker and oxygen tank into the Pilates studio so you could give me a lesson. I remember how you would get mad at me if I ever told you I felt guilt about anything at all because you considered guilt "wasted energy." I remember how much you loved it when Zack called you "Drandma." I remember how when you had a problem with a customer service representative, you'd tell them your daughter was going to write a front-page Wall Street Journal *exposé on their company. I remember how much you loved Bob to rub your feet while you watched* Law & Order *reruns. I remember how you loved mandarin orange Arizona Iced Tea and wild berry Tofutti and drank coffee so strong that Lizzie and I called it sludge. I remember how you always said that the key to good matzo balls is this: when you think you've beaten the egg whites enough, beat them some more.*

Mom, your body broke—just betrayed you horribly despite the loving and respectful way you treated it—but I thank God that your spirit has been set free. You are in the heavens, most likely dancing to hip-hop.

When I was going through some things on your desk the other day, I found that you had jotted this down on a stray piece of paper:

To open heart:
Ignore what is irrelevant to who you are.
Choose beliefs that align with how you want to feel
And what you want to create.

And it instantly hit me that that is how you lived your life, particularly once Lizzie and I had grown up and moved off on our own. You shunned convention, you gave the finger to conformity. And there were consequences sometimes to that, but you really didn't seem to be overly concerned by what other people thought. Despite the fact that your illness really defied all rational understanding, maybe you knew subconsciously that your life would be cut short, and so you lived in the moment even before you knew those moments were fleeting.

Mom, I had no idea how much you valued the sanctity of life. Even up to the very last weeks that you could really talk, you told me that you'd rather be alive as you were—broken, battered, in unimaginable pain, a prisoner to cells that wouldn't stop dividing—than separated from your family.

The possibility that you might get to see your grandchildren grow up was reason enough for you to endure the unrelenting pain. Mom, you got screwed big-time. As did I, and Lizzie and Bob, and your stepkids and all your grandkids, and your mom and your brothers, and the many, many friends who mourn today from Tucson to Detroit to New York. We have all been wronged. What has brought everyone together today is an injustice.

You made me promise you about three weeks ago that I would live a happy life. You said it was the only way I could properly honor you—to laugh with my husband, to love my family and my work, to become a mother. Mom, I will find a way to do those things one day soon—however unimaginable happiness is to me right now. I promise that Lizzie, Bob,

and I will take care of each other and of Grandma. And I
promise to be the kind of woman that you raised me to be.

My heart literally aches right now. And I think it will for
a long time to come, Mom. Nothing I can do about that—
the void you leave is massive. But when I'm lonesome and
depressed and feeling alone, I will conjure you, my brave
mama. I will remember you. And I will remember that I am
the baby daughter, the living legacy, the flesh and blood of
Ariella Chaya. I will follow the example you have set. I will
pick myself up and soldier on in hungry pursuit of love and
happiness.

Love, Katie

I TOOK A week off from work, during which time I delivered
that eulogy, sat shivah, and began the complex process of shifting
from caring for a terminally ill parent to mourning her death. My
boss at the time suggested I take a second week before returning
to the Manhattan newsroom of the *Wall Street Journal*. I declined
her offer because I thought work would be a good place to direct
my focus.

My mom had been very proud of my accomplishments.
When I told her that I had been offered a job at the *Journal* in
2004, she sent an e-mail to all of her friends. In the subject line
she wrote "Wall Flower" and then she described to an audience
of about seventy the new gig. I hadn't even gotten the chance
to accept the job yet. But for Mom, maternal pride trumped
discretion.

She routinely e-mailed my recent articles to everyone she
knew. But she didn't brag about all of them equally. As does so

much parental satisfaction, Mom's was influenced by the pull of reflected glory.

In the fall of 2003—at a time when Mom hit a rough patch and was really sick—I was working as a freelance journalist, writing for a wide swath of publications. My most reliable stream of work came from *Elle* magazine, for which I was contracted to write in a year's time four substantively reported pieces on politics, culture, or sociology. Aware of the strain Mom's illness was putting on my schedule, my editors at *Elle* assigned me a story that wouldn't require too much time-intensive reporting but would still fulfill one-quarter of my contractual obligation. The "gimme" assignment: I was to attend, at a Manhattan "school of womanly arts," a workshop devoted to one-hour-long orgasms (yep). Steve and Vera Bodansky—a husband-and-wife team, each with a PhD in sensuality; they are self-described "cliterologists" (not making this up)—would cap their tutorial with a live demonstration of the "Extended Massive Orgasm," or EMO. After attending the seminar, I was expected to write about the experience. I made Joe join me in attending the seminar (which he dubbed "Pussy U"). I described part of the experience on the pages of *Elle* thus:

> *EMO comes in manual transmission: Since it requires acute dexterity, intercourse can't bring the truly Big O. And because EMO requires communication, it's harder to execute during oral sex. "You don't see many brain surgeons using their penis to operate," Steve points out. I'm fairly tickled by Steve's reasoning. Joe—who has by now five times muttered, "This is complete and utter bullshit"—is less amused.*

Although writing about sex was not my bailiwick, I was incredibly grateful to my editors for the assignment. This was not the sort of piece they had in mind when they gave me a contract, and we all knew it. I expected my mom to be equally appreciative that a national publication was willing to help me fulfill my professional obligations and keep my career alive while I was devoting ever more time to her care. But no.

"You're writing about orgasms now?" Mom said, making no attempt to hide her disapproval. "I hope no one who reads it knows you're my daughter."

I suppose part of me should have been happy that she wasn't too sick to be a bitch.

And as if cancer wasn't a big enough cross for Mom to bear, many readers did make the connection. I heard from a number of her friends who, while sitting in a hair salon flipping through *Elle*, were surprised to read of my and Joe's matriculation from orgasm school. Somehow—more than one person noted with amusement—Mom had for the first time failed to e-mail them about my latest opus.

AND SO I thought it best to return quickly to work after Mom died and report pieces she would have been proud to promote. At the time, my mandate at the *Journal* was to write for the leisure section on a range of cultural trends and the quirky subcultures upon which they reflected: elite book clubs with stiff membership requirements; reality TV stars trying to transform a willingness to lay themselves bare before cameras into legitimacy in the business world; "extreme philanthropy," whereby philanthropists seek to experience the hardship they're helping others to overcome. (For that piece, I visited a prison in Sugarland, Texas, with a bunch of business executives teaching white-collar skills to inmates.) But from the day I returned to work, I felt so weighted by my sadness that it was a struggle to focus on the pursuits of others.

I hadn't realized how much my mom's disease had become the frame of my life. Though I felt incredible relief that Mom was gone, I didn't know what to do with the absence of worry—worry that had sucked up so much of my life for so long. When I set out to come up with a story idea, my thoughts invariably wandered to Mom. And the worst part was that the Mom I conjured was not the vibrant ass-kicker, the energetic woman who on any given day might climb to a mountaintop before 7:00 a.m. When I closed my eyes, I was seeing the cancer victim—gaunt, bedridden, labored in breath, drugged into obliviousness. I was haunted by the idea that I would never again be able to imagine her as she would wish to be remembered.

Even as I was starting again to report trend pieces for the paper, I became increasingly obsessed with what I didn't know about Mom's life and what I feared I would never understand about the way she approached her death. Much more than that, I anguished that unanswered questions would prevent me from overcoming the emptiness I felt. My depression wasn't just about Mom dying, it was about how she died: in emotional distress and with a complete unwillingness to reflect on her life. As much as I wanted to care about my own life, I was haunted by her obvious lack of peace at the end. My mom would have hated that she in some way stood between me and my future. But that, in fact, was the reality.

One night, while driving on the West Side Highway with Joe,

I said, "I hate the story I'm on now. I just wish I could report on Mom."

"You don't need an assignment from the *Wall Street Journal* to write something," Joe said without looking away from the road. "Just come up with a linear idea and go for it.

"Do it on the weekends," he said. "Do it for yourself."

TWO YEARS AFTER my mom died, I finally took my husband's advice, setting my sights on Mom's collection of vintage Steuben and Venetian glass art. She started to collect it, in earnest, around the time she was diagnosed with cancer, and her interest accelerated as the illness progressed. Thus Lizzie and I had inherited all sorts of vases, candlesticks, wine stems, and objets d'art. I knew nothing about the import of this bounty, unsure of both its historical significance and why it all meant so much to Mom. Ironically, because of Mom's refusal to discuss matters of nostalgia or mortality, it was only once she was dead that I could search for answers.

I approached the endeavor as I would any story, making dozens of phone calls and sorting through hundreds of e-mails. My grieving process—my entire life, really—was upended by what I learned. Retreating into the online community of glass collectors as her life was unraveling, Mom was confiding to her electronic acquaintances the fears she refused to discuss with us, her family. It was a stunning realization.

Over coffee with Marcus Brauchli, then a top editor at the *Journal*, I mentioned my project and early findings. Instantly, he urged me to write about the experience for the paper. I did so, in a story that ran on Page One. It generated hundreds of e-mailed responses—immensely poignant and personal letters from readers who had lost parents, siblings, lovers, and even children. These readers took solace in realizing that there were ways to continue learning about loved ones well after they had died—and to seek the sometimes elusive sense of closure. In the aftermath of that response, the urge to learn about my mother intensified. Finally, about a year later, I began in earnest to call and e-mail strangers—people who had been involved with Mom on the golf course, in the Pilates studio, in the haute couture section of clothing boutiques in Detroit, in the pursuit of ecological living in Arizona—asking them to tell me about a woman to whom, I thought, I couldn't have been closer.

As I began to talk to people who knew Mom in many of the ways that I didn't, I began to see how the communities and subcultures she belonged to connected to the narrative of her life, her illness, and ultimately, her death. And because I am a writer, I began to envision a book that shows what a family goes through when a member is struck by illness, in a manner that's not macabre, airbrushed, or prescriptive. As a daughter, I could consider my mom as it hadn't occurred to me to do before—as someone who could be defined by more than motherhood. At the same time, I could test a theory I've long held as a reporter: that when you're willing to spend the time to peel back the layers, even seemingly conventional players are revealed to be complex; that ordinary people can lead quietly extraordinary lives.

It seems only fair to note that my stepdad and sister would never put the family's experiences on paper in a public forum. But if they did, they each surely would tell different stories. What I set out to do was to draw as factually accurate a portrait as I could, knowing full well that the facts would still be refracted through my eyes and my experiences. My memoir of Mom is just that.

I had two overarching goals in reporting on her life. The first was to see if I could learn to understand better why she approached her death as she did. More important, I was desperate to reconnect with my healthy, vivacious, free-spirited, moody, pain-in-the-ass, nurturing, imperfect, perfect mother.

I hadn't considered that in doing so, I might heal myself.

THE JOURNEY BEGAN with Mom's green leather Filofax. And it occurred to me quickly that it reflected her, almost uncannily.

Mom was no Luddite—she loved technology—but she always carefully maintained a paper address book. First it was a square white plastic ringed binder (which sits on Bob's desk in Tucson as a keepsake). Then it was the Filofax. As with most address books, these both are organized—a generous use of the word—alphabetically. Though not in the traditional sense. If Mom had a plumber named Ned Smith, she could have listed him under S for Smith, N for Ned, P for Plumber, H for Household, R for Repairman, or B for Bathroom. And wherever she had decided to list him, Mom would list him as simply Ned Smith, or even as Ned—but never as "Ned Smith, plumber."

Lizzie and I had long gotten a kick out of Mom's system—when we weren't frustrated by our inability to find the number we needed in her absence.

Flipping through these jumbled pages, three years after Mom's death, I was surprised by the feeling of comfort and even euphoria. She had her way of doing things, and she didn't give a shit if it made sense to anyone else.

Thus, having no idea why most people were in her address book, I began cold-calling numbers. I reached a handful of answering machines and left long, convoluted messages like, "My name is Katie, and I am the daughter of Suzy Rosin. I found your name in my mother's address book. Unfortunately, she died a few years ago, and I am trying to learn more about her by reaching out to people who knew her. So if you have any idea who I am talking about and care to share your recollections of her . . ."

I also found myself on the other end of a lot of this-number-has-been-disconnected recordings. But when Mom had written down peoples' last names—which she did infrequently—I did Internet searches to try to track down their current listings. On my very first day, this stab-in-the-dark reporting yielded some amazing results.

To get a quick sense of what I might find, I randomly flipped to P, where I assumed Mom recorded the numbers of her Pilates students. For about a decade before she died, Mom taught Pilates, most often in the studio that adjoined her house. She excelled at doing so, and it brought her tremendous pleasure. She loved the movement, but she was also really compelled by the relationships with those she taught.

Mom had scribbled the full name and telephone number of a woman whose name I didn't recognize. I called the number; it had been disconnected. On a Web-based white-pages site, I found a number for someone in Tucson who shared her last name. I called—it was the home of the woman's brother and sister-in-law. I told the sister-in-law what I was doing, and she relayed the message to her husband, who called his sister on my behalf. She called me to say that she did remember Mom.

Jennifer had been a student of Mom's for several months. They talked a lot during their one-on-one sessions, and she found herself confiding to Mom about the difficulties she was facing in a troubled marriage.

When we spoke by phone, Jennifer shared with me one of her favorite stories about Mom: One day, during a lesson, Jennifer lamented that she had a work event coming up to which she was expected to bring her husband. She was excited about the party but felt anxious that her husband would be moody and might embarrass her. "I'm worried he's going to ruin it for me," she told Mom.

Mom listened and continued on with the lesson. When they finished the workout, she put her hand on Jennifer's shoulder and said, "This is what you do: twenty minutes before you have to walk out the door, have sex with him. It'll buy you two or three hours of him being relaxed and in a good mood." (Jennifer said to me of Mom's advice: "It worked!")

My mom said this? *My* mom?

I considered the significance of this story from all sides. It told me a lot about Mom's view of marriage and the role that sex can play. In Mom's consideration, sex could provide a woman with happiness in her marriage—and not just in the obvious way. It also implied a lot about how Mom navigated her own thirty-one-year marriage to Bob.

Obviously, a daughter—even an adult daughter—doesn't want to think of her parents as sexual beings (yuck). And I'm pleased to report that this was the sole instance in which my search led me into the realm of Mom's sex life. But if my goal was to learn about her in a more holistic sense, I suppose sex might be a part of that.

If Mom had a good sex life with her husband, I'm happy that she did. And if she used sex as a tool to manipulate her husband, I don't know why I'm surprised.

But the impact this story had upon me transcended what it told me about Mom's values.

To hear a funny story about her three years after she had died—from a complete stranger, no less—well, it was exhilarating. That's the only word for it.

I thought about this little anecdote constantly for weeks, and dined out on it for much longer. That was the first time in a long time that I fixated on a story about my mom that had nothing to do with cancer or death. It was such a relief.

Chapter Four

"... Love Like Your Heart Has Never Been Broken, and Dance Like No One Is Watching"

At her fiftieth birthday party in 1994, my mom performed a well-choreographed, extensively practiced, slightly naughty hip-hop dance routine for the one hundred friends and relatives who had assembled at Ventana Canyon Golf & Racquet Club in Tucson to fête her. She wore a black velvet vest, with her toned arms bare and much of her back exposed by a low halter. With it, she paired black leggings and cool combat boots. A smile engulfing her face, Mom did this routine that was funky and sexy and sort of Janet Jackson. My fifty-year-old mother was doing a circa *Control*, "Janet, 'Miss Jackson' if you're nasty" dance.

She looked absolutely fantastic. The way she moved was astonishing. Lizzie and I were totally mortified.

Before she began, Mom stood on the dance floor, holding a mic. Bob stood next to her as she said, "To get things going tonight, we have a little entertainment planned." Someone in the crowd screamed, "Go Suzy!" Then the DJ put on rap music, and Mom fixed herself into starting position: her hips cocked, her elbow bent as if pretending to file her nails out of boredom. Then she was approached by her dance partner, Jerome Weinberg. He was dressed in white pants and a white shirt under a brown vest. A brown beret kept his chin-length hair from falling in his face. In the dance that he choreographed, Jerome played the suitor who courted her despite her indifference.

Almost fifteen years later, and several years after Mom died, my uncle Eddie sent me a copy of the video he made at Mom's birthday party. Since then, I've watched the dance a number of times, and the dance of my memory holds up. Her talent was incredible—truly MTV-worthy. Her outfit was sexy, funky, and adorable. Her body was killer. I am no longer embarrassed. Far from it. I am proud, thrilled even, for Mom and for me to have this as my example of what middle age can mean. That said, I don't feel guilty about being horrifed at the time of the birthday party. Children, no matter the age, are meant to be mortified by their parents. It's part of the natural order.

MY MOM LOVED to move to music. As a girl and teenager, she was a talented figure skater and ballet dancer. As a young mom, she started teaching aerobics even before Jane Fonda did. At the YMCA, she would arrive resplendent in a leotard, tights, and a pair of Reebok high tops (which she owned in every available color: pink, white, light blue, royal blue, black, yellow . . .). She also loved to jog and was disciplined about completing her six-mile route several times a week. Even in the numbing conditions of the Michigan winter, she could be seen slogging down Long Lake Road in layers of thermal underwear and sweats, her Sony Walkman clipped to her waistband. She kept abreast of popular music and maintained an ever-changing roster of favorite songs. It was not unusual to come home from school to find Mom focused on the buttons of her stereo system to the exclusion of all else: PLAY, PAUSE, REWIND, PLAY, PAUSE, RECORD. She never cut off the beginning or end of a song. She always left an equal number of seconds between songs. Her mixed tapes were masterful.

Mom had slews of albums stacked vertically in the slots of the mirrored bar built into our living room. Peter, Paul & Mary, the Beatles, and Harry Belafonte Jr. But what she most often played was disco. The Bee Gees. Gloria Gaynor. Donna Summer (toot toot . . . ahhh . . . beep beep!).

When I was about six or seven, Mom and Bob decided to host a disco party in the private room of the Vineyards, the restaurant at which they had their first date. In advance of the big night, they hired a dance instructor to come to our house on Tuesdays—the night that Bob's kids, Natalie, Tommy, and Jimmy, came for dinner. The instructor's name was Michael Angelo. For many years, I thought he was the guy who had painted the Sistine Chapel. What a multitalent.

At the party, Michael Angelo was in attendance to teach some moves to Mom and Bob's guests. We danced the Hustle, as performed by Van McCoy and the Soul City Symphony, all together as a big happy disco-dancing family. Afterward, Mom and Bob rocked out to Rod Stewart's "Do Ya Think I'm Sexy?" to which Bob knew all the words. I wore an outfit I had gotten a few months earlier as a Hanukkah present. It was a pants-and-vest ensemble in ice-blue satin. I called it my Olivia Newton-John.

Most nights Mom cooked elaborate dinners, using what seemed like every pot and dish in the kitchen. The unenviable task of cleanup fell to Lizzie and me. We hated it. But often Mom would play DJ, spinning "Tainted Love" and tunes from Barbra Streisand's album *Guilty*, and the three of us would dance around the kitchen, shimmying our shoulders as we filled the dishwasher.

Mom performed more traditional dances beautifully as well. One of the best things about being invited as a family to bar mitzvahs or weddings was being able to watch Mom and Bob dance together. The state of their relationship had no impact on their ability to glide around a dance floor. Bob could be annoyed with Mom because she took too long to get ready and made us late, or Mom could be annoyed at Bob for daring to be annoyed with her for being late. No matter. On the dance floor, they were in sync, in step, in love. With their eyes locked, Bob's arm easily guiding Mom about the floor and Mom's dress swaying like a flag unfurled, they were the parents you wished were yours.

Off the dance floor, it wasn't always so. Mom fought depression when I was young, and our house could be a dark place. During her bouts, she napped a lot and went to bed early. I remember tiptoeing around the house, even in the light of day. She would be quick to anger and ill tempered, erupting sometimes for no good reason. There were occasions when she slammed doors and screamed with a lack of control that scared me.

But music was usually an antidote to the moodiness. It transformed her. Her posture loosened. Her face relaxed. She moved her shoulders and hips, ever so slightly, with an effortlessness unique to those with a sense of rhythm.

It almost didn't matter the place or the circumstances. When music played, Mom would dance, and dancing made her happy.

HER RED CURLS drenched with sweat and pinned off her face with a barrette, and her strong, petite body clad in a rhinestone tank top, tight black athletic pants cut off at the calf, and black rubber-soled combat boots, Mom waited for a chance to introduce herself to Chris Toledo, the teacher of Street Jams, the trendy dance class held at Voight Fitness and Dance Center on the corner of Santa Monica and La Cienega boulevards in Los Angeles.

It was a total Hollywood scene. The hour-and-a-half class took place at night, in a studio packed with body after hard body. The stereo vibrated with songs from Naughty by Nature, Lighter Shade of Brown, and Johnny Gill. Casting agents watched from the windowed hallway. The mirror-lined walls fogged up from the body heat. Lithe, professional dancers and glistening, barely dressed starlets—most of them half Mom's age—clamored for space close to the front of the studio. She had carved a spot for herself in the back corner.

It was the early 1990s, and word of this dance class had traveled all the way to Tucson, where Mom was spending much of her time. She heard so much about it from other dancers and fitness instructors that she finally decided to try it herself, taking the fifty-minute airplane flight for a three-day visit to L.A., during which she'd attend a few of Chris's classes. After the first class, when the studio finally emptied out, Mom wedged herself close enough to Chris to say hello. "I'm Suzy," she said. "I came in from Tucson for this class."

"I grew up in Tucson," Chris told her.

She was excited and earnest. "Here's my number," she said, and she scribbled on the back of an envelope she fished from her purse. "If you're ever in town, I'd be interested in working with you."

Chris told me that Mom rocked on her heels as she spoke. He sensed that it took confidence for her to approach him. But her timidity waned over the next several months as she flew in about once every six weeks to attend Chris's classes. Within six months, she had inched her way from the back of the class to the middle to the very front row. "You had to be aggressive to find a spot in front," Chris told me. "There were some hungry wolves."

But even when tucked away in the back, Mom had caught his eye. "I can watch someone for ten seconds and know if they know how to dance," Chris said. "Your mom knew how to dance."

MOM AND BOB had come to Tucson to build a house—to live in the mountains and to allow Mom to spend more time with her parents and brothers. But Mom was also looking to escape the conventional life of a suburban Detroit mom. Looking back, I now see that her fiftieth birthday party—a party that she herself hosted and planned—was her coming-out. And nothing said "fuck you" to formality and appearance like putting on public display her friendship with Jerome, her co-performer and choreographer.

In the late 1980s, when Mom was about forty-five, she met Jerome in Tucson. Ten years her junior, Jerome was a fitness instructor at Canyon Ranch, where Mom hung out a lot. He started as her dance teacher. But their friendship lasted years, and through them, Jerome became a kind of life coach, a yogi figure. There was nothing indiscreet about the relationship. If anything, Mom was sort of a mother figure to Jerome, who despite his guru-ness is very childlike. He'd hang around Mom and Bob's house a lot. Though he had lived a far-flung life across several continents, he was in some ways an unworldly puppy dog looking for guidance. Bob was a good sport about their friendship. When Mom told Bob that Jerome was coming over for dinner, Bob would tease, "I haven't seen our son in days!" But he respected that the relationship mattered to Mom. Bob has gone out of his way for Jerome even since Mom died, because he knows he meant a lot to her. Lizzie and I have always been less dutiful when it's come to Jerome. We were skeptical. And we were jealous. But much more on Jerome later.

First, back to Chris Toledo, another guy whom Mom and Bob might not have met at the country club in suburban Detroit. Mom used to say, "Chris is a cool dude." Those words—*cool* and *dude*—get thrown around a lot, but in this case, they are apt.

Chris Toledo was born on September 11, 1960, in the hallway of a hospital in Tucson. His father, of Mexican descent, supported the family as a football coach—first at a juvenile prison facility a few hours from Tucson, and then at a local community college. Chris and his two sisters were born before his mom was twenty.

Chris was a gifted basketball player as a boy. He spent every second he could on asphalt courts in the black and Latino neighborhoods of Tucson. There, gaggles of teenage girls would watch at the sidelines, blasting early hip-hop and rap from the Sugarhill Gang and Kurtis Blow from their boom boxes. Under the tutelage of these neighborhood kids, Chris learned to dance.

After graduating from high school, he moved to Mexico to play ball in a pro league for about three years. When his team cut him, he returned to Arizona to interview with Club Med. The company hired Chris to head up the sports program at a location in the Bahamas. By day he played basketball with guests. At night he began to take small parts in the staged musical revues. "There were some of the most dynamic performers I had ever seen," Chris said. "I was learning about choreography, getting used to changing backstage in front of women. It was an immersion in a whole different culture." Soon, organizing the sports program became almost a sideline to dancing. He moved on to Club Med's Playa Blanca resort in Mexico. Then to Tahiti. Then to Eilat in Israel.

From Club Med, he made his way to Los Angeles to teach his wildly popular street dancing class. After a few years, he caught the eye of marketers at Reebok, who hired him as some sort of dance ambassador. To help the label penetrate markets abroad, Chris traveled around the world—to places like Singapore, Finland, Chile, and Colombia—leading hip-hop dance classes. In each country he visited, he sought out dancers to teach him the local folk dances.

ABOUT A YEAR after Mom first attended his class, Chris's wife got pregnant, and they decided to quit L.A for Tucson. Their son, Elijah, was born there in 1997. Though Chris had opportunities to re-create his Street Jams classes in Tucson, he was looking to branch out into different forms of dance he had learned abroad. "All people wanted me to do was the latest hip-hop street dancing stuff," he said. "I was having difficulty crossing over and was worried about money." He remembered my mom's offer of work. He called her from a pay phone down the road from his dad's house. "Come over and give me a lesson tomorrow," she said.

Mom and Chris met in the studio that she and Bob had built right off the master bedroom. Chris recalled, "I told her I wanted to do something different. She said, 'I'm game.' If it had something to do with movement, she was all over it."

With Mom his guinea pig, Chris began to mesh hip-hop dance steps with the new forms of movement he'd learned during his travels, methods like tai chi and Capoeira, a Brazilian style that disguises martial arts in dance. He called his creation the "flow," for "focus love on the world." "She let me experiment—and then paid me for the time we danced together," he told me. "She really helped me make ends meet. But she continually made me feel proud of our time together. She let me know that my creating this side by side with her was exciting for her. It made her feel included and important."

Soon, they were dancing together three times a week. It wasn't merely exercise for Mom. She lost herself in the music and movement. Often, when she transitioned from the up-tempo hip-hop portion to the meditative tai chi, she would become overcome with emotion. Unlike me, Mom was not a crier, and at first she fought the tears.

When I was in college and would visit Mom in Tucson, she'd often ask me to join her during her lessons with Chris, or at least watch her do the "flow" with him. I'd occasionally oblige her by sitting in the dance studio for about five minutes with a bored, distracted look on my face.

Looking back, I don't know why I refused to watch a full lesson, why I wouldn't join her and Chris, why I treated the moments that meant something to her with disrespect. I was a kid, or really, worse than a kid: I was in college and totally self-absorbed.

Mom always said that "guilt is wasted energy," so I don't let it consume me. But when I consider what I missed in sharing with Mom, I'm hit with a pang of loneliness.

It's a bummer that so often when we learn a lesson, it's too late to put it to good use.

WHEN CHRIS WAS supposed to give Mom a lesson but couldn't find a sitter to care for his infant son, Elijah, he would bring him to Mom's house. She quickly grew smitten with the boy. She would talk about him to Lizzie and me endlessly, as if he were her grandson. Mom had an infinite capacity for love and held to a beautiful and inclusive definition of family.

Before long, Mom was babysitting Elijah on a fairly regular basis, and she became emotionally invested in his development. Mom worried about him—a lot. Elijah's mom didn't believe in childhood vaccinations and was adamant about raising Elijah as a strict vegetarian. Though Mom ate very little meat herself, she was concerned about Elijah's nutrition.

"Your mom drew a good balance of respecting that things were my decision but being persistent in reminding me what signs were important to pay attention to," Chris said. "At the time, I had no idea how to parent. And Elijah's mom wanted everything to be antiestablishment. Your mom wouldn't criticize any of that. She'd just say, 'With the girls, this is how I did it. . . .' I needed my hand to be held. I didn't have the hang of it yet. She really helped me learn how to be a good father." (Mom may have been less respectful than Chris knew: When she was babysitting Elijah at various stages of toddlerhood, she would sneak him a scrambled egg here and a chicken drumstick there. "He seemed *starving*," she would tell Lizzie and me.)

Even when Mom was openly meddlesome, she tried to be subtle. When she really became concerned about Elijah's nutrition, she suggested to Chris that he have their son's health evaluated by a physician she knew who incorporated alternative and holistic medicine into his Western practice. He agreed to take him (without telling Elijah's mom), and my mom paid the bill. "I believe that she really, truly loved Elijah," Chris said of my mom. She did.

Chris and his family moved to San Diego in 1999. They kept in contact until Mom got sick and disconnected herself from so many people she cared about.

I tracked Chris down by e-mail, and we subsequently spent hours on the phone, talking about his experiences with Mom. Chris is still in San Diego, where he oversees a fitness program for a drug rehabilitation center and works as a life coach. He and Elijah's mom split long ago, and he's raising Elijah on his own.

For all of our discussions about dancing, I was most struck by something he said at the very beginning of our conversation about his son, who is now a champion skateboarder. "Elijah has gotten all his shots and eats a normal diet. He goes to public school, goes to skateboarding practice, comes home, does his homework, then goes to bed. He has a lot of structure in his life. He's a really happy kid." And then he added, "I guess I just wish your mom could see that I'm a real good father."

I HAD DECIDED to really dig into my reporting by talking to people who were connected to Mom through dance for a reason. I thought it would be a gentle start, a cotton-candy entry, an easing in before confronting some of the more gripping, emotional material that I suspected might overwhelm me. But just in reconnecting with Chris, I was struck by his comments about Elijah and his own abilities as a father, and how it signified the extent to which he cared about how he was perceived by Mom. I knew that Mom was close to Chris for a time, but her lasting impact upon him startled me. He was still yearning for her approval.

I was also struck by a realization that Mom mothered a number of people beside Lizzie and me. I had a sense of this before interviewing the scores of people I tracked down, but it was in talking to Chris that I first sensed the breadth of Mom's influence. The relationships tended to fall into certain patterns. There was often a client/service provider element, an age difference, and ethnic, religious, or class differences. The people she took into her hold all joined her in some sort of physical activity or sport. It's as if she connected to people best when she was sweating, moving, and asserting her physical strength and grace. And since I felt burdened by the memory of her deterioration, that was just the sort of image of her I was yearning to rediscover.

SOON AFTER INTERVIEWING Chris, I went to a dinner party at the home of close friends. I sat next to a guy I had never met before. The conversation made its way to what I was working on. I told him about this book and how I was using my skills as a reporter to learn more about my late mom's life.

He told me he had lost both of his parents in the last decade. I knew he was going to have strong opinions about what I was doing, and I was eager to hear them. He thought my premise—to use his term—was bullshit. "You're assuming the things you find out about have underlying meaning," is what he said, more or less. "But you really have no way of knowing what, if anything, any of your discoveries signify."

He wasn't necessarily wrong: I can't be sure, because I can't interview the one person who could connect all the dots for me. But as this guy aired his cynicism and anger at me—literally, he was indignant about what I was doing—I came to decide that I rejected his take and further decided that, in fact, I had been underestimating the importance of some of what I was being told by people . . . people who, in almost every case, hardly knew Mom compared to how I knew her.

I had changed since my mom died, and it took a guy who was pissed off and drunk to make me realize that. I had become less cynical and more like the sort of person who believes that if you are open to finding meaning—which is almost always an exercise in faith and almost never an exercise in certainly—you might find meaning.

The day after this wine-shellacked dinner-party conversation, I was convinced that I could, in some cases, glean real insights into my mom even when talking about hip-hop dance lessons, fashion choices, and country club golf championships. I went back to my notes from several interviews, including one of those I had done with Chris. I came across a little notation that had previously escaped my focus: "I had a nickname for your mom," Chris had told me. "I called her Suzy Rosecakes."

That is just the sort of fact that the dinner-party guy would call trivial. But I was floored. I was *incredibly* close to this woman. And yet she had a nickname I didn't even know about. She wasn't just my and Lizzie's mom. She wasn't just Bob's wife. She was Suzy Rosecakes too. That's who I was in search of. And already, I was finding her.

IN SEPTEMBER 2002, in the bright and happy kitchen of Lizzie and Mitchell's house in Los Angeles, Lizzie and Mom were doing what Jewish women do in kitchens on Rosh Hashanah: basting juices on the brisket to keep it moist, putting cloth napkins through golden rings, arranging peonies in crystal vases on the dining room table.

I was doing what I tended to do when in the kitchen with Mom and Lizzie: staying out of the way. They always expressed some level of irritation that I wasn't contributing, but the unspoken truth was, they didn't want my help. My mom was an absolute artist with food and flowers. It's a gift Lizzie inherited. Whatever she touches in a kitchen becomes beautiful. But much of what I touch becomes burned.

So I hung back from the bustle, laughing to myself as I watched

Mom trying (unsuccessfully) to assert authority in Lizzie's kitchen. I had gotten married a few months earlier. Lizzie was two years married, and already a mother to one-year-old Zack. No longer just Mom's girls, we were women now, and we were feeling our way around our changing dynamic.

There is a spiritual rhythm created by women in a kitchen on a holiday, and I let it wash over me. It was a rare moment for me— serenely suspended between a comforting sense of nostalgia and a confidence in my future.

Then Mom coughed.

Since I had returned from my honeymoon in late June, Mom had been fighting a nagging cough. At first she thought she had bronchitis or some sort of respiratory infection. She was such a healthy women and so disdainful of traditional practitioners of medicine, she didn't even have an internist she regularly saw in Tucson. So she got a prescription for antibiotics from her holistically inclined gynecologist.

The antibiotics didn't work. Her cough, in fact, grew worse— morphing from a little rasp in the back of her throat to a nasty chest rattle.

"I have asthma," she had asserted to Lizzie and me by phone, diagnosing herself.

One of Mom's Pilates students was married to a radiologist. She urged Mom to let her husband do a chest X-ray and a CAT scan. A huge spot on her right lung showed up.

"It can't be cancer," Mom relayed to us, " 'cause the doctor says the spot is so big that I'd already be dead if it were." Somehow, I initially believed her when she said that this was reassuring. Each time I spoke to her, she had another moderately compelling explanation for the lingering cough. Among them: Bob had recently been diagnosed with valley fever, a respiratory condition caused by a fungus often found in desert environments. Since Mom breathed the same Tucson air as Bob, it was possible that valley fever was the root of her problems as well.

I had spent a lot of time with Mom in the months and weeks leading up to my wedding. She seemed to me as she always had: happy, filled with energy by day, ready for sleep by about nine. By Rosh Hashanah, I hadn't seen her in person for a couple of months, though we spoke by phone several times daily. As she described it to me, her routine hadn't changed much since the cough surfaced. So I hadn't been too worried.

But then, standing in the kitchen with Lizzie, I heard Mom cough. That *cough*. My God. It was ferocious—a bark from an angry German shepherd. I darted my eyes at Mom. She quickly looked away. I locked glances with Lizzie, searching for reassurance from my big sister. She had none to give. Her eyes were frozen with terror.

RATHER THAN FLYING back to New York with Joe after Rosh Hashanah as planned, I headed to Tucson. I was, at the time, working as a freelance journalist, and this arrangement afforded me flexibility. Lizzie had one-year-old Zack, so she had less of it. Banded in sisterhood, Lizzie and I decided I would accompany Mom to the hospital for an upcoming test. Called a bronchoscope, the test involved a pulmonologist threading a camera down Mom's throat and into her airways to get a better look at the mass that had showed up on the scans.

After the test, the pulmonologist repeated the dubious reassurance that the spot was so large that it was almost unthinkable to imagine it was cancer. "See," Mom said to me in the car in a voice made scratchy from the invasive test, "I'm fine." There was a pleading in her tone; she was implicitly begging me to agree. I nodded and said nothing.

A few days later, I sat in my mom's den, whiling my time away on her computer. As I did, I was listening to Macy Gray's *On How Life Is* on my iPod—then a novelty item that was not yet ubiquitous.

"What are you listening to?" Mom asked as she walked by, toward the kitchen. "I wanna hear the sound quality on these things."

I handed her the iPod. She put the buds in her ears. As she would do when listening to music, she started to groove—making slight, staccato movements with her shoulders, balancing on her heels as she tapped her toes.

Within seconds, her breath became audibly labored. She yanked out the earphones. Her complexion turned ashy. "I have to sit down," she said.

I knew we were in trouble.

In late February 2003, I sat in my "office"—a desk in a cubicle rented for cheap from my friend Tad, who runs a television production company in the Flatiron District. I stared at the computer screen. I wrote nothing. I was expecting a call.

Since Mom's bronchoscope test was inconclusive, she underwent a series of other tests. Each one ruled out one disease or another—except for cancer. We were told repeatedly that the size of the spot (no one was calling it a tumor then) was so significant that if it were cancer, she'd surely be dead. (People: Not comforting!) Finally, in late February, the pulmonologist and radiologist decided Mom needed to have a biopsy. So a needle was shoved through her back and into her lung. Cells were drawn out and studied.

The phone on my desk rang.

Without preamble Mom said, "Sweetheart, it's cancer." Then she did something she rarely did: she started to cry. When she said, "Will you come here?" she sounded like a little girl.

Lizzie left Los Angeles for Tucson that afternoon. I boarded a plane the next morning.

FOR SEVERAL MONTHS before our May 2002 wedding, Joe and I took dance lessons at a small studio on the second floor of a gritty building on Third Avenue. The studio's co-owner and our instructor, Carlan, was an over-the-top former chorus dancer with long legs, red hair, and a wicked laugh.

We knew we didn't want to dance a standard wedding dance. Carlan was a woman who seemed to like a little drama. She suggested we tango. We needed tango-friendly music, so we selected the slightly unconventional wedding song "Whatever Lola Wants," from the musical *Damn Yankees*. (We favor the version sung by Sarah Vaughan, and I like to ad lib during the chorus: "Whatever Katie wants, Katie gets. . . .")

For about four months, we went to dance lessons every Wednesday night at eight thirty. Under Carlan's tutelage, we learned to communicate through the placement of Joe's hand on the small of my back and the shifting of weight from left to right. I came to think of dance lessons as premarital counseling. When one steps forward, the other must step back.

After the cocktail reception that followed our wedding ceremony, our 135 guests took their seats in the ballroom. The lights dimmed. We glided onto the dance floor—Joe dapper in his tuxedo, me looking good (*really* good) in my like-a-glove strapless gown and white gloves that stretched past my elbows. Joe twirled me into his arms and dipped me provocatively.

The band struck up our song. We theatrically pressed our bodies together, extended our opposing arms and strutted down the dance floor. Joe spun. I twirled. The crowd went nuts.

As the song ended, Joe dipped me one last time. Ebullient, we walked off the floor and toward our roaring guests. Mom and Lizzie, who had no idea Joe and I had prepared this performance, were standing right on the edge of the dance floor, and they quickly engulfed me in an embrace. They both were shrieking with laughter. Mom kept repeating, "Oh! My! *God*!" Her eyes appeared backlit, and her mouth was fixed in an uncontained, open-jawed smile.

About a year before Mom died, Lizzie took Mom and Zack to the Santa Monica pier, and the three of them rode the Ferris wheel. Suspended above the ocean, her hair whipping in the wind and her grandson seated next to her screeching with glee, Mom appeared in a state of ecstasy. That is what Lizzie has told me, and I love conjuring the image.

But I wasn't there to absorb it myself. So for me, the moment I try to freeze in my mind is Mom's reaction to my wedding tango. It was the last time I witnessed a look of unbridled pleasure on her face.

As so often is the case, what I see most clearly comes only in retrospect: it took my writing about Mom's dancing, and my own, to realize that as she did at her fiftieth birthday party, so too did I at my wedding. We are so much more alike than I had ever understood.

ON A RECENT spring day—procrastinating when I was supposed to be writing—I logged into an e-mail account that I infrequently check. In it was a promotional blast from the Alvin Ailey American Dance Theater touting its Ailey Extension program. "Real classes for real people," it promised. The offerings included a Latin-influenced fitness class, West African dance, and ballet. I scanned the list and I saw this: "Hip Hop—Learn upbeat choreography to the beats of today's hottest songs."

Every day I receive dozens of e-mails from companies and organizations promoting their products in the hope that I will write about them. Frankly, I delete a lot without even opening them. I don't know why or how this one from Alvin Ailey caught my eye.

A few weeks later, I headed to Ailey's headquarters near Lincoln Center and paid $17 for a hip-hop lesson. I'm in fairly decent shape and try to work out a few times a week. But I'm not very hip, and I'm even less hip-hop. Yet after I rolled my eyes through Mom's performance on her fiftieth birthday and refused to get excited about the funky moves she learned from Chris, taking a dance class felt like an important thing to do.

In a state-of-the-art studio—mirrors extending from floor to ceiling, barres lining the walls, wood floor scuffed by dancing shoes—I stood at the very back. I was one of about thirty women (and two men). I wore black shorts, a turquoise tank top, and sneakers. I wasn't the oldest person there. I prefer to think of myself as second-to-least-youngest.

The teacher's name was Tweetie. She wore sweatpants that were baggy throughout the legs but fitted at the waist. Her New York Yankees baseball cap was obscured, but for the brim, by the hood of a gray zip-up sweatshirt that had a rhinestone dog on the back. The cap sat low on her head. If she had eyes, I wouldn't know it. The music came on. It was loud. Like, really loud. Like, I thought for sure it was a mistake, and that Tweetie was going to race over to the stereo to turn it way down in a rush of apologies. But she just started stretching. She oozed cool. (I oozed old.)

Everyone in the class got down on the ground and started mimicking Tweetie's warm-up moves: we stretched our hamstrings, we shimmied our shoulders. The song "Can't You See" by Biggie Smalls blasted from an iPhone that was plugged into the sound system (No, silly, I didn't recognize a Biggie Smalls song—I'm way too uncool for that—but I asked the DJ about it after class). Tweetie started taking two steps forward and two steps back, again and again. Her knees would bend deeply and she'd crouch her torso low over the thighs. "Pretend you're trying to creep into a room without being noticed," she hollered over the music. We tiptoed forward; as we took our steps backward, we leaned away from the front of the room and threw our hands up as if to say, "It wasn't me!" I say "we" did this, but what I mean is, most everyone in the studio did it, and I tried to do it. It was hard! I was creeping forward and "It's not me!"–ing back, and my body was stiff where it was supposed to be flexible, and it was flexible where it was supposed to be stiff. I looked ridiculous, and I couldn't have cared less. It was so much fun. I felt *joyful*. From the back of the room, I caught a glimpse of myself in the mirror. I had a massive grin on my face. I willed myself to stop smiling—just to see if I could do it. I couldn't.

In the moment, I thought about how thrilled Mom would have been to see me taking this class. I felt her presence in me. It was like I was her host in some sort of spiritual way—I was only dancing so she could dance. It sounds all Whoopi-Goldberg-in-*Ghosts*, I know. But that's how it seemed. I physically felt my mom's elation.

But then I started thinking about how much Mom would have loved to attend these classes. The Ailey Theater is a few blocks away from the studio where her Pilates guru taught, and right across the street from her favorite restaurant in New York. Several times a year she would have come to the city to visit, and would have spent most days doing Pilates, taking a lesson from Tweetie, and then meeting Joe and me for pizza and spaghetti at Fiorello. "I study hip-hop at Alvin Ailey with Tweetie," she would tell people, very serious and proud.

When Tweetie called a break, I crouched in the corner, pretending to look for water in my purse. The music muffled my sobs.

AFTER CLASS, I needed a chance to digest the emotional boomerang that had come at me. So rather than hopping on the subway, I walked uptown through the muggy evening. I felt joy in knowing how much it would please my mom that I was taking a dance class. And I felt sadness in knowing how much my mom would have loved to take such a class herself. The sweetness of the experience was connected to the bitterness. I couldn't have felt one without the other. It occurred to me that sometimes bittersweetness might be as much as a person reasonably can hope for.

I was hungry after the rigorous workout, so I stopped at a pizza place for a slice. As I munched, I read a gossip column that had been clipped from the newspaper and taped to the countertop.

I took as a sign of progress that one moment I could be thinking such Big Heavy Thoughts—and the next, I'd be texting my friend Liz to tell her that I was eating pizza where Madonna just recently had done the same.

Chapter Five

She Wore Missoni to Her Biopsy

In March 2003, when Mom woke up from her surgery at Tucson Medical Center, Lizzie and I were next to her bed in post-op, and we were wearing ridiculous, massive, shit-eating grins. Our stepmom, Carolyn, has been a nurse forever, and she told us that it's comforting for patients to see teeth upon rousing after an operation—that in a post-anesthetic haze, teeth connote smiles, and smiles connote You're Alive.

Things had been pretty glum in the days leading up to the surgery. A man we took to calling "Dr. Doom" had told us that a scan indicated that the cancer might have spread to the left lung. The spot on the left side was precariously located near an artery, making a biopsy—let alone surgery—very risky. "Inoperable," he said.

Some doctors seem to take the approach that since lung cancer is so deadly, staging an aggressive fight is a waste. We thought the life of our vibrant fifty-seven-year-old mother was worth fighting for, despite this doctor's flippant pessimism. So we found an oncologist we loved, Dr. Robert Brooks. He said that if Mom wanted to wage a battle, he'd help her.

Dr. Brooks hooked us up with a surgeon, Dr. Douglas Lowell. Handsome and intense, Dr. Lowell sat down with us in his office and gave us a no-bullshit assessment. He saw the same spot on the scan that led Dr. Doom to suppose the cancer had spread. He agreed it couldn't be biopsied easily, not without cutting Mom open. And he agreed that if, in fact, the cancer had spread, surgery wasn't called for. But he offered this compromise: he would take Mom into surgery, cut open her left side, and perform an expedited biopsy that would have a high-but-not-100-percent accuracy rate. If that biopsy showed that the spot appearing on the X-ray was *not* cancer, he would sew her up, flip her over, open up her right side, and remove the tumor we all knew for certain *was* cancer.

The day of the surgery, a big crowd sat nervously in the waiting room at Tucson Medical Center: Lizzie and me, Bob. Jimmy. Uncle Eddie and his wife, Teresa. Lots of people Mom had taught Pilates to. When a nurse approached us after about two hours to say that the quick results from the biopsy on the left side had come back negative and that Dr. Lowell was about to operate on Mom's right lung, we exploded, cheering and crying and carrying on amid other clusters of families who probably were annoyed and wishing that we would quiet down. We would come to learn waiting-room etiquette—one tenet being, you don't flaunt your good fortune. We didn't understand that yet. But even if we had known the rules, I'm not sure we could have abided by them. Our response was instinctual, guttural, uncontrolled, and uncontrollable.

About four hours later, Dr. Lowell came out to the waiting room to let us know that he had removed a lobe of Mom's right lung. The tumor was massive, but he got it all.

So when Lizzie and I were crowding around Mom in the recovery room, with its beds lined up right out of a scene from *M*A*S*H*, we had a lot to be glad about. That's a big help when you're trying to freeze your face in a cheek-flexing, teeth-clenching, jaw-locking smile. When Mom's eyes fluttered open, Lizzie and I began to dart the good news at her in happy, smiley, short strokes: "Mom, you did great!" "The biopsy was negative!" "They took out the tumor on the right!" "The margins were clear!" "The lymph nodes looked good!"

We were spouting medical jargon we barely understood, attempting to engage Mom in some sort of cogent conversation. She wasn't up to it; she lay there impassively—or, some might say, postoperatively—fighting to keep her eyes open.

Then, for a moment, she seemed to gather herself. Her eyes looked like they were getting oriented to the room. She turned her head and aimed her glance up at Lizzie. My sister and I took a sharp breath and held it. We were anticipating a deep proclamation from a woman who was just told her life had been saved.

This is what Mom said: "I wore Missoni to my biopsy."

SO HERE IS the backstory: The morning of the operation, Lizzie had grabbed a sweater from Mom's closet to keep her warm against the anticipated chill of the waiting room's A/C. The buttonless Missoni cardigan was in a signature style of the Italian label, famous for its bold, patterned knits. It was the same sweater Mom apparently had worn about a month earlier when she first had the lung biopsy that led to her cancer diagnosis.

Under the influence of the anesthetic, Mom made a simple identification: she saw the sweater and connected it to the moment when it last had been worn. I'm not saying that when coherent, Mom thought the most memorable part of having a growth in her lung biopsied was that she had arrived at the hospital turned out in Missoni. Yet in her drugged state, that's the first place she went. It signaled to me that, subconsciously, Mom cataloged events in her life by what she was wearing.

MOM WASN'T SOMEONE who liked to spend a day at the mall. Not at all. Shopping in all but a few favored boutiques made her tired and cranky. But clothes mattered a lot to Mom.

She wasn't about looking overly done or trendy. She dressed quite casually, more frequently than not. Still, she liked using clothes and jewelry to express her moods—she had sporty stuff (yoga pant upon yoga pant), youthful stuff (tight, tight, tight jeans), funky stuff (Vivienne Tam mesh tops), and plenty of options for when she felt she needed to look like a demure grown-up (Jil Sander suits). She liked to look pretty, and clothes helped her do that. She didn't dress for others as much as she did for herself. I think she saw fashion as a creative outlet.

When she was young, Mom's pull toward fashion impacted some of her most formative relationships, notably with her mother, Charlotte. Having grown up in the poverty of the 1930s, Charlotte looks at "things" for their utility and function. A shoe shouldn't be about "Who made it?" or "Do you have a purse to match?" To Grandma Charlotte, what matters is "How long it will last?" and

"Is it very comfortable to walk in?" This philosophical difference didn't result in some huge schism in Mom and Grandma's relationship. But it was, in fact, a philosophical difference.

There was no such disparity in approach between Mom and *her* grandma—Charlotte's mother, Rose Wyman. They were very close, and fashion cemented that closeness. "Grandma Rose was Suzy's clothier," Uncle Eddie explained to me. "Grandma always talked about how beautiful Suzy was. She loved that Suzy looked the way she looked, and she bought her all the things our mother wouldn't buy." When my mom wanted something and her parents said no, she went to her grandma. "Grandma Rose would always say, 'Honey, go do it,' " Eddie said. While Mom's relationship to her grandma wasn't merely superficial—they were extremely emotionally connected until Rose died in the early 1980s—they certainly bonded over "girly-girl" stuff that was of less interest to Grandma Charlotte.

Mom wanted everyone around her to look good. Before she had daughters to dress, she played the role of stylist for Eddie. In 1965, when he was about to enter eighth grade at an elite prep school in suburban Boston, Eddie told his mom that he wanted a pair of expensive penny loafers to fit in with the other boys at school. Grandma Charlotte refused, telling her son, "Your feet are still growing, so I'm not buying you expensive shoes." At the time, my mom was back in Boston before returning to Ann Arbor for the school year. "Eddie," she said, "get in the car." She took him to Brooks Brothers in downtown Boston and bought him a pair of Bass Weejun penny loafers for $19. "That was a lot of money for shoes in those days," Eddie said. "I don't know how she had the money."

After she graduated from the University of Michigan and married my dad, Mom moved with Dad to New York City so he could take grad-school classes at Columbia University. Mom helped to support them by landing a job as a secretary at Lehman Brothers on Wall Street. As she liked to tell the story, she was the extra in the pool of partners' secretaries. No, they didn't hire Mom for her typing. She was more of a front-of-the-office presence: a young, pretty, educated married girl who greeted the clients before meetings. Once, Lehman's managing partner had to leave town on the opening night of the New York City Metropolitan Opera. He gave his fifth-row center tickets to Mom. She and Dad got dressed up: Dad in a tuxedo, Mom in a black Audrey Hepburn cocktail dress. At the time, Dad's younger brother, my uncle Hank, was in New York, visiting from Cambridge, Massachusetts, where he was attending Harvard University. Hank put on a suit and played the chauffeur, driving Mom and Dad to Lincoln Center from their rent-controlled sublet at the corner of West Ninety-third Street and West End Avenue. Neither Dad nor Hank recall with certainty what car they drove in. But it might have been the 1960 Plymouth Valiant that my great-aunt Adele sold to Uncle Hank in the late 1960s for a buck.

There is a photograph of Mom and Dad from that night: Dad is impossibly young and handsome. Mom, with her hair piled high and her strand of pearls falling primly around her neck, is stunning. Her dress is sleeveless and perfectly tailored—the sort of dress that looks timeless and smart and makes other women feel foolish for having spent so much more on trendy frocks they'll never again wear. When I was a little girl, I would look at that photo and imagine the night when my mom was the most beautiful woman at the opera.

After their year in New York, Mom and Dad moved into Lafayette Park, an apartment complex in the Mies van der Rohe Residential District in downtown Detroit. Mom's serious interest in fashion took root in a little boutique called Hattie that was run out of a historic farmhouse in a suburb about half an hour north of the city. Hattie was a threadbare space with a closet used as a dressing room, opened by a woman then called Hattie Belkin. The store didn't have much in the way of staff, so customers who stopped by would help her cart big cardboard boxes of inventory from the back porch into the "store." My mom would come by at least once a week. Even though she just bought something now and then, she'd stay for hours, trying everything on. "Your mother understood fashion in a fundamental way," Hattie told me. "She was one of the best dressed women in Detroit."

Many women who were born in the mid-1940s were married by the mid-1960s and thus missed out on the explorations of freedom that marked the hippie culture of the late 1960s and early 1970s. Born in 1944, my mom grew up in the genteel 1950s. Throughout college, she lived a preppie kilt-and-penny-loafers existence. She was married in 1966 and pregnant in 1968. There wasn't a lot of pot-smoking and bra-burning for her. So some women of Mom's age (and class) started to experiment with feminism and freedom through fashion. Designers like Yves Saint Laurent were pushing the conventions of what was appropriate for women—offering women pantsuits and other male-inspired fashions that were a break from tradition. Previously, it had been unusual for a woman to wear pants in any way other than casually, around the house or among friends.

Hattie jumped headlong into what she rightly saw as a burgeoning market to service these women. She was born in Brooklyn in 1943, and after attending college at New York University, she landed a job at the United Nations. One night out on the town, she met a handsome doctor from Michigan. At twenty-five, she moved to Detroit to be with him; they married and had two daughters.

Many women in suburban Detroit who didn't need to work didn't. Hattie wanted a career, though. When she took note of the money flowing through the area—and the fact that local women were flying to New York and Europe in order to buy high-end fashion—she decided to bring New York and Europe to them. She recruited as a partner Linda Dresner, a housewife whose fashion experience was mostly limited to modeling clothes on the floor of Bonwit Teller and other local department stores. Together, they turned Hattie into a cutting-edge boutique. The store was among the first in the Midwest to carry designers like Giorgio Armani, Yves Saint Laurent, and Sonia Rykiel.

Linda and Hattie's foray into fashion was well timed. After the riots of the late 1960s and the subsequent white flight, Detroit's suburbs were flush with cash. In the early and mid-1970s, the auto industry was booming; a lot of people were making and spending lots of money. Detroit was hurt by the oil crisis of the late 1970s. But upper-middle-class suburban Detroit still enjoyed prosperity well into the 1980s and beyond. Nowhere was this prosperity felt more keenly than in a handful of suburbs that abutted one another, among them West Bloomfield, Bloomfield Hills, and Birmingham.

In and around cities like New York and Chicago, a stereotype paints women from the suburbs as provincial and uncultured in comparison to their city-living counterparts. But in the metro Detroit area, that is false. The city's upper middle class was almost completely nonexistent by the 1980s—nearly everyone with money (and nearly everyone who was white) was in the suburbs. In Birmingham and Bloomfield Hills, and other suburbs in metro Detroit, there were trendy stores, fancy restaurants, chic nightclubs, well-funded museums and cultural institutions. There were true sophisticates—people living on the vanguard of art, culture, and fashion.

"Everyone would go out on Saturday nights, and they got *dressed*," Hattie said. "Whatever the women bought from us that week, they would wear. It was very glamorous. We knew who was going where, and we made sure no two women wore the same outfit."

In this milieu, the business thrived. By 1975, Hattie and Linda had moved the store to Birmingham, to the cool shopping district that attracted both destination shoppers and those who came to stroll by the windows of all the specialty stores selling home furnishings, expensive knickknacks, and clothes.

In the 555 Building on Old Woodward Avenue, the boutique really took off. Most of the regular clientele had store accounts. They would come in and pick out a few outfits, and the bills would be sent home to their husbands. "No cash changed hands. No one ever asked the price of anything," Hattie said. "We just couldn't keep enough in the store."

She did a lot to keep her customers happy. When women overspent, and feared their husband's wrath, sales clerks would send a portion of the bill home and then spread the remaining amount among a slew of credit cards. The store even indulged various neuroses and naughty habits of its clientele: one well-to-do kleptomaniac seemed to get a kick out of buying several thousand dollars' worth of clothes and stealing several thousands' worth more. Hattie and the sales clerks let her walk out of the boutique with the stolen goods shoved into her purse—and then they would simply send a bill to the woman's husband. "Detroit, at the time at least, was a lot like Peyton Place," Hattie told me.

Hattie knew the dirt. Plenty of men underwrote both their wives' and their mistresses' shopping excursions. Hattie would send a wife's bill to the house and a mistress's bill to the office. She was discreet. Why wouldn't she be? Infidelity would make one source of revenue double into two. Once, a wife came into the boutique a day after her husband's mistress had gone on a wild shopping spree. The wife looked at a blouse and said, "I just can't spend so much money!" Hattie recalled. "You wanted to slap her and ask, 'Do you have any idea how much the other one spends?'"

Hattie, the store, was something of a club, and Hattie, the woman, was sometimes forced to operate as a maître d'. She told me that my paternal grandmother, Mae Rosman, used to come into the store and bitch about my mom when she and my dad were still married. And Mom would complain to Hattie that she felt like Gran didn't like her. Once, when Mom was trying on clothes, Hattie spotted Gran pulling into the parking lot. Hattie said, "Suzy, your mother-in-law is coming in! Hide!" Mom stayed in a closet during Gran's forty-five-minute stay.

I learned all of this when I met with Hattie in Palm Beach, Florida, where she now lives. We sat first next to the pool at the waterfront home of an old friend of hers from her Detroit days. Then we moved on to her sprawling apartment atop the tony Worth Avenue shopping district. Hattie is now in the purse business, and there were dozens of sleek clutches in her living room. On the wall was a drawing of her that, to judge the hot pink accents around the face, was done in the late 1970s or early 1980s. As she smoked one Marlboro Red after another, Hattie and I had a wonderful talk about her career highs and lows, and about my mom. She hadn't seen or spoken to my mom more than once or twice in probably twenty-five years. And she only knew her in the context of the boutique. But she obviously had been paying attention.

We talked a lot about Mom's style. "Your mom had an appreciation for clothes," Hattie said. "It was like having a passion for art. She loved trying things on. Her style was offhand. She liked to look as if she didn't try hard. It did help that she was so beautiful and had such a great figure. She liked a casual look. One that appeared she hadn't put much thought or time into it." Hattie mentioned that Mom loved Sonia Rykiel. I described to Hattie a Rykiel sweater of Mom's: pink, with a black tie around the neck. Hattie knew just what I was talking about. "She bought one in every color," she said.

By the time the store moved to Birmingham—and, not incidentally, by the time Mom had gotten married to my stepdad—she was at Hattie's a lot. "She was one of our best customers," Hattie told me. It's a distinction, I imagine, Bob might have preferred that Mom not earn.

For customers like Mom, Hattie and Linda would maintain specially designated bins and racks in the back of the store. When inventory that they thought Mom might like came into the stockroom, they set it aside. When she "popped in," as she so frequently did, someone would bring the earmarked clothes into a dressing room. Mom bought what she liked. What she discarded was then put out on display for other shoppers to consider. (How much money might she spend in a given month or year? I asked a number of times. "A lot," is all Hattie would say. *"A lot."* As much as I wanted an answer, I appreciated Hattie's instinct to protect a customer's secrets.)

As I was packing up my notebook and getting ready to leave Hattie's apartment, she stopped me. "Let me ask you one question," she said. "Did your mom have friends?"

That's quite a question. "Tell me why you ask," I said.

"Your mom always came in by herself," she said. "Really, no one else did. Most women came in groups. They would go to lunch and then come to the store. Everyone needed to know what everyone else thought about how they looked. 'Does this look good on me?' 'Do I look fat?' But not your mom."

Hattie's comments really struck me. Essentially, she was saying two things: first, that Mom had a lot of self-confidence—but also that Mom was alone a lot.

"She was very close to a handful of women in Detroit," I said, "and she stayed really close to about three of them until she died. But I do think she was something of a loner when she lived in Michigan."

Hattie shrugged her shoulders. "Maybe. But I always liked that about your mom," she said. "She didn't need anyone's approval."

That's one way to look at it. But I felt a little sad. Mom didn't fit into suburban Detroit, and even the woman selling her clothes knew it.

SO THE WOMEN who lived in suburban Detroit were more sophisticated than stereotypes of suburban women might suggest. Still, they also could be insular, cliquish, and narrow-minded.

Lizzie and I longed for Mom to insinuate herself into the circle of friends formed by the parents of our classmates. Many of them grew up in and around Detroit and had known each other for years and years. Mom never felt totally comfortable in their midst. She often felt they shunned her. When she decided around 1986 to start Suzanne's Kitchen, a dessert catering business, she organized a tasting at our house, inviting all the mothers of my school friends. Mom planned the event for weeks—scrubbing the floors, filling each room with flowers, and slaving in the kitchen for hours and hours to create a couple of dozen beautifully presented cakes, pies, and sweet delicacies.

No one showed up.

I remember coming home from school that day.

"How'd the tasting go, Mom?" I asked.

"It didn't," she said. Then she went into her room and shut her door. I didn't see her again until the morning. I was about fourteen years old, and I was devastated for her. I longed for her to share her sadness with me, to let me snuggle her and say, "I love you." But instead she closed herself off. To this day, I find the whole dessert-tasting incident an excruciating memory. When I try to imagine how she might have felt, I am crushed.

To be sure, I think Mom bore some responsibility for her outsider status: her occasional awkwardness could be misinterpreted as aloofness. There were certainly times when Mom didn't try that hard to make nice with the parents of Lizzie's and my contemporaries.

We frequently shopped for groceries at a market in a shopping center with the very creative name Shopping Center Market. Getting a good parking spot was a big focus of Mom's. Often, on the way to the store, Lizzie and I would see Mom moving her hand oddly, as if she were writing, despite the fact that she wasn't holding a pen.

"What are you doing?" Lizzie asked once.

"Reiki," Mom responded, referring to a Japanese method of meditation. "I'm doing Reiki for parking spots."

Outside Shopping Center Market was arguably the greatest parking spot in the history of suburban shopping malls. It was in the very front of the lot, just a few steps from the store's entrance. Yet it wasn't designated handicap. We called it "the special spot."

Rather than parking in the nearest spot that she could find and taking a forty-five-second walk to the door, Mom would drive around the parking lot for five or ten minutes—loop after loop—waiting for a great spot.

Following this exact protocol (Reiki and then fifteen circles around the parking lot), one day, when I was accompanying her on a trip to the market, she landed the special spot. After shopping, she and I were loading the grocery bags into her trunk when a man started shouting at us from a few spots away. "You parked in a handicapped spot!"

Mom ignored him and continued transferring bags from her cart into her car.

I recognized him, and she did too. The father of boys who attended the same school as I did, he was an attorney who frequently advertised on television. This was well before DVR technology allowed viewers to skip TV commercials, and this guy seemed to blanket the airways, soliciting business from anyone involved in any incident that could potentially be blamed on someone else.

He continued to call out to us: "You parked in a handicapped spot. You should be ashamed of yourself!" Other people were craning their necks to see what the commotion was all about. It was embarrassing.

Finally, Mom turned toward his car and in a voice loud enough to be heard miles away, screamed, *"It's not a handicapped spot, you fucking ambulance chaser!"* The lawyer rolled up his window in a huff and drove off.

What a delicate rose, my mom.

Mom initially built her social life in the suburbs around the country club and golf. But she gave up the sport when I was a preteen and grew even more socially adrift and lonesome.

During my junior year of high school, Mom and Bob bought a small condo in Tucson. Mom began traveling there more and more—spending her time with her parents and brothers. There, she busied herself with two pursuits: hiking in the mountains and taking dance lessons.

I busied myself with having parties when she and Bob were both out of town. Once, in an effort to clean up after a particularly raucous bash, I went room-to-room at around one in the morning looking for stray beer cans. In the guest bedroom, I found so much more: a friend of mine was riding the stationary exercise bike while a member of the varsity football team lounged in bed, watching TV. Shortly thereafter, my friend threw up all over the bedroom carpet. The football player and I tossed her into the bathroom, where she puked more and then passed out for the night.

Not surprisingly, my friend—we'll call her Julia—returned home in the morning to a frantic and angry mother who wanted to know why she had stayed out all night. Julia told her mother that she had had "two sips of a wine cooler" at my party and then fell asleep while watching a movie at another friend's house.

Mom and Bob returned home from Tucson later that evening. Because of the vomit on the carpet, I had to come up with some feasible explanation. Even with the irrefutable evidence left on the carpet, I told Mom that I had had a few friends over, and that Julia had arrived at our house already drunk. I swore to Mom that no alcohol had been consumed in our house.

But calamity struck: the phone rang, and it was Julia's mother (let's call her Nance) calling for my mother. My mom and Nance were not friends. During the height of Mom's depression, I had confided in Nance my anxieties about her—something I never told my own mom I had done. Ever after, Julia's mom treated mine with disdain and sanctimony. Mom couldn't bear her—and she motioned for me to pick up an extension of the phone to listen to the call.

"Hi, Suzy, it's Nance," she said. "I have some things to tell you, from one mother to another."

"Yes?" Mom replied, archly.

"Well," Nance continued, "from one mother to another, I think you should know that Katie had a huge party last night, and she was serving alcohol to everyone"—not true: as a teenager, you don't share your alcohol; it's too hard to come by—"and there were orgies going on in every room"—again, not true: with all the Quarter Bounce, who had time to fool around?—"and Julia had two sips of a wine cooler and left. I just thought you should know that, from one mother to another."

Have you ever seen someone so mad it looks like their eyes might explode out from their sockets? I have.

"Well, Nance," Mom began, her voice barely containing rage, "from one mother to another, you should know that Katie found Julia riding our exercise bicycle before Julia threw up all over our carpet. And from one mother to another, I thought I'd just let you know that we'll be sending you the cleaning bill."

Nance was silenced. She gathered herself enough to say, "Thank you," and then both women hung up.

Mom turned to me. "You're grounded," was all she said.

Julia and I had put our moms in a terrible situation: they were having a conversation that was based on lies fed to them by their respective daughters. Yet Nance was so righteous, and through my mom's fury, I could see how humiliated she was.

A few weeks later, Mom said to Bob, "When Katie graduates, I'm moving to Tucson. I hope you'll come. But that's where I'll be living."

TEN DAYS AFTER Dr. Lowell removed a third of Mom's lung, she was back in the Pilates studio. I sat on a mat on the floor watching her do a modified workout. She wore blue yoga pants and a tight floral-print tank top that hid the long wound along her side and back. Her hair was pulled back into a ponytail at the nape of her neck. One clump of curls had broken free from the elastic band, and it was stuck to her sweaty face. She had no makeup on—and I know it's a celebrity-profile cliché to say, but she couldn't have looked more beautiful if she were primped and coiffed for a fancy ball.

I had admired Mom's beauty throughout my life.

When I was little, I loved seeing what Mom was going to wear on Wednesday and Saturday nights, which were the nights she and

Bob went out. And when they were out, I loved snooping through Mom's closet, brushing my hand past the silky blouses dangling delicately from a rack and shuffling around the house in open-toed, four-inch high heels. In the top drawer of her built-in drawer set, next to her vanity (all white Formica, it was the 1980s!), Mom kept all her jewelry. This top drawer had a lock. She "hid" the key in the drawer beneath the jewelry drawer, nestled under the balled-up golf socks. Lizzie and I spent a lot of time rifling through the jewelry, holding up diamonds to our not-yet-pierced ears.

I loved having a gorgeous, stylish, slender mom. I never resented her beauty, even as I felt mine didn't equal it. And I never felt jealous of her figure. But I still did blame her for the way I struggled as a teenager and young adult with a negative body image and an emotional relationship with food.

I had my heart broken after a breakup with a high school boyfriend, and for the first time in my life I turned to food for comfort, gaining fifteen pounds the summer when I was sixteen. I had been away for six weeks at a summer-school program at UCLA. The day I got home, Mom looked at me and said, "I just feel so bad for you." That devastated me.

It made me mad too. What a mean thing for a mom to say! That she expressed such disappointment in me based on something so superficial stung. Wounded and defensive, I decided I could get back at her by getting fatter and dressing in a slovenly way. On Sunday nights, when it was time to go to the country club for dinner, I delighted in coming downstairs dressed in ragged jeans and an untucked, sloppy, oversize shirt. "Ready!" I'd say cheerfully (angrily), enjoying the look on Mom's face as she fought to keep her mouth shut.

She didn't keep her mouth shut when I was putting food in mine. The kitchen was right next to Mom's bedroom, and anytime she heard the pitter-patter of my feet walking into the kitchen, or when she heard the pucker of the refrigerator door opening, she would dash in after me, breathless. "What are you getting into?" she would ask.

We had no junk food in the house (except for crushed Heath Bars that Mom baked with and the ice cream she herself ate each night after dinner), so I was never pigging out on chips and cookies. But if I were making a grilled cheese sandwich, Mom would insist I use fat-free cheese (the sort of thing I referred to in my journal as "phood"). If I wanted a bowl of cereal, she'd suggest a smaller portion. I felt I could never eat without being eyed critically by my mom. I started sneaking food. I would tiptoe into the kitchen and try surreptitiously to take a pint of ice cream upstairs to my room.

In my early college days, I became increasingly nuts about eating in front of people. I felt like everyone was surveying what was on my plate, counting calories, looking at my double chin. I'd starve myself all day, consuming massive quantities of cigarettes and diet Coke. Then I would be so hungry at night that I would stuff myself, always on the stealth, with crap food that I consumed furtively, quickly, and with self-hatred. It was a dark time in my life, and I blamed my mom.

But when I turned twenty-one, I had something of an epiphany in which I realized I could reasonably blame my parents for a whole lot . . . but then I would be spending all my time being angry about my past rather than looking to my future. It took several years, but I pulled myself out of the grip of body-obsession.

Throughout most of my twenties, Mom and I took an annual trip together, just the two of us. For a number of years, we went to Park City, Utah, and hiked amid the wildflowers.

On July 15, 1997 (I remember it was the day Gianni Versace was murdered), Mom and I had a truly honest conversation while hoofing it up a trail. I wasn't angry. She wasn't defensive.

I said, "You made me feel ugly and like I had to sneak food so you wouldn't be disappointed in me."

She said, "I could see you punishing yourself with food, and I wanted you to stop."

She said, "I am so, so sorry."

She said, "You and your sister are the most beautiful things I've ever seen."

She said, again, "I'm so sorry, sweetheart."

It felt liberating to forgive her. And after I did, the excess pounds started a slow melt. I struggled again for a few years when I first moved to New York City. But it's been a long time since then.

Spending time with Hattie, and, afterward, thinking a lot about Mom's beauty and the role it played in her emotional life, I was finally able to see more than merely a superficial explanation for what I saw as her absolute need for me to be thin. It had a lot to do with her own vanity. But it wasn't merely about that. Mom wanted her daughters to enjoy the special place that attractive people have in our culture. She undoubtedly never considered the cost of her misguided approach. It was about wanting the best for her girls.

I find it revealing that during her Detroit years, Mom believed that beauty and happiness were inextricably linked. As she got older, she overcame a lot of that insecurity, and that was a beautiful thing.

BUYING THINGS, HOWEVER: that remained a passion. (Poor Bob.) In fact, as Mom got sicker, it grew into a coping mechanism she relied on more and more. You didn't have to be Freud to see that she was desperately trying to buy an image of what she wanted her life to be again. The acquisitions represented symbols of wellness, as well as providing her with a sense of control: perhaps she couldn't stop the cells from multiplying, but she could buy that gunmetal gray quilted purse from Chanel.

That's exactly what she did a few days before an operation she was undergoing in New York City in September 2003. She saw the purse advertised in the *New York Times* Sunday Styles section. The purse is, at once, edgy and ladylike. Very Mom. She simply picked up the phone, credit card in hand, and called the Chanel store on Fifty-seventh Street in Manhattan.

Mom had never bought a Chanel purse before. She always told Lizzie it was the sort of thing that represented the apex of style and luxury, something to aspire to. When she saw young women in Michigan wearing fancy furs and big diamond rings, she would say to us, "What does she have to look forward to?" That's how she thought of a Chanel purse: something to look forward to.

When Mom told Lizzie, the day before surgery, that she had called the Chanel store and bought a purse—just like that, as if it were no big deal—it signaled to Lizzie how terrified she must have been. And *that* scared the hell out of Lizzie.

Of course, Mom never addressed it straight out. But I don't

imagine the purchase did much to quell her fear. And I don't think she ever carried the handbag.

A few days before that, Mom and I went out to lunch with one of Mom's best friends, Maxine, and one of Maxine's daughters. After lunch, Mom, Maxine, and I went to Bergdorf's. On a mannequin, Mom spotted a black jersey long-sleeved to-the-floor Michael Kors dress that was ruched along the entire right side. The dress was totally Mom's style: demure in that very little skin showed, but incredibly va-va-voom. Also, it had versatility. I could picture Mom wearing it with high heels and a sparkly red strand around her neck, or paired with a chunky pair of biker boots and a cropped leather jacket. "I'm going to have Bob take me out to dinner in New York one night after I've recovered from surgery, and I'm going to wear this dress," Mom said to me and Maxine. But that night on the town never came.

Several months before she died, there was a Prada incident that reflected the total chaos and lack of control in her life. It was spring of 2005, and every glossy magazine was running ads for an oversize Prada watch—a round timepiece encased in a large plastic bicolored square affixed to a clunky-looking wristband. Mom was obsessed with this watch, agonizing—as she lay in the bed she, by that point, rarely left—as to whether she should buy it or not. I firmly said, "Don't do it." I thought the watch was ugly. But more than that, it was just too trendy. Usually, she preferred not to blend into a crowd.

But she kept obsessing. Finally, she called a Prada boutique. A sales clerk told her that the watches were selling out, and if she wanted one, she'd better buy one soon. This sent Mom into a frenzy. The idea that she might be precluded from owning this watch created all sorts of anxiety for her. She called the store back with her credit card. But for some reason that was never quite clear, they refused to let Mom pay for it over the phone with a credit card. They wouldn't even set it aside for her so that Mom could be sure that no one else would buy "her" watch.

Mom called me from Tucson and said, "You have to go to Prada tonight before it closes and get the watch for me." I was incensed. My whole life was devoted to going to work and flying to Tucson to take care of Mom. Now I was expected to dash out of work and then run all over the city to buy her some ugly, expensive watch? I was furious with Mom for her inability to see past her own crisis, to consider anyone but herself. But I never said any of that to her. Instead, I went to Prada that night and bought the watch. When I brought it to Tucson a few days later, I sat next to Mom as she laid the watch over her bony wrist, all bruised from IVs. Forget her wrist: the watch probably could have fit around her upper arm. She admired it, looking pleased and as though she had no sense of how this watch was swallowing her arm. I had to turn away.

The watch never saw daylight.

Around that time, when packing my bag at the end of a visit to Tucson, I tiptoed into Mom's closet while she slept and took a black Prada sweater set. I didn't ask permission. I just took it. It was not sweater season in Tucson. She wasn't going out, except for doctor appointments. She wasn't wearing much more than sweats and T-shirts when she did. She'll never miss it, I thought.

A few days later Mom called me. Ballistic.

"Did you take my black sweater set?" she asked.

"I borrowed it, yes," I replied.

"How dare you go into my closet and take something without asking permission," she hissed, and for good measure, she added, "You know, I'm not dead yet."

Then she hung up.

It hadn't occurred to me that she might connect my taking her clothes with the fact that she was dying. Stealing clothes from your mom is a part of the very DNA of a mother-daughter relationship, and I was fulfilling my genetic destiny. But my mom saw my sneaking off with her clothes without permission as a sign that I considered her impotent. I returned the sweater set to her closet as soon as I arrived at her house on my next visit to Tucson. But before I did, I wore it to work twice and admired my sophistication every time I gazed in the bathroom mirror. Goddamn right I did. My stealing the sweater set wasn't about cancer, and I wasn't going to be bullied.

HATTIE BELKIN WHITEHEAD and Linda Dresner parted ways in the late 1970s. Neither woman wanted to tell me about the breakup. All Hattie would say was, "It was one of the most painful things to happen to me. Linda was like a sister to me." No one I asked in Michigan remembered the particulars.

Regardless, Hattie went on to have a multifaceted career in retail. She oversaw a few Yves Saint Laurent boutiques, in Michigan, New Jersey, and Arizona. Then there were boutiques in Palm Beach—Krizia and Giorgio Armani. She was tapped as president of Elizabeth Arden for a time, but she found the job too corporate. She returned to the Detroit scene for a while, working to bring her high-end clients to Neiman Marcus. Now she's selling her purses and is an active figure on the Palm Beach scene.

Linda has stayed on a more stable path. After splitting from Hattie, she opened a boutique of her own. Called Linda Dresner, it first opened in a mall in Troy, Michigan. In 1978 it moved to a beautiful, minimalist space right in the walking-shopping district of Birmingham. By 1983, Linda had opened a boutique on Park Avenue in New York City. When she closed it in late 2008, *Women's Wear Daily* profiled Linda, referring to her as a "retail icon." The flagship boutique in Birmingham remains.

Mom was a loyal customer of Linda Dresner. She shopped there all the years she lived in Detroit—and even after: when she moved to Tucson, Linda and other salesclerks just mailed to Mom the things they thought she would like. She kept what she liked and mailed back the rest.

When I wrote to Linda, about three and a half years after Mom died, and said I wanted to talk to her about Mom's relationship to clothes, she called me and said, "Come see me at the store."

On only a few other occasions had I felt such anxiety over what to wear. I wanted to do Mom proud by putting together something stylish and pretty. When I packed my suitcase in New York before heading for Michigan, I narrowed the possibilities to about four different looks. But as I was getting dressed in advance of our meeting, I agonized. The brown V-neck Jil Sander dress was feeling a little too snug. The black pants with the Kristensen du Nord corduroy blazer with distressed seams came across as too dark and New Yorky on this sunny Michigan spring day. I put the brown dress back on and tried to channel Mom's confidence. But I couldn't do it. So I ended up in a no-name but very nice pair of khaki slacks I had bought a few years back in New York with a thin, gauzy white T-shirt and a thin black like-buttah leather jacket that Mom had bought from

Linda a long time ago. One thing I didn't have to worry about was my shoes. I had packed only one pair: my black leather boots. They looked a bit bulky and heavy for the pants I was wearing. But who would notice that when the rest of me looked so cute?

I arrived at the store at about two in the afternoon and walked to the back corner that is, oddly, the focus of the store. Linda was there, looking stylishly disheveled. She was wearing cargo pants and a sweater with big round iridescent sequins sewn on to the bottom. It was an outfit I couldn't have pulled off without looking mismatched. But for Linda, it worked. Her tousled hair was thrown back off her face. Her eyes were so pale blue I tried to catch a glimpse of her eyeballs from the side to see if she was wearing colored contacts. She wasn't.

She was rushing about, thumbing through short stacks of clothes, selecting items for a trunk show she was hosting later that week in New York. But she couldn't have been warmer to me. When I asked if she was too harried to talk, she said, "I am too busy, but I promised you I would do it, so let's do it." I followed her down a staircase to an employees-only area where we sat at a large, modern block of a table.

In her younger days Mom loved the French designers, like Lagerfeld and Sonia Rykiel, but in her fifties she became more taken with minimalist looks. "She was attracted to Jil Sander, which is all about classic lines and refinement," Linda said. "And she loved the Japanese designers, with their elegant silhouettes. She was perfect for them. Her demeanor was serene and quiet." (Unless you pissed her off in a parking lot.)

After we chatted, Linda and I returned upstairs, to the store.

"Why don't you show me some stuff Mom might have liked?" I said. We looked at a few things, including a long blue retro dress that had an empire waist, with a scene from the Sistine Chapel hand-painted upon it. Much more her style was a long grayish green jersey gown by Tuleh. I could envision Mom wearing this to a wedding or a big event. It had three-quarter-length sleeves, a wee bit of a train in the back, and a little sequined sash. It looked like it would cover everything but would fit very snug: modestly revealing. "This dress is for a very confident woman," one of the sales clerks said to me when she saw me admiring the gown. Exactly.

Then I saw something I liked for myself: a gray, menswear-inspired jacket with cap sleeves and two buttons. I tried it on—it cost $1,590; I was just playing dress-up—and turned toward a massive mirror to admire myself.

"I look good!" I said, smiling and rather pleased that I was at Linda Dresner with Linda Dresner, looking sharp.

"Your shoes are wrong for what you're wearing today," Linda said. "They're too heavy."

Oy! Mortified!

"You need a shoe like this," she said, and she walked to another side of the store, grabbed a shoe from its display setting, and brought it back to where I stood, still in front of the mirror but now focusing on my feet. Linda handed me the shoes. They were oxfords—black and white spectator shoes in very pliable leather. They were the absolute most "me" shoes I had ever seen. "Oh, my God," I said, as I flipped them over, looking for a price tag. "Dare I ask how much, or is it a 'If you have to ask you can't afford it' situation?" I said.

"Probably," Linda said. She dispatched a saleswoman to a back room to look up the price. She returned with a sheepish look on her face. "They cost about $700," she said. That's what I consider too heavy.

I hugged Linda and ventured out onto Maple Road. On my way to my rental car, I popped into a casual wear boutique and bought a flouncy white blouse with black polka dots. It cost $32, and it's just my style.

IN 1991, MOM and Bob's house in West Bloomfield burned down. There was a bad thunderstorm one night, and a bolt of lightning struck the fuse box attached to the outside of the house. It was close to midnight, and Mom and Bob were asleep in their bed. The sound of the lightning connecting with the fuse box produced a prodigious crack; Mom woke up before the fire alarm even went off. She smelled smoke and shook Bob awake. He grabbed the phone to call 911, but the line was dead.

They raced outside in their robes and called for help from a car phone. Several fire trucks arrived with their sirens roaring. Standing on the street, surrounded by neighbors, Mom and Bob watched as their home was gutted by fire.

Whatever wasn't completely turned to ash by fire was badly damaged by smoke or by the water from the firefighters' hoses. All of my mom's clothes were destroyed. All the couture, the vintage, the alligator bags and tweedy suits and fancy shoes and beautiful lingerie . . . gone. But I never once heard her bemoan that loss. Not once.

I guess her brand of materialism was sort of Zen: she loved things, but she didn't care about things.

The only loss she mourned was the ring her late grandma Rose had gotten for her fiftieth-wedding anniversary from her husband, Grandpa Barney—a ring that had been passed down to Mom. Mom wore it daily, and the night of the fire, she took it off and laid it, as she always did, on her bedstand. In the chaos, Mom didn't grab it as she raced out of the house.

I was nineteen. Though I was technically on summer break from college, the night of the fire I had been in Ann Arbor with my friends. In the days after the fire, I stayed with Mom and Bob at our neighbors', the Weisbergs. During the day, I hung around the neighborhood with Mom and Bob, who needed to be nearby to deal with the folks from the insurance company. Among the personnel who showed up each day were men who searched the rubble for any surviving items of value. They would take handfuls of ash and run it through a sifter to see if anything was hiding among the ashes. They were very decent guys, and they listened sympathetically as Mom described her grandmother's ring.

At the end of each day, Mom would approach the crew and give them a hopeful, expectant look. They'd shake their heads silently. Mom would drop her head in disappointment.

By the fifth and final day the crew was working though the remains of the house, Mom had pretty well given up on Great-Grandma's ring. As she said good-bye to the crew and thanked them for their hard work, one of the guys reached behind him and said, "Is this of any interest?" as he pulled from his jean's pocket the diamond ring. In their five days of going through the rubble, it was the only thing they found.

Mom wasn't a crier, and I hadn't seen her break down in the

days after the fire. But as the ring was handed to her, she burst into tears. "I'm not crying because my ring was found," she said to me and the guy who found it. "I'm crying because this tells me that my grandma is watching over me."

And now that ring belongs to me.

TOWARD THE END of Mom's life, she was in bed all the time, and she lay in the same position—on her back, supported by a slew of deliberately placed pillows. The back of her head was constantly pushed against a long, firm pillow. As a result, her hair was matted, dreadlock-like, into a massive snarl.

One day I was hanging out next to my mom's bed, surfing the Internet on a laptop while she dozed in and out of drug-induced naps. A nurse's aide, whom Bob had hired, walked in.

She was a very nice, totally well-meaning woman with a rear end a little too big for her white polyester, standard-issue nurse's aide pants. The aide headed toward Mom with a comb in her hand and said, "Oh, *honey*, look at your hair. It looks like a total mess!" She spoke in the tone people use with really old people. Even to me, the comment sounded patronizing.

Mom wasn't able to talk without a lot of effort. But she summoned some energy and very slowly spoke three one-word sentences:

"YOURS," she began.

"LOOKS," she managed.

"WORSE," she said.

It was a great moment. At certain points in a woman's life, there is something about vanity that reflects upon dignity, strength, and hope.

* * *

IN A LARGE nook off their bathroom in Tucson is a closet that Mom and Bob shared. It's not the biggest or fanciest closet I've seen, but it was well designed and allowed for their clothes to be neatly displayed and easily accessible. There was a long rack for Mom's dressy stuff—suits, gowns, long skirts. There was another full-length rack where she hung her jeans and casual pants. There were three racks for shorter pieces—blouses, T-shirts, and sweaters. Running the full height of one wall was a footwear rack where Mom placed her shoes, the nice ones neatly stored in felt bags within the storage slots. In her built-in drawers, she had dividers that allowed her to maintain her exercise wear, bras, and panties meticulously. She had an entire drawer of pristine Cosabella underwear, folded immaculately, as if on display at a lingerie store.

We cleaned out Mom's side of the closet over the course of a year and a half. It took a long time because there was too much stuff and too many emotions to do it all at once. Between Lizzie and me, we tried nearly everything on. Lizzie took a few selected pieces that had a lot of emotional value—the dress Mom wore to her wedding to Dad, the dress Mom wore to my wedding, the famed Missoni sweater. I went for volume: I took pretty much everything I could fit in, including her underwear.

If Mom looked to fashion to help her stand out, she'd appreciate my wearing her clothes to work in the *Wall Street Journal* newsroom. When I need to prepare myself for big days—when I really need to kick ass—I will put on a Jil Sander dress and a piece of Fuck You Jewelry (baubles that are too big for someone of my age and means). Sometimes I look inappropriate. But I always feel powerful and sophisticated and like I've got Suzy Rosin juju pumping through my veins.

On occasion, someone at the paper will admire my too-expensive-for-a-journalist Comme des Garçons suit or the modern, funky ring with a big blue chunky stone in an artsy setting. "That ring is gorgeous," a colleague might say as we're standing in the elevator. I'll then take a coy glimpse of my fabulous ring with self-admiration and say, "It's from the Dead Mother Collection." That usually makes people uncomfortable but it's funny to me somehow.

Nearly any time I dress up, I wear something from the DMC. Most often, it's something she bought from Mark Keller, a Birmingham clothier Mom loved who added a funky element to her wardrobe. I love the purple silky skirt by Rima that is draped like a Roman shade, and the sequined pencil skirt from Collette Dinnigan that I sometimes pair with the sleeveless black silk Dries Van Noten top with the plunging neckline. When I dress fancy, I almost always wear Great-Grandma's diamond ring.

To COMMEMORATE BOTH the second and third anniversaries of Mom's death, Lizzie and I talked with a spiritual medium named Rebecca Rosen. A lot of people I've told of these conversations with Rebecca have looked at me askance or otherwise have been dismissive. That's their right. But I believe in Rebecca's abilities to help me connect with Mom. I guess that's the definition of faith: believing in something not because you can absolutely prove its truth but because it gives you comfort.

Anyway, the second time we talked to Rebecca, she said, "Your mom says that you both are wearing her clothes and her jewelry."

"Yes," Lizzie said, "that's true."

Neither of us were particularly blown away by that assertion: presumably, lots of daughters wear their late mothers' clothes and jewelry. But then Rebecca zeroed in on something specific.

"I'm getting some image of lingerie," Rebecca said. "I think your mom is saying someone is wearing her lingerie, or maybe even her *underwear*. Could that be right?"

"Katie, wanna answer that one?" Lizzie said, amused.

"Um, yeah," I stammered. "I have Mom's underwear and, uh, like, yes, I do. I sometimes do wear them."

Rebecca paused for a moment. Then she said: "Your mom says she thinks that's a little much."

Chapter Six

Bed One Rules

On September 17, 2003, Lizzie and I were curled up spoon-style in a double bed at the Surrey hotel in Manhattan. The phone woke us. It was Bob: "The doctor says Mom may have pneumonia."

Two days before, Mom had part of her left lung removed by a thoracic surgeon at the renowned Memorial Sloan-Kettering Cancer Center in New York City. The tumor was precariously located near an artery.

She had resisted being treated there. If she needed another operation, she had wanted to do it in Tucson, near her home, with doctors she knew and trusted. Her surgeon in Tucson—who had successfully removed the first tumor—told her and Bob that he was willing to consider performing the second, riskier operation, but that they needed to understand the peril. For a second opinion, we all went to meet with a surgeon in New York, someone people flew from all over the world to be treated by. He lacked the warmth of Mom's Tucson surgeon. But he came off as supremely confident. I got the impression that, for him, this operation would be almost routine.

To me it was a no-brainer: if one guy who says he can't promise that the operation will be a success and the other gives the air of invincibility, you go with the second guy. I now see how idiotic I was: there are no guarantees in life, and fewer in Cancerland. Regardless, I was taken with the name-brand reputation of Sloan-Kettering. Mom wasn't so convinced. She believed there was real value in being close to home. And she didn't get a good vibe from the New York surgeon. Despite having been warned earlier by the Sloan-Kettering oncologist who referred him that this surgeon could be gruff, Mom was put off by his demeanor in their first meeting.

"I don't think we connected," Mom said afterward.

I rolled my eyes. This is no time for your touchy-feely bullshit, I wanted to say to her. Instead I said, "You're having the surgery at Sloan-Kettering"—as if I made the rules, as if I were the boss, as if I had all the answers. And then I pressured Lizzie and Bob to help me pressure Mom into caving. They did. And then she did.

A few days before the surgery, Mom had a meeting with the surgeon, Dr. Toppen, in an examination room at the hospital. He was nearly an hour late for the appointment, which he then rushed through—quickly telling Mom he'd be removing the majority of her left lung's bottom lobe. Just before Dr. Toppen raced back out of the room, Mom had a question: "After the surgery, um, how will my breathing be?" she asked, stumbling for words. "I mean, will I still be able to dance?"

Dr. Toppen's eyes narrowed and darkened. "You're worried about dancing?" he asked, his voice icy and incredulous. "You're lucky I'm willing to operate on you at all," he said before storming out of the room.

There was a moment of shocked silence. Then Mom burst into tears. "What'd I do wrong?" she asked. Her jaw started to chatter. "Now he's gonna be mad at me when he's operating on me! What am I gonna do?"

Instantly, I was besieged by guilt for ignoring Mom's concerns about the doctor's bedside manner. It matters, of course it matters! Her mental and emotional state will affect her recovery. It will, of course it will! And here she was, crying and afraid of someone who, in just a few days, would be cutting her chest open.

Mom dashed out of the examination room with Bob and me in tow. She headed for Dr. Toppen, who was making notes on a chart in a hallway. "Can you please forgive me? Please?" Mom pleaded. He nodded. "You need to focus on getting through this surgery," he said.

As much as I hated him in that moment, I forgave him two days later. That's when he walked into the hospital's main waiting room to tell us that Mom's surgery had gone well—the tumor was very deep and hard to access, but he got it all, and the lymph nodes appeared, pending a pathology report, free of signs of metastasis.

Back at my apartment that night, I was relaxed enough to consider matters other than cancer. Like my career. In an entry on a blog I had recently started, I wrote:

> *For the second time in six months, my mom had a malignant*
> *tumor, along with a chunk of her lung, removed.*

She amazes me. She is so tough, so beautiful, so intent on living.

Early in the evening, we had a celeb sighting in the Memorial Sloan-Kettering waiting room: Mort Zuckerman, engaging in some sort of business convo with a similarly dapper man. It was a strange scene: families, like mine, faces tear-stained, bodies exhausted and spread out on uncomfortable chairs amid half-completed crossword puzzles and mostly eaten bags of potato chips. Then there's Mort Zuckerman power-chatting.

Briefly, I wondered if I should approach Mr. Zuckerman, show a little gumption in this venue of grief. I considered introducing myself to him, asking him if he was, in fact, going to buy New York *magazine, at which point I would offer him my unmatched editorial abilities.*

I felt this collision of lives—my pre-My-Mom-Who-Is-the-Cleanest-Living-Person-in-the-World-Has-Lung-Cancer life, when nothing could get between me and my ambition, and my life now, when nothing can get between me and my determination to see my mom through this ghastly disease. My once insatiable thirst for bylines has given way to an impenetrable focus on lifelines—namely a long one for my sweet mama, who has done nothing to deserve the physical and emotional battery she has bobbed and weaved her way through this year.

I'm still there for you, Mr. Zuckerman, should you buy New York. *But more than anything or anyone else, I'm here for you, Mom, you lioness of life.*

* * *

THE DAY AFTER surgery: sweet relief. We spent the day with Mom, in her room on the hospital's fourteenth floor. She was awake and alert.

Lizzie was in the untenable position of being pulled in two very important directions. She had just given birth to her son Michael about six weeks earlier, and rather than nesting with him at home on the West Coast, she had him holed up in a hotel with a babysitter on the East Coast, where her mother was undergoing major thoracic surgery. For two days poor Lizzie had been racing between the hotel on East Seventy-sixth Street, where she would nurse her child, and the hospital off East Sixty-eighth Street, where she would tend to her mother. She had resolved to return back to California with Mikey the following day. And why not? Mom was going to be fine.

That's what Lizzie and I thought, at least, when we went to sleep that night. I had decided to sleep at the hotel with her, and the two of us curled up together like little girls. But then the phone rang.

I would come to dread the ringing of the phone.

AS IT TURNS out, postoperative pneumonia is a relatively common complication after lung surgery (which doesn't mean it's not usually serious, just that when there is a post-op complication, it's often pneumonia). It was really scary. We watched Mom in her hospital bed struggling to breathe, with diminishing success as the day progressed. Her lungs were filling up with fluid. There were even little pockets of liquid bubbling up just beneath the surface of her back. She was getting panicky.

Lizzie would buzz the nurse through the intercom. In a terse voice that betrayed her own terror, Lizzie would say, "My mom can't breathe, can you come here right now, please?" A harried nurse would dash in, turn up the concentration of oxygen filling the mask over Mom's mouth and nose, and fiddle with the tube that had been inserted into her chest to help drain excess fluid. "The ICU is full," the nurse would tell us. "Your mom will be transferred there as soon as there is a bed."

Late that afternoon, a bed became available. I didn't let myself think about what might have happened to result in the sudden vacancy. I was filled with relief that Mom would be getting more specialized attention and care. Quietly, though, I considered the implications. My mom was intensively ill.

A critical-care team came up to her room to collect her. It felt like a scene out of *ER*. There was a rush, an air of urgency. Bob, Lizzie, and I followed her as she was quickly rolled on a gurney to the second floor. Mom was clasping her oxygen mask. Her eyes were wide.

In the ICU, there was a pit crew waiting for her. It was a well-choreographed frenzy: the nurses and doctor moved her from the gurney to the bed and began hooking her up to a wall of machines that beeped and buzzed, hissed and whined. I mostly remember how tiny and fragile Mom looked as she was handled and prodded by a team of gowned, all-business nurses.

They asked us to leave. We told Mom that we loved her, that she was in great hands, and that we would see her first thing in the morning. We left—Lizzie and Bob went back to the hotel. Joe and I returned to our apartment.

There, my phone rang. (Ugh.) It was the resident. "Your mom isn't doing well," she said. "She's very agitated, and we can't do what we need to do. We need you to talk her down. We're going to pass the phone to her right now. Get her to calm down. And then you'd better get here quickly."

The phone was passed to Mom; I heard nothing but a frantic struggle to breathe. It was terrifying.

"Mom," I said, "It's Katie. You need to calm down. Just close your eyes and focus on your breathing. We need to let the doctors do their job. I am going to get in a taxi and come there right now."

I ran—literally sprinted—down the street toward a taxi. Joe ran behind me. We pulled up in front of the hotel; Bob and Lizzie (with Baby Mikey nestled in her arms) hurried in. When we arrived at the hospital, Bob, Joe, and I tore inside, passed security without stopping, took the stairs two at a time to the second floor. Lizzie waited in the lobby, trying to protect her weeks-old son from a hospital's germs.

When we got to the ICU, we could see Mom surrounded by a crew. She looked so tiny amid the bustle. The resident broke away for a second and told us that Mom's breathing had gotten worse. Much worse. They needed to intubate her—meaning they needed to put her on a ventilator by sticking a large tube down her throat and into her air passages. They would also need to medically induce her into a coma. Mom was in a state of panic, the doctor said, and was resisting. They needed permission to medicate her. They needed us to calm her down.

We need to let the doctors do their job, Bob and I told Mom as we crowded around her bedside. We need to follow the doctors' instructions. We need to let them take care of you.

She shook her head. Bob said, "I love you," and ducked away. He was sobbing.

I stood next to Mom, my hand on her shoulder. She pulled her mask away for one moment. "Promise me you won't let me die," she said.

I promised.

WHEN I SET out to report upon Mom's life and write a book about what I learned, I had in mind a very clear focus (on the pockets of her life that I wasn't that connected to) and purpose (to better understand how and why she approached her death as she did). But from the very beginning, I felt drawn to revisit the circumstances surrounding Mom's coma. Ironically, it was an experience that only peripherally involved Mom. In fact, it was the first time Bob, Lizzie, and I experienced what life might be like without Mom, how our dynamic might operate without her at the center. We were allowed to emote openly, speak freely—to focus on our own devastation, our own exhaustion, our loss.

Sitting in the waiting room, sampling a reality without her in it, I felt a strange combination of emptiness and rage. For the first time, I realized that the situation with Mom wasn't going to work out so neatly, that "She worked out ten days after her first surgery and is cancer-free!" was no longer our narrative, that it wouldn't become that again.

Against the backdrop of that hopelessness appeared a doctor who gave me a sliver of hope—an offhanded remark, the sort of thing that can give an unexpected, even unintentional, soul-saving boost. The doctor said, "I know how you feel"—signaling to me something that at the time seemed unthinkable: that people before us had experienced this, that people have the capacity not just to overcome loss, but to transcend it.

When I think back upon that brief interchange in the ICU

waiting room so many years later—as I try to make sense of my need to revisit that experience and to reconnect with that doctor—I realize that my journey isn't just about what happens when a person dies. It's about how those left behind survive their sadness, or at least, find a way to live their way through it.

IF A HOSPITAL is a self-enclosed community, a biosphere that operates separate from the world outside its walls (and it is that), then an intensive care unit is a subculture within a subculture. When you spend a lot of time there, you don't know the day of the week, if it's night or morning, what's going on at the office or in the lives of your friends, what the president is up to, what happened on *American Idol*. It's a bubble. It has its own hierarchies. And there are rules that don't make sense, laws that you are powerless to impact. For instance, every week in the ICU, good people, young people, and people who have taken care of themselves die.

In the fall of 2003 at Memorial Sloan-Kettering, the ICU was a dizzying swirl of people who would never otherwise intersect. There were hardened doctors and harried nurses. There were emotionally raw visitors trying to make sense of beeping machines, insurance forms, and dire prognostications. And there were mostly comatose people of varying ages lying in the unit's twenty beds. Mom was in Bed One.

There was a reason it wasn't called "Room One." It wasn't a room. It was a bed surrounded by machines in a narrow space—and it was separated from Bed Two on one side and from the nurses' station on another by a hanging sheet with a tropical scene printed upon it.

Technically speaking, ideally speaking, it was a place of healing. But Mom wouldn't have seen it that way if she were conscious. So Lizzie and I tried to incorporate elements that we believed were important to Mom's overall wellness. We bought a little CD player with speakers, and we played a constant stream of classical music in the hope of drowning out the mind-numbing white noise of the heaving ventilator, the beeping monitors, the mechanical doors to the unit that opened and shut, opened and shut, all day and night. To various surfaces, we attached with Scotch tape and straight pins photographs of Mom from when she looked healthy—at my wedding and at Zack's second birthday party, where she climbed into the bouncy house with ten sugar-crazed toddlers. We wanted to force the staff to see that they were treating more than another body in Bed One.

Mom had a very bad case of pneumonia, "the worst we've seen in probably five years," the doctors told us a few times. That's never the sort of distinction you want to hold. Whether or not she was going to live became a day-to-day—sometime hour-to-hour—question. The ventilator was doing all of the breathing for her. And the induced coma shut her body's energy exertion to a minimum. The doctors wanted all of her energy to be directed to building an immuno-response to the pneumonia. She lay there motionless, but for the mechanized heaving of her chest.

Lizzie, Bob, and I—and an ever-changing cast of relatives and friends who rotated in and out, flying to New York from around the country in support of us—were at the hospital about eighteen hours a day. Among the people who spent the most time with us were my dad and his wife, Carolyn, who flew in from Michigan repeatedly during the ordeal. When Mom became even more ill

on the day that would have been her and my dad's wedding anniversary, I pointed this out to Dad. "Maybe as a final 'Fuck you,'
she'll die on your anniversary," I said to him. We both thought
that was pretty funny.

Day after day, Lizzie, Bob, and I held Mom's hand. We sat
in an uncomfortable chair next to her bed staring at the stock-
photo tropical beach scene. As the days turned into weeks, and
when the nurses weren't watching, Lizzie and I would pull out a
tweezer and pluck Mom's brows, because a gal still needs her arch
even when she's in a coma. We said prayers over electric Shabbat
"candles" on Friday nights. We sang her favorite disco songs.

We could handle the heavy emotion that came from sitting
bedside only for so long, so we spent a lot of time in the designated ICU waiting room right outside the unit. It was a boot-
shaped space, drab and institutional in feel. A TV was mounted
high up on one wall. With the volume muted, it flickered images
from *Jerry Springer* and soap operas as the families sitting beneath
it lived their own. On a desk by the stairwell, two computers were
set up for the use of waiting-room denizens. We rotated turns
checking our e-mail. Long obsessed with food, Bob busied himself by absorbing every word in a Zagat guide to New York City
restaurants that my friend Rachael had bought for him. ("You
see, this place has a 25 for service, but the decor is only a 19," he'd
say while pointing to a listing.) I did a lot of crossword puzzles
and downed a lot of Diet Dr Pepper. In lieu of eating, I nourished
myself with the countless pills I found in a black canvas makeup
bag in Mom's purse. If it was morning, it must be time for half a
Ritalin. Mid-afternoon, Xanax took some of the edge off. Before
bed, I'd partake of a little Clonazepam, unless I had drunk too

much wine. I tried to be responsible in my irresponsible pill-popping.

We sat in that ICU waiting room long enough to see a number of families come and go. With no privacy afforded any of us, grief was expressed publicly and pain became communal. The Catholic mother of a seventeen-year-old boy who had just recently been diagnosed with cancer and whose condition deteriorated quickly would pray loudly for her son's liver function to normalize—she'd repeat the term *bilirubin* frequently, and any time I've heard it since, I've thought of this woman whose name I never knew. When one morning we arrived in the waiting room and noted her absence, we knew the news was bad. There was another woman of Asian descent who spoke no English. She wailed all day long—just sat in a chair and wailed until her wails became white noise. Then one morning she too was gone.

When new families arrived, I greeted them and tried to prepare them for the oddities that would become normal for them if they stuck around long enough. I don't know why I thought I had been elected mayor of the ICU, but I assumed the mantle. I guess it gave me something to do. We grew close to a few families. There was one family—a lovely group from New Jersey whose mother was in a bed across the unit from Mom's. She had six children, three of whom were waiting-room regulars I grew to know, however briefly.

There was another family—the Lippmans. They were there near the beginning of our tenure. Like ours, their family had two daughters, but Amy and Donna were about ten years older than Lizzie and me. Their dad, Kenny, was a bit older than Bob. Their mom, Lillian, was in the ICU. She had liver cancer. When they knew their mom wasn't going to make it much longer, the three Lippmans approached me, Bob, and Lizzie in the waiting room. "We'd like to give my wife's lungs to your mom," Kenny said. We had previously been told that a transplant wouldn't save Mom. But the offer saved *us*, for at least a moment. Lizzie, Donna, Amy, and I clasped each other, connecting with hands made chapped by frequent use of the hand sanitizer. Bob and Kenny, virtual strangers, held each other and cried—two men of a generation that didn't encourage such displays of emotion, clinging to each other. When your world is crumbling, an act of altruism is a very powerful thing.

It was from these other families—our temporary community—that we sought emotional solace. The hospital did have some programs in place meant to help families like ours. Bob consulted with a hospital rabbi. We applied for a "patient representative." But we found most of the support superficial if not ineffectual. Certainly, we had no use for the social worker whose office was located just off the waiting room. She reeked of cigarettes and reminded us of the hypertanned Magda from *Something About Mary*. Imagining her smoking while Mom fought for life felt like a slap in the face.

A number of the nurses smoked too. They took care to scrub themselves after a break, but you could smell a hint of the odor on them still. For me, witnessing on a daily basis the destruction caused by cancer would have been a motivator to quit smoking. But it was hard to begrudge the nurses their habit. If anyone could make the argument that they *need* to smoke, it's ICU nurses. Twelve-hour shifts of screaming machines. Numbers dropping or rising precipitously. Tubes clogging. Organs stopping. Relatives crying. I hate smoking, but I considered most of what these nurses did beyond reproach.

Several times a week Lizzie and I brought dozens of doughnuts for the morning shift and a few fresh pizzas for the night shift. We would decorate the boxes like high school seniors might decorate the back windshield of their cars at homecoming: "Bed One Rules!" we'd write.

We were trying to show our appreciation but also to buy some goodwill. We stayed diligently on top of Mom's care, which is to say that we were high-maintenance pains-in-the-ass. We had questions, we wanted to see the ICU doctor on call, we wanted a specialist, we wanted assurances that couldn't be given. And when we weren't there, we called. A lot. When you are keeping a close vigil over someone who is in the hospital for a long time, you have to learn to deal with a lot of different personalities. We loved some of the nurses. Others, we found a way to work with.

The situation was more fraught with some of the doctors. We were very unhappy with the manner in which we all were treated. It seemed to us that once Mom's treatment went awry—once she could no longer help the research-minded staff to prove its hypotheses or further its studies—we were no longer on the radar. Sloan-Kettering would perform the surgery no other hospital staff would perform. But when it came time to getting care for Mom as a woman with pneumonia, we worried that we were in the wrong place.

To be fair, when someone you love is sick, and when the illness strikes in a way that seems particularly unjust (i.e., a health-conscious person developing lung cancer), you look for something or someone to blame. In lieu of obvious targets, it's easy to project the anger onto the doctors who don't (can't) fix what is broken and who are the messengers of bad news. Had we witnessed Mom miraculously recovering from cancer as a result of doctors' actions at Sloan-Kettering, we would have overlooked the bedside manner. But this was not our lot, and some of the doctors gave us reason to channel our rage in their direction.

We didn't see Dr. Toppen, the surgeon, for at least a week after the operation because he had gone out of town the morning after performing it. (We didn't see him for weeks after his return, either, but we were eventually told that he had come to see her, very early in the mornings before we had arrived at the hospital.) The oncologist who originally referred her to Dr. Toppen (and of whom Mom and I were both originally quite fond) sort of dropped us as well, disappearing when Mom went into the ICU. When I finally contacted him to inquire about the pathology results of tests taken of Mom's lymph nodes during surgery—tests that would determine if the cancer had metastasized—he informed us, via e-mail, that that cancer had, in fact, spread. Days later, after I had sent him a number of e-mails all but begging him to come talk to us, he came down to the ICU to tell us what this meant. (It meant bad things.)

Finally, there was Dr. Daniels. As an ICU doctor, his job was to care for the hospital's most vulnerable patients. Yet he showed to us a bedside manner that can only be described as atrocious. He was impossible to pin down for updates on Mom's condition. He seemed annoyed when talking to us. He snapped at us for having too many visitors in the waiting room. He was blasé when Mom showed signs of improvement.

Lizzie, Bob, and I all worried that he perhaps excessively depersonalized his work. We knew this might have felt like an occupational necessity to him. But we wanted him to know Mom and to take some investment in her well-being. That was a big part of the reason we plastered pictures around. Once, when I stood in Mom's area, I flagged Dr. Daniels as he walked by. "Look at this picture of Mom taken at my wedding," I said as I pointed to a snapshot of Mom walking down the aisle in a gorgeous black chiffon dress with spaghetti straps that tied behind her neck in a halter. He stopped. With a put-upon look on his face, he cast his eyes over the photo. "*This* is what a mother of the bride wears?" he said. Then he walked off.

One day, while idling in the waiting room, Dr. Daniels charged through the door from the stairway. I knew what time his shift was to begin, and he was late. "Is everything okay?" I asked as he passed. "Actually, no," he replied. "I had to get an MRI. The machine broke, and I got stuck inside it." This thrilled me. I'm a bitch, but so is karma.

In fact, Lizzie and I were very concerned about karma. We wanted to make sure that we did nothing to hurt Mom's chances for survival. So as we discussed our disdain for various doctors, we would wish them well too. For instance, after an update from Dr. Daniels, we might say, "What a mother-fucking, cock-sucking, dickwad, asshole shit-for-brains." We might, and we frequently did. But we always followed up by adding, "May he live to be a thousand." This parlor game—unleashing a torrent of verbal bile against Dr. Daniels and Dr. Toppen, and then wishing them a long life—helped pass a lot of time. Whatever gets you through the day.

* * *

DR. LOUIS P. Voigt got us through a lot of days. Even on the days that, strictly speaking, he wasn't the doctor in charge of Mom's care (which usually meant Dr. Daniels was), Dr. Voigt was a calm, kind, knowledgeable, and reassuring presence. When he merely walked past me in the waiting room, I drew comfort from knowing that he was around, keeping an eye on Mom and us.

Dr. Voigt introduced himself to us a few days after Mom was admitted. He was, at the time, the unit's assistant attending physician. From the outset, he had an authoritative air that engendered a lot of confidence. He wasn't arrogant or unapproachable. But without being saccharine or overly solicitous, he was a gentle man, and we could tell he cared.

We were desperate for an authority figure we could believe in, who we could trust—and for a source of information. Dr. Voigt became all of that.

Every single day that Dr. Voigt was responsible for Mom's care, he would sit down with me, Bob, and Lizzie in a closet-sized room situated right next to the ICU. He updated us on Mom's condition. He answered questions. He didn't rush. He didn't sugarcoat. He told us it was likely that Mom would not survive the pneumonia. But he allowed us—encouraged us, even—to hold on to the hope that he would be proved wrong. As he told me years later, "I am careful not to give a family false hope, but I can't take all the air out of a room either."

One evening, about a week or two into Mom's stay in the ICU, Dr. Voigt sat down with us and gave the daily State of Suzy download. These numbers were up. Those indicators were strong. This wasn't a good sign, but that wasn't so bad. On and on. He let us vent our frustration, our fear, our exhaustion. He listened patiently. Then he said, "I know how you feel."

Numb, I had been only half tuned in, but his comment shook me awake. His father had been ill and had died, Dr. Voigt went on to say, and the experience of being a son to a man who had been seriously ill and hospitalized motivated him every day to be a more compassionate doctor—not just to patients but to their relatives too.

I remember the moment so vividly. And though he never again mentioned this circumstance to me, I replayed it in my head. Dr. Voigt was showing me that he was able to take something positive out of the experience of watching his parent die. Maybe that would be my experience too.

About a year earlier, I had reported a story to coincide with the first anniversary of the September 11 attacks. As part of my research, I conducted an interview with a grief counselor who had lost her own son in a plane disaster—the bombing of PanAm Flight 103 over Lockerbie, Scotland—a tragedy that eventually led her to go back to school and become a therapist. Her life, she told me, was richer for her son having died. That didn't mean she wouldn't prefer to have her son alive—of course she would—but she was offering herself as an example that people can rise from the ashes of their burned-down worlds, and live lives that are somehow enriched by tragedy.

I remember that during the interview this woman told me that her comments would make a lot of people angry—the trauma of September 11 was still too fresh. But she said that she believed that eventually, many survivors of those lost in 2001 would come to see the truth of her remarks.

I thought about these comments throughout Mom's stay in the ICU. I think about them still.

Louis Voigt was born in the mid-1960s in Fort Liberté, a town in north Haiti, near the border of the Dominican Republic. His father was a teacher, his mother a homemaker. Young Louis was the middle of five children, and the only boy. The family lived in a three-room house. They were poor, but not more so than most people in Haiti. "I considered myself privileged," Dr. Voigt told me.

When he was of school age, Dr. Voigt's family moved to Cape Haitian, the country's second largest city. His family was devoutly Catholic, and his father scraped money together to send his kids to private Catholic schools. During these years, Dr. Voigt said, he was taught the principles of discipline and compassion. As long as he can remember, his teachers put an emphasis on taking your natural gifts and determining how to exploit them for the common good. "The Jesuit philosophy was one of raising men for others," he said.

He graduated as class valedictorian with a baccalaureate degree and decided upon medical school. In Haiti, there was one free medical school. Ten thousand people applied for a hundred spots every year. Admission was based solely on the score of a standardized test: the top hundred got in. Dr. Voigt was the twenty-fifth highest scorer. "I was surprised," he remarked. "I thought I was the smartest person in Haiti." He said this with a straight face. When I cracked up, he did too. But he didn't back down. "Honestly, I thought, 'Wow, those twenty-four people must be *really* smart.' "

Dr. Voigt loved medical school, but political unrest in Haiti was a distraction. Classes were canceled so frequently that he lost his entire third year. When the turmoil quieted down, he was able to resume his studies. He also began traveling around rural parts of the country, going into schools and giving lectures on HIV and other infections.

As dictated by the Haitian medical schooling system, Dr. Voigt capped his education with a year devoted to a "social residency," whereby those completing their training spend time administering to those living in areas without medical professionals. He chose to work at a hospital run by the Salvation Army in the southern part of the country. He was obligated only to give a one-year commitment, but he ended up staying three years. During that time, Dr. Voigt practiced general family medicine, delivered babies, performed circumcisions, and did minor surgery. But he was on the frontlines of abject poverty and as a result functioned as a public health advocate as well. He worked with the United Nations' UNESCO agency on issues of water potability—overseeing the construction of wells. He partnered with a U.S. agency to increase immunization coverage in the rural area in which he was living. As a native son—not some American do-gooder who would be treated with skepticism—Dr. Voigt was able to convince community leaders of the importance of vaccinations and other immunization therapies.

When his school was shut down due to political violence, Dr. Voigt traveled to New York. There he met, courted, and eventually married an American woman, a pediatrician. They had two children who were born in New York but were being raised in Haiti. Growing worried about raising their boys in an unstable political climate, the Voigts chose to relocate to New York in early 1995.

After studying for and passing the U. S. medical board exams, Dr. Voigt completed a three-year residency in internal medicine at Methodist Hospital in Brooklyn. Then he did a two-year subspecialty residency in pulmonary medicine. Then he underwent a year-long training in critical care medicine at Memorial Sloan-Kettering Cancer Center. At the end of the year's tenure, the hospital offered Dr. Voigt a full-time position, and he accepted.

I DIDN'T KEEP an active journal during much of Mom's illness. But when she was in the ICU, I posted regular entries on my blog. On October 6, 2003, I wrote this:

> Today is the twenty-first consecutive day that my mom has spent in the Intensive Care Unit at Memorial Sloan-Kettering Cancer Center, and it's the twenty-first day that we, her indefatigable entourage, have camped out in the second-floor waiting room.
>
> Last Wednesday, using awful hospital euphemisms like "We do not expect your mother to survive this hospitalization," Dr. Daniels told us that Mom was going to die. My husband, Joe, asked, "Is there any hope?" and Dr. Daniels shook his head no. So we adjourned to the familiar waiting room, where we were encircled by friends and engulfed by the horror of losing our mom.
>
> But Mom's still here, and so are we.
>
> In the six days since the doctor ruled Mom down for the

count, Lizzie and I have allowed ourselves moments of deluded, guttural humor. We envision the whole of Ira Kaufman Funeral Home in Southfield, Michigan, packed with hundreds of people who were friends with Mom at various stages of her life. In our reverie, they are dressed in dark suits; some are locked in stunned silence, others are crying softly as they await the beginning of the service. That's when Mom makes her big entrance.

In our dream, she is in her casual-chic uniform of yoga pants paired with a bright, snug Vivienne Tam–type top. Her red hair is loose to her shoulders, her face fixed with her big, toothy smile. From the back of the chapel, she starts strutting down the main aisle, and she is belting out that wonderful female anthem "I'm Still Here."

She is here, and for now she is singing loudly—notes coming from deep in her belly—simply by staying alive. The doctors have told us in the last several days that while Mom remains very critically ill, she has made "subtle" improvements. I like Lizzie's response to those reports: "There is nothing subtle about the fact that Mom is alive when these brilliant doctors had her death certificate all but signed six days ago."

You underestimate Suzy Rosin at your peril. Just like her daughters, she is fueled by spite and loves nothing more than proving doctors wrong. After Dr. Daniels came to speak to us on Friday, when he shrugged his shoulders and said that he was surprised Mom hadn't died on Wednesday, I raced to Mom's bedside and recounted the moment for her. She heard me—I'm sure of it—and her pride from defying expectations

propelled her to make plodding but steady gains throughout
the weekend.

When I close my eyes, I see Mom in her natural state. She
is dancing and laughing. Then I place my hand over my own
heart and I feel her. Because she's here.

OVER THE DAYS and weeks, Mom's lungs steadily improved. But
each improvement ushered in a new obstacle: every time the doctors tried to lessen the dosage of medicine that was keeping Mom
comatose, her heart rate would accelerate to dangerous levels.
There were a few days when we weren't sure if she'd ever come to
again. Over the course of a very long week, she was weaned from
the drugs that were keeping her comatose and brought back to
consciousness. (It is my recollection that Dr. Voigt created the
action plan that finally worked.) When Mom "woke up," though,
she was out of it. Of course, she wasn't expected to be able to
talk—she was prevented from doing so by the tracheotomy tube
threaded through a hole that had been poked through her neck,
just above the collarbone. It connected her respiratory system to
the ventilator and had been inserted during Mom's second week
in the ICU, when doctors realized she would need the support
of the vent indefinitely. The problem was, when she awoke, she
was loopy—swatting at bugs that weren't there, trying to take a
bite out of a rubber ball as if it were an apple. She also was mostly
unresponsive to doctors: she didn't respond to requests that she
nod her head and give other nonverbal gestures. All the medical personnel (physicians and psychiatrists alike) assured us that
Mom was not taking any sort of narcotics that could have led to
decreased cognition. Neurological specialists who came to evalu-

ate her speculated that she might have had a stroke at some point. Lizzie and I weren't buying it. On my blog, I wrote:

> *Lizzie and I both think that when Mom appears unresponsive, she really is just holding on to her power and autonomy. She will shake her head yes and no when she feels like it, thank you very much, not necessarily when a team of doctors that doesn't even bother to look at her name on her chart implores her to do so.*
>
> *On Friday, a cabal of neurologists came to Mom's bedside. They were poking the bottom of her feet with sharp instruments, pulling up her nightgown to grab at her knees. Using diction and volume usually intended for a deaf, retarded person, the lead neurologist told Mom to blink her eyes. (She declined.) Then he turned to me and said, "What's her name again?" I thought I might throttle him. Instead, I looked Mom in the eyes and said, "Don't you hate all these doctors barging in on your privacy and then poking at you?" To that, Mom responded with a huge smile and an emphatic nod of her head.*

The doctors' concern with her mental cognition wasn't the only big issue. Her continued dependence on the ventilator was of real concern too. Even though it seemed her lungs were capable of breathing again, Mom would get agitated and panicked whenever technicians or therapists drastically reduced the vent's function. We asked again and again if Mom was being given a proper dose of Prozac—a drug she had been taking for about five years prior to the cancer diagnosis—and we were assured she was. But we felt that no one but us seemed to take seriously the role an antidepressant might play in her recovery.

Almost six weeks after her surgery, we arrived one morning at the hospital and were told by a nurse that Mom was being prepared for a move back onto the fourteenth floor. She was no longer among the most critically ill patients. It was an incredible triumph not just for Mom but for Bob, Lizzie, and me too. We felt that our perseverance, as much as Mom's, helped her come through the pneumonia and coma.

But the joy was very short-lived as it became quickly evident that physically, Mom was stuck on a breathing machine, and mentally, she wasn't all there. The benefit to being in the ICU was that Mom had round-the-clock, one-on-one care. Up on the fourteenth floor, she was back in the hospital's general population—one of several charges of harried, overextended nurses. Sometimes Mom's vent would get clogged, the tubing would pop off, or in a moment of confusion, she would tug at the tubes. The machine would start to beep loudly, and Mom would totally panic (both because of the sounding alarm and because she was disconnected from her mechanized oxygen supply). The nurses would respond as quickly as they could, but it often wasn't instantly. Seeing how run-down Lizzie and I were, our stepmother, Carolyn, flew to New York and spent ten days perched by the bedside of her husband's ex-wife. A nurse, Carolyn is among the most patient, truly nurturing people I've ever known. After watching Mom's frustration at not being able to talk (which she couldn't do because of the ventilator), Carolyn taught Mom signs to help her express her needs.

As the burden on all of us grew, Bob hired two private nursing attendants, who took shifts in Mom's room through the night and early morning, when none of us could be there. Unfortunately, the two women—both of South Asian descent—didn't get along.

One morning, Lizzie came to the hospital around the time that the baton was to be passed between them. "I can't work in these conditions," one of the aides told Lizzie. Apparently the women's ancestors had once been at war, centuries ago.

"Her people tried to eat my people," the other aide said.

Lizzie knew that if one or both of them quit, even more of the onus would fall onto our shoulders. So in addition to zigzagging the country to care for a toddler, an infant son, and an ailing mother, she had to negotiate peace between factions. "We need to put our ancestral differences behind us and come together in common purpose," Lizzie said, as if she were a UN envoy or President Obama.

When Mom was in the ICU, our crisis played out in black and white: Would Mom live or die? Once she was out of the ICU, the situation was in many ways even more treacherous: Would she have any quality of life? The enduring strain was wearing on all of us. On October 27, I wrote this:

I really wanted to write something normal today—a musing of some sort on a topic other than my mom, pneumonia, cancer, ventilators, ICUs, or hospitals. But beeping machines, frantic nurses, and distraught families have surpassed the surreal and bounded into normalcy in this Memorial Sloan-Kettering Cancer Center community of which I've become an unwitting citizen.

I am an ambitious person, and the past eight years of my life have been defined by professional striving. I have cajoled, maneuvered, charmed, manipulated, and begged my way into the milieu of New York City journalism.

This city does not always follow the rules of meritocracy. It's often about whom you know. I grew up in Michigan, and soon after moving to Manhattan at twenty-three, I realized the disadvantage of not belonging to an East Coast, Ivy League network. I'm not ashamed of the combination of brass-knuckling and eyelash batting I've employed simply to secure opportunities to prove my work ethic and talent. And by some standards, I've actually achieved quite a lot.

Today was meant to be my day to get back to all of that, or at the very least, to dip my toe back in that world. I promised my husband—and I promised myself—that for the first time in seven weeks, I would make an appearance at my office, flip through some mail, even make a few calls.

But how do you go back to "normal" when "normal" has been completely eviscerated from your life? Right now, normal seems like a state of being to which I cannot even aspire. Sheer will and chutzpah can get my work published in Elle *and the* New York Times. *But they can't effect normalcy for my family.*

The fourteenth floor of Memorial Sloan-Kettering operates on murky, ill-defined rules. Professionally, I thrived on attempting to report on, understand, and then relay with written words the mores of rarified subcultures. Here, on Sixty-eighth and York, such tea-leaf reading is more difficult—and much more painful.

For instance, families we left behind in the ICU last Tuesday have lapped us. Literally, they can be found walking gleeful circles around the fourteenth-floor respiratory ward, tagging behind their once critically sick mothers and sisters, who are now freed from ventilators like the one that continues to hold my mom captive. I am ashamed to admit that sometimes I have to remind myself that life (and quality of life) is not a zero-sum game. Someone else's wellness does not need to falter in order for my mom's to flourish. Still, I frequently find myself looking enviously at patients who are much older than Mom—people who were in much worse shape than she was before surgery, people who smoked and disrespected their bodies in ways that are anathema to Mom—and wonder, Why them? Why not Mom?

Yesterday was physically and emotionally grueling for Mom. There were no serious medical developments (as far as I know), just a lot of arduous, frustrating housekeeping tasks. Swelling arms mandated that new veins be tapped for IV fluids. But Mom's veins, teeny and defiant like the rest of her, were not compliant with the stream of (largely unfriendly and impolite) doctors and nurses who entered our room, intent on jabbing at Mom's body and dignity with needles and brusque manners. Then a rash mandated a visit with a kidney specialist. The ensuing exhaustion from such matters (and I've cited only a few) kept Mom from undertaking the tasks of physical therapy—from the completion of which she derives so much well-deserved self-satisfaction. Thus far, her attitude has been amazingly positive. But yesterday she was very discouraged—and helplessly watching her struggle made me ache inside.

Today will be better. I promised Mom that it would be, and I'll jump through whatever hoops necessary to make it so. Then, with some luck, tomorrow will be even better. And soon—maybe, hopefully, please God, haven't we earned a break?—good days will feel normal again.

A few days later, Lizzie and Bob shipped me off to California for a respite. There, I stayed at Lizzie's house with her husband and my older nephew, Zack. I ran errands. I brought the snack for Zack's preschool class. I sat in the sunshine. I didn't set foot in a hospital. It wasn't nearly so relaxing for Bob and Lizzie. While I was gone, they were alerted that a rehabilitation hospital in upstate New York was willing to take Mom on as a patient. So Lizzie and Bob followed the ambulance north as it carted Mom to Helen Hayes Hospital. If Mom was ever going to have another day with quality of life, Helen Hayes was our last, and our greatest, hope.

AROUND 1997 DR. Voigt's father, Calvin Voigt, was diagnosed with prostate cancer. Already suffering from diabetes, Calvin traveled to New York with his wife for treatment in 1999.

At the time, Louis was fulfilling the obligations of a residency, meaning he routinely worked thirty-six-hour shifts. Exhausted and dead on his feet, Dr. Voigt would call his dad several times a week to check in. His dad always said he was feeling fine. But Dr. Voigt would hear from other relatives that his father was sharing with them his suffering and fear. It made Dr. Voigt angry. "He was breaking the code of trust," Dr. Voigt told me. "I was his son, I was a physician. And he was making it look like I was uncaring. So I confronted my dad. He said, 'I don't want to be a distraction to your education and your training.' In his view as a parent, it was his responsibility to protect me."

On a Saturday in the spring of 2003, Dr. Voigt got a panicky call from his sister: their father had passed out. She had dialed 911 and begun administering CPR. Dr. Voigt rushed to the hospital where his dad had been taken and joined his family in the ER. They waited for eight hours before a doctor sat down with the family to explain the implications of the fact that Calvin had suffered a massive stroke. "It was an eight-hour blackout in terms of information, and this is when I started to experience—for the first time from the other side— how unfriendly the system is, particularly in a time of crisis," Dr. Voigt said. "The physicians were overwhelmed. The ER was overpopulated. I found a resident, but when she learned I was a physician, she refused to talk to me," perhaps out of insecurity, perhaps out of arrogance. "I felt I could have helped them—both because of my background and because we could have told the doctors about my father's history. At one point, my mother looked at me and said, 'Is this how you treat your patients?'

"I made a promise to myself from that moment that I would do everything I could to make sure that no one related to a patient of mine would have the same experience."

In July, a few months after the stroke, Calvin Voigt died. Six weeks later, my mom ended up in his son's care.

"I was very mindful of my family's experience when I was caring for your mom," Dr. Voigt told me when I interviewed him more than five years later. "I remember sitting down with you all and explaining the situation, organ by organ."

He did so with us, and he does so with other families, not merely to be a nice guy. Dr. Voigt says it's good health-care policy. "One of the biggest problems is a failure to communicate, and by that I mean physicians and nurses, and physicians and family members. If we meaningfully addressed these problems, there would be a significant impact on health care. The number of tests that are done twice—we could eradicate that. And in an ICU type environment, where the family is often bedside at the time of a crisis—that relative might have witnessed something we did not, or they could have information about the patient that is absolutely relevant. That is why I seek out the family. I mean, who knows someone better than family?"

Dr. Voigt is on hospital committees meant to address such concerns. But he also emphasizes the unparalleled value of Sloan-Kettering—a hospital that attracts patients from around the world for good reason. When doctors at other hospitals might consider a cancer beyond treatment, the faculty at Sloan-Kettering is often willing to take a shot. It's just this approach that drew us to the hospital and that caused me to believe it our best chance.

"The philosophy of this hospital is 'Why not?' " Dr. Voigt explained. "That frees you to push the envelope. And that is how progress gets made."

I asked him, "Is it fair to say that a different skill set is needed for innovation than for bedside manner?"

"Yes," he allowed. "I'll stop myself there."

We both broke into laughter. But Dr. Voigt's demeanor quickly grew serious again. "Listen," he said, "you can't teach humanity. You have it or you don't."

WHEN LIZZIE FIRST saw Helen Hayes Hospital (or H-Cubed, as I took to calling it), it seemed to her like something out of *Wuthering Heights*. It is atop a long winding driveway in a working-class upper–Hudson River town. Bob and I had checked out the hospital a few weeks before and were told by nurses at Sloan-Kettering that it had a good reputation for weaning people from ventilators. But moving Mom in there, amid the desolate, leafless trees and gray skies of mid-November, Lizzie and Bob felt anxious, uncertain, and guilty for leaving Mom in this unfamiliar place.

Mom would be staying in the "vent unit" on the second floor. It was a giant square room with four beds, near the center of which was a desk manned twenty hours a day by a nurse. The hospital was clean, but there was no gloss. Unlike Sloan-Kettering—a private institution with a global reputation for research excellence and the support of the social set that hosts galas throughout the year to benefit the hospital—Helen Hayes is a public hospital run by the state of New York. Its doctors, nurses and therapists don't necessarily publish lots of studies; it's not world-renowned.

And yet it was there that Mom got the "compassionate care" to which Sloan-Kettering lays claim in the advertisements it runs on NPR and in the *New York Times Magazine*. At Helen Hayes, every single doctor, nurse, therapist, and aide listened to our concerns and answered our questions. And the impact of this was not superficial.

Seeing that Mom was in emotional distress, the doctors instantly enlisted the care of a staff psychologist. Dr. Bruce Lowenstein spent time with Mom privately, but with our whole family as well. He listened carefully as we stressed to him the powerful role Prozac had played in Mom's life—helping her combat depression and anxiety for years—and that we were surprised it wasn't having a bigger impact in helping her relax during the process of being weaned from the ventilator. When we emphasized the huge calming effect Prozac had on Mom and asked if we could up her dosage, the psychiatrist at Sloan-Kettering responded with a patronizing "It's not that simple." When we explained the same to Dr. Lowenstein, he consulted with physicians who instantly took this information as vital. They played with her dosage, and as soon as they did, everyone noted a marked change in Mom's demeanor. Almost immediately, she began to snap out of the haze. Her mental health properly taken into consideration, she chilled out and began to tolerate it when the respiratory therapists turned down the vent. Wednesday, November 26—the day before Thanksgiving—I posted this entry onto my blog:

> Let's not bury the lead with any stylish metaphors: Mom is off the ventilator.
>
> In less than two months, she has gone from being diagnosed with total lung failure (which we were told was irreversible) to completely breathing on her own. The amazing doctors, nurses, and therapists at Helen Hayes Hospital tell us they expect to remove the tracheotomy tube altogether in the next couple of weeks.
>
> A lot of people have classified Mom's recovery as a mira-

cle, and it is. But from witnessing the process, I've come to learn that miracles don't transpire like magic—Poof, you're better! Miracles result from a heap of toil mixed with a lot of good luck. It's only through Mom's unimaginable and endless expending of blood, sweat, and tears (literally) that this "miracle" has occurred. A couple of days ago, one of the therapists asked her how she did it, and she shrugged her shoulders and said simply, "When the cancer pushes me, I try to push back harder." She truly is amazing, this woman, my mom.

We were so used to the glacial pace of improvements that Mom's very accelerated progress at Helen Hayes has stunned (and completely delighted) us. It was only last Monday that Mom finally got comfortable wearing a speaking valve, a small tube that rerouted her exhaled air so that it would pass over her vocal cords. The experience of hearing Mom—and from the get-go she sounded like herself—was truly over-whelming for all of us, including Mom. We called Lizzie in California (who was absolutely and jubilantly dumbstruck when she realized she was on the phone with Mom) and then dialed up Grandma Charlotte. Gram was off at her mah-jong game, so Mom left a message that sort of said it all. "Mom," she said, "it's your daughter Suzy. I found my voice!"

Once Mom had been successfully weaned from the ventilator, there were other hurdles to surmount: her body had so atrophied that she had to regain the strength first before she could even try to relearn skills like walking. But untethered from a breath-

ing machine, she committed herself to physical therapy with exhausting determination. You couldn't get her out of the physical
therapy room. I had borrowed a car from my in-laws and drove
up to the hospital each day. By this time, I'd bound up the stairs
to the vent unit with a spring in my step. Nurses and therapists
would stop me along the way. "Your mom is so inspiring," they
would tell me, and I would bask in the thrill we all shared from
witnessing her glory.

Mom was a bossy Jewish mother to the core of her being, and
it wasn't long before she was taking over the joint. One evening,
I was walking down the second-floor hallway at H-Cubed, my
arms holding grocery bags filled with snacks meant to fatten up
Mom. From the vent room, I heard the strains of a monologue
that sounded familiar yet out-of-place:

"And pump two three four five six seven eight . . ."

"Scoop that powerhouse! Pretend your bellybutton is pinned
to the floor! And scoop two three four!"

I made it to the vent room entrance and craned my neck to
catch a stealthy glimpse of the action. The night nurse—an overweight, middle-aged woman who wore the beleaguered look of a
working mom with little time to care for herself—was lying on
the floor at the foot of Mom's bed, her head curled off the floor,
her straightened legs at a forty-five-degree angle from her "powerhouse," her feet configured on a V-shape connected at the heels,
her planked arms pumping vigorously by her side.

"Reach your fingertips toward me thirteen, fourteen, fifteen!"
my mom howled.

She was in the hospital bed, giving the nurse a Pilates lesson.

There was another significant sign that she was recovering.

She started bitching about the gray in her roots. Since vanity is an indulgence of the healthy, I was elated. I called Danuta Benjamin, my longtime hair colorist and friend. The following Sunday, on Danuta's day off, I picked her up outside her midtown apartment, and together we took the hour-and-a-half drive to H-Cubed. The nurses watched with amusement as Danuta set up her mobile Borja Color Studio in a handicapped-accessible shower stall.

After a month at Helen Hayes, Mom was breathing on her own and walking without assistance. She was ready to go home. The staff at the hospital treated her impending release with excitement. All the technicians, nurses, and doctors who had worked with her came by the vent unit to congratulate her on her amazing strides and to wish her well. Before heading to the airport on December 17, I asked a nurse to take a photo of Mom and me beside her bed. We both had our chins jutting forward, proud and a little defiant. Joe and I accompanied Mom and Bob on the flight back to Tucson. She made it home a couple days before her fifty-ninth birthday.

A few months later, I took a photo of Mom and Bob on their thirtieth anniversary. Mom looked beautiful, relaxed, and remarkably vital. I e-mailed the picture to Dr. Daniels and to Dr. Voigt. Dr. Voigt responded. He wrote: "I am very happy that your mother (my patient and friend) Suzy is doing well. She should be grateful to have such a wonderful family. Please send her my regards. Louis."

IN JANUARY 2009, nearly five and a half years after my mom's stay in the ICU of Sloan-Kettering, I returned to the hospital to interview Dr. Voigt. In my twelve years as a journalist, there were few interviews that I worked harder to get. It took me eleven months of wooing (via handwritten letters) before Dr. Voigt would agree to talk to me. He's busy. He's doesn't seem to like a lot of fuss and attention.

We met at his office. Dr. Voigt sat behind a desk lined with three computers, in front of a credenza holding medical books and a few family photos. We had a conversation that lasted more than two hours and touched on a gamut of topics. He shared details—with precise diction and a heavy Haitian-French accent—about his life in Haiti, his medical education, his career goals. We talked a lot about my mom, about health care and the role of bedside manner. He told me about his family: his wife the pediatrician, and their two sons with whom Dr. Voigt dreams of running a marathon. He has gotten really into rugby, mostly because his sons play. "It's not exactly a sport I grew up with," Dr. Voigt said. "As you may have noticed, I'm not Irish." (He's black. We laughed.) He was just as warm, patient, articulate, and funny as I remembered.

We talked a lot about his father too, and about how soon after his dad's death my mom had come into his care. Despite the timing, he said that my mom's case was not the one that personally impacted him the most.

The one who truly got to him was a man who landed in the ICU several years after Dr. Voigt's father had died. The man was a seventy-something man, and after less than a day in the ICU, his condition was deteriorating. So Dr. Voigt picked up the phone to make what, for a critical care doctor, is something of a routine call. He flipped through the man's file, found the emergency contact number, and dialed the man's son. "You'd better get here quickly," said Dr. Voigt. The son arrived in time and raced to his father's bedside. His dad died three hours later.

After, the son approached Dr. Voigt. He was crying. He said, "I got to say good-bye. You gave me that opportunity, and I am grateful."

That night, while driving from the hospital to his house in Brooklyn, Dr. Voigt pulled off the FDR Highway and onto a side street. He hunched over the steering wheel for fifteen minutes. It was the first time he had cried since his dad died.

"Until you've gone through it," Dr. Voigt said to me, "you can't realize that when your parent dies, part of you goes away."

As we wrapped up our interview, Dr. Voigt mentioned that in the ensuing years since Mom was there, the ICU had been moved to a different floor, expanded, and completely revamped. "I'll give you a tour," he said casually. Briefly, I froze. I hadn't considered walking back into an ICU, certainly not this ICU. Had I a chance to mull it over, I might have begged off. Instead, I took a deep breath and tried to hide my tentativeness.

We walked down the hall from his office and into the waiting room. It was much airier than the waiting room I had spent so much time in; cleaner and more comfortable, it had more dedicated space for families to have private conversations with doctors.

We walked past two women staffers, who cheerily greeted Dr. Voigt. "I have a guest with me right now," he said, motioning to me. "So I'll catch up with you later."

"Oh, Dr. Voigt is the best!" one of the women said to me.

"Please put a good word in for me," the other said, teasingly. "I would love to work for him!"

I laughed politely.

As Dr. Voigt and I pivoted back toward the ICU, I locked eyes with a woman who was slouched in a chair and had been watching us approach. She looked absolutely spent, with greasy hair, dark circles beneath her eyes, and tearstains on her cheeks. She glared at me as I must have glared at so many—with an anger in her eyes that said, *How dare you laugh.*

I wanted to rush to her side, to apologize, to tell her I knew what she was going through, to throw my arms around her and assure her that she was not alone. Instead, I looked down—feeling ashamed, even disgusted with myself.

Dr. Voigt was continuing apace toward the unit, so I shook off my self-contempt as best I could and followed him inside. This new ICU on the eleventh floor bore no resemblance to its predecessor on the second. It was sleek, modern, and much larger, with accommodations for twenty beds instead of the twelve downstairs. Each bed had a discrete room with an actual door and glass walls that, with a flip of a switch, could be made to frost over, affording privacy.

"Let me show you this one," Dr. Voigt said as we stood at the threshold of one room. On the outside wall was a sign: "Bed 1."

"My mom was in Bed One," I said.

"I remember," he replied.

We walked in. To my shock, I felt very little.

I first had come to Dr. Voigt the distraught daughter of a very sick patient. But half a decade later I found myself standing beside Bed One a detached journalist, an observer brandishing a notebook and emotional distance. I guess that it took reentering the ICU to notice all the ways I had healed.

Chapter Seven

Playing Golf at Augusta National, Kindness from Strangers, and Other Impossibilities

Like almost anybody who has picked up a golf club, my stepfather, Bob, has always had a fantasy: to play at the Augusta National Golf Club. The legendary Georgia course is home to the Masters Tournament, and admission is strictly limited to its closely guarded roster of members and their invited guests. Neither Bob nor I knew a soul there.

It was early 2004, and Bob's seventieth birthday was approaching in the spring. Just home from rehabbing at Helen Hayes Hospital, Mom wasn't well enough to attend a big party, let alone plan or host one. Instead, Lizzie and I tried to get her to focus on a special gift, something we could give to Bob that would befit the occasion. We all decided upon a golf-themed present. We thought about setting up lessons, or bringing in a pro to play eighteen holes with him. But we decided that would be something he would do for himself if it truly appealed to him. Then my mom spoke up: "He's always dreamed of playing golf at Augusta National."

There was something about the way that Mom presented it that irritated me. She wouldn't be doing the work that might culminate in Bob landing an invitation to play at Augusta. And yet, as our discussions about the birthday continued, she kept coming back to it. Though she didn't explicitly say so, I felt like she was hinting that I'd be lazy for not trying.

So I began to seriously consider the challenge, first by discussing it with friends and colleagues who played golf. Without exception, everyone I shared this idea with had a one-word response: impossible.

Playing at Augusta is probably the toughest ticket in golf. In order for guests to play "the National," they must be accompanied by an active member. Why, my friends asked, would an absolute stranger invite a seventy-year-old suburban Detroit real-estate developer to Georgia to tee off at one of the world's most secretive and exclusive clubs?

But my mom had just overcome pneumonia and come out of a coma, despite the expectations of most medical experts. She then relearned to walk, swallow, talk, eat, and breathe without assistance. So I was growing tired of being told of impossibilities.

MOM AND BOB'S was not a perfect marriage. It lasted thirty-one years, and it rode the waves as decades-long unions do. Bob is not a saint, and Mom could be a real pain in the ass. But they loved each other. And when my mom got sick, Bob was the man my mom needed him to be.

Bob is a gentleman. Solid, old-fashioned, he doesn't always have the right words, but he knows the difference between right and wrong. That's what you can say about Bob: he almost always tries to do the right thing. Not every man would marry a woman with two young children. But he did so without hesitation (he first proposed on their second date), and he truly embraced Lizzie and me as part of the package. This wasn't necessarily a simple matter, because he had his three children—my stepbrothers and -sister, who experienced normal, understandable jealousy and insecurity in the face of their dad's remarriage.

Bob tended to us all. He stopped by his ex-wife's house after work to see Jimmy, Tommy, and Natalie pretty much every day until each of them graduated from high school. All the while, he helped potty-train me, attended Lizzie's and my recitals, and paid the bills.

Bob Rosin is as much a father to us as is our real dad, Bob Rosman, to whom Lizzie and I are also very close. (The Bobs, incidentally, have an interesting relationship: little in common but a woman they married. Yet they both appreciate and respect the role the other plays in Lizzie's and my lives.) At each of our weddings, Lizzie and I walked down the aisle with Dad at one side and Bob at the other.

So Bob has always been a good guy. Still, you never can be sure how someone is going to react to a life-and-death crisis. This is how Bob did it: He went to every doctor's appointment with Mom. He sat with her during every infusion. He was at her bedside every single day during every single hospitalization. He told her what she wanted to hear—that she was going to beat the cancer, that there was no chance it could end any other way—and he did so not to indulge her denial but because he truly couldn't imagine living in this world without her.

And that's just the emotional stuff. Bob also took to huge logistical and organizational tasks with initiative and dedication. Mom was treated at several hospitals across the country and consulted with an even broader range of doctors. There was a constant need for blood test results and CAT and PET scan films to be trafficked; there was always a big wad of red tape from which to get unstuck. He oversaw the Herculean job of dealing with insurance companies and hospital billing departments. (Cancer may be the great equalizer, but it's still easier for those who have money. We were lucky.) He orchestrated the hiring and management of the overnight nursing aides. This was an unending chore. My mom was angry that she needed help and resented those who gave it to her. She was demanding and unforgiving of many of the aides. Mom fired some. Others burned out. Then Bob would hire a new batch, train them, and massage relations between them and Mom for as long as possible. He tended to the house, too, hiring someone to maintain (with only moderate success) Mom's peony plants and rosebushes. Of course, Lizzie and I helped a lot. But Bob deserves tremendous credit. When Mom was diagnosed, he didn't know how to boil water or toast bread (like, literally). Computer-illiterate, he was used to having a secretary and a wife take care of a million daily details. Yet he figured out how to juggle all of his new responsibilities, and did so without complaining.

So when his birthday came, Mom, Lizzie, and I felt like the time was ripe for a grand gesture. And once Mom got so excited by the idea, I had no choice but to push forward.

But I wasn't doing it just for them. I very consciously felt the need for a huge challenge, something that might restore a belief in the possibility of unexpected victories.

AUGUSTA NATIONAL IS shrouded in institutional silence. It has been at the center of controversy over the years because it is has admitted no women and few black members. The club comments publicly only through an official spokesman, and only about the Masters; it refuses to disclose its members' names, or even how many there are. Published accounts place the membership at about three hundred.

Founded in 1932 in eastern Georgia, Augusta National was conceived as a winter club for northern industrial leaders and friends of cofounder Robert T. "Bobby" Jones Jr., the era's premier golfer. According to people familiar with the club's history, a small percentage of the membership would be drawn from the Augusta and Atlanta area. The club's founders started an annual invitational tournament that became the Masters, the sport's elite event. While professional golf's other three major tournaments—the U.S. Open, the British Open, and the PGA Championship—are played at different courses every year, the Masters is always played at Augusta National. Every significant player since 1934 has walked its fairways.

So veiled in secrecy is Augusta—and so intent are sports aficionados and historians on staying in the good graces of the club's powers that be, in case they might be considered for membership—that even those who spoke to me about benign matters like the club's history (ignoring its controversial stances on women and minorities) would do so only if I promised them anonymity.

* * *

I CALLED MY dad and told him that I wanted to try to get Bob an invitation to play at Augusta for his seventieth birthday. Did he have any ideas? Dad suggested I call a colleague of his—an Atlanta-based guy who can trace his southern roots to his grand-daddy's granddaddy, or something. (Side note: I give my dad a lot of props for being so enthusiastic and eager to help me in my endeavor to make a big show of thanks to my stepdad.)

I called Dad's friend. He told me—as so many others had—that what I was trying to do was impossible. But he also gave me a very helpful tip: he told me that a list of members had been leaked to the press a few years back. I found a copy posted in the archives of a blog. (Love the Internet!)

Since I knew that a member had to be on the golf course with Bob in order for him to play—and since I was willing to admit it was unlikely that some Silicon Valley CEO was going to jet into Georgia in order to play golf with a random guy from suburban Detroit—I decided to focus on members listed as living in Atlanta or Augusta. On the Web, I found the home addresses for some forty such members.

I wrote to them. I explained my mom's illness, my stepdad's role in our family, and our desire to surprise him with a memorable round of golf. I said I lived in New York and worked as a freelance journalist. Joe read the letter. He thought it was too long—more than one typewritten page—and pulled too hard at heartstrings. "Heartstrings are my only hope," I told him.

Lizzie thought it was important that I include a photo or two. "They should know we're pretty," she reasoned. I saw her point, and I even went wilier: on the outside of the envelope I wrote,

"PHOTOS—DO NOT BEND." I figured that my appeal might reso-
nate with some member's wife—and that a good way to attract a
wife's attention would be to send her husband a letter, with pictures inside, addressed in a woman's hand.

The first response came swiftly. Boone Knox, a retired banker
from Georgia, called within a week. He and his son were planning to play soon, and Bob could join them if he could get to
Augusta in two days. My mom had a medical test scheduled, and
we knew we couldn't make the arrangements in time. We had to
decline, but in thanks, Lizzie and I sent him flowers. Then we got
another response: a woman called to say she had opened the letter
on behalf of her infirm husband. She wanted to help, she said, but
her husband wasn't physically able to escort anyone to the club,
and she was not a member.

Mostly my mailbox began filling up with polite regrets. "I
appreciate your letter," wrote Carl E. Sanders, who was Georgia's governor from 1963 through 1967. Mr. Sanders wrote that he
couldn't play golf due to an injured back. "I wish you and all your
loved ones the best," he wrote. Another member wrote: "As you
may imagine, requests for a round of golf from friends, clients,
friends of friends, old school mates, relatives, etc. use the time
I can devote to golf entertainment. I am sorry." When I called
to ask him about the letter, he declined to be identified in print.
"I wouldn't want to encourage anyone else to try your trick," he
said.

About a month passed. Lizzie and I made plans to fly to
Tucson to mark Bob's birthday and Mom and Bob's thirtieth
wedding anniversary. We were crestfallen at the thought of showing up without a gift. My mom told me to compile a scrapbook

with the letter and pictures I had mailed, plus the responses I had received. "Just showing him what you tried to do for him will be present enough," she said.

I WAS PUTTING the letters into an album one evening in my New York City apartment when the phone rang. In a thick southern accent, the caller identified himself. "This is Dessey Kuhlke from Augusta, Georgia," he said. He told me he had read my letter over and over since it arrived the previous month. Each time, he told me, he thought of another reason why he should say no. "But none of the reasons seem good enough," he said.

It was as if someone had given me a gift. I was filled with unbridled excitement. I did a teenybopper dance around my apartment.

Dessey express-mailed a formal letter of invitation for a round of golf at Augusta National for Bob and two others of Bob's choice. He included a photocopy of a photograph showing the club's then chairman, William "Hootie" Johnson, handing the Masters Trophy to Phil Mickelson, who weeks earlier had just won the 2004 tournament. Standing behind Hootie was a group of members wearing the famous Augusta National green jackets. With a black marker, Dessey had drawn an arrow toward one man's face and wrote "ME."

I rearranged the order of the scrapbook I was compiling. First came the letter I wrote, followed by the photos included in the envelope. Then the letter, and photo, from Dessey. Then all the other rejection letters, nice and otherwise.

All together in Tucson, we gathered in the living room. I watched my mom. She beamed, freed from the impotence she felt as a wife who was not throwing a party for her husband's seventieth birthday. It felt great to have a family moment that wasn't created by a crisis. We had gathered for something besides cancer for the first time in a long time, and the air in the room felt easier to breathe.

Lizzie and I presented Bob with the book. He looked confused, but started flipping through it. No one said anything. We let him take his time to read through the letters, to grasp just what he was being given as a birthday present. He stared at the book for about twenty minutes, muttering again and again: "Say, 'Honest to God.' Say, 'Swear to God.' " Then he picked up the phone and called his close friend. "Don," he said, "are you sitting down?"

For two weeks, Bob carried the book with him everywhere.

DESSEY WAS BORN in Augusta, like his father and his grandfather. After high school, he joined the army in 1959 and about a year later began his studies at Georgia Southern University. He met his wife, Barbara, on a blind date in 1961. She was in high school in Decatur; he drove there on weekends to see her. They married in 1963, the same year Dessey graduated from college with a degree in business.

They settled in Augusta, where Dessey took a job with his family's construction business. He and Barbara had three children: David in 1968, Kathy in 1972, and Brian in 1975. Dessey retired in the mid-1980s, when he and his brothers sold their business. Since then, he's focused on private investing.

He was invited to join Augusta National in 1993. When he was at the top of this game, Dessey wasn't a bad golfer. His best round at Augusta National was in 2000, when he shot a two-over-par 74. "It was an aberration," he told me.

Joe and I got the opportunity to meet Dessey and Barbara a few months after Bob's birthday when they traveled to New York to see friends. We had dinner at a loud steak house in Midtown. Despite the din, Dessey and I talked a lot about my mom. This began a dialogue that continued for months, over the phone and via e-mail. Our conversations weren't light: he asked me a few times if I, as a Jew, believed in an afterlife, and he shared his Christian views with me. I felt that he took a pleasure in comforting others. A few months before Mom died, he wrote to me: "There is one thing I can tell you for sure—one of the greatest gifts of all is the gift of endurance. I am so sorry for the suffering all of you are dealing with and I pray for you every day. Please know that you are not alone."

When you're sad a lot—and when your parent is dying slowly, you're sad a lot—you sometimes worry that your sadness makes other people uncomfortable. With Dessey, I felt the opposite. He helped me confront the inevitability of Mom's illness. Even though I was nearly half his age and from a different walk of life. Even though I was a virtual stranger.

In the spring of 2004, when Dessey first agreed to host Bob at Augusta National, we had settled on a to-be-determined date at the end of the year. But Mom got worse over the summer, and in September, when I asked Bob what he thought of flying in a few months to Augusta, he winced. I told Dessey that Bob was reluctant to leave Mom. Dessey assured me that his invitation wouldn't expire.

After Mom died in June 2005, I sent Dessey an e-mail to let

him know. He let some time pass before he called me and said, "Let's get this trip planned."

NEARLY SIX MONTHS after Mom died, on December 5, 2005, Bob flew into Columbia, South Carolina, a seventy-minute drive away from the golf course. Dessey was waiting to pick him up in his car. The two of them, meeting for the first time, talked all the way to Augusta.

As far as my stepdad knew, he would be staying at the Radisson Hotel in town. On the way downtown, Dessey told Bob that he needed to take care of something at the club before dropping Bob at the hotel. They walked through the club's main house and onto the grounds, which has ten cabins that serve as accommodations for members and their guests. Dessey led Bob to the Jones Cabin, a bungalow near the tenth tee named after the club's cofounder. Dessey showed him the living room, dining room, and two bedrooms.

"Do you ever stay here?" Bob asked.

"I'm staying here right now," he told my stepdad. "And so are you."

"I was dumbstruck," Bob said later.

Dessey had told Bob he could decide who would round out their foursome; my husband, Joe, and Bob's close friend Don Kwasman were the lucky two. They arrived a few hours after Bob, and in the evening the four convened in the Jones Cabin. At a table set up in the living room, a staffer served them fried chicken, collard greens, corn on the cob, and apple-bread pudding. After the meal, the men adjourned to the living room. Sitting beneath a portrait of Bobby Jones that had been painted by

President Dwight D. Eisenhower, they drank Grey Goose vodka and Famous Grouse Scotch until one a.m.

Before his first hole the next morning, Bob took in the scenery. In front of him was a perfectly groomed fairway. To his right was the sprawling white clubhouse—originally an antebellum plantation—with its two-story porches and blooming pansies. To the left was the eighteenth green, where earlier that year Tiger Woods had sunk a fifteen-foot birdie putt in sudden-death play to win his fourth Masters.

Bob drew back his club and uncorked about a 215-yard drive, landing his ball at the top of a hill on the fairway. "I hit it straight down the middle," he told me. "I felt good." Over the next two days, Bob, Joe, and Don played thirty-six holes, plus a round on the course's nine-hole, par-3 course.

If for a moment the foursome forgot the course's history, there were reminders. On the thirteenth hole, Joe landed his ball in a swale between a semicircle of sand traps and the green. Joe expected to reach the green with a pitching wedge. His caddie—all golfers at Augusta National are assigned one—advised him to wedge himself out with a putter. "Really? A putter?" Joe asked. The caddie responded: "When Jack Nicklaus had his ball in the exact same place, he used a putter. But you do what you think is best." Joe did as told, and missed the cup by about fifteen feet.

IT WAS WELL after Dessey initially extended the golf invitation—and his emotional support—that I learned why he was so inclined to do so. Dessey and Barbara have survived unimaginable loss—the deaths of two of their children. In 2002 their eldest child, David, died at thirty-four after a long illness. Sixteen years earlier, their younger son, Brian, died at ten years old after a playground accident.

Dessey was helped in his grief by the kindness of strangers. After Brian died, he received a letter from Jack Nicklaus. The golfer had won his historic sixth Masters championship on the day of Brian's death. Dessey was not yet a club member, but Nicklaus had learned that a local couple had experienced tragedy on the day of his triumph. "He said that he was writing as one parent to another and expressed sincere sympathy," Dessey said. "I think more of him because of his compassion than all of his golf victories."

Even more powerful was the solace he found from a man named John R. Claypool IV. "Outside of my family," Dessey said of Claypool, "he was by far the most instrumental person in my coping with these losses."

JOHN CLAYPOOL WAS an associate rector at an Episcopal church in San Antonio, Texas, when Brian Kuhlke died in 1986. Reverend Claypool didn't know the Kuhlkes, but he heard about the death through a mutual friend, a man whose child had been in Brian's class at school. Claypool wrote the Kuhlkes a letter. He shared his sympathy and his empathy, explaining that it had been twenty-one years since his daughter "moved from one room in God's house to another."

"That phrase stuck with me," Dessey told me. "It was a very comforting thought."

A week later, another family friend brought Dessey a tape of a recent Claypool sermon. Dessey listened to it, and then he bought one of Claypool's books. "I started reading everything of his I could get my hands on," Dessay said. He felt that Claypool was putting words to his own sorrow. Dessey became a devout member of Reverend Claypool's flock. "For twenty years," Dessey told me, "I got his sermon every week on tape and I listened to it in the car when I was driving."

A NATIVE SON of Kentucky, Reverend Claypool was ordained in 1953 and settled into a career as a pastor at postings across the South—first in the Baptist tradition before becoming Episcopalian. He and his wife had two children, Rowan and Laura Lue. (He and his wife ultimately divorced and he married his second wife, Ann, in 1982.)

In the late 1950s and early 1960s, he was asked to oversee "discrimination reduction" within his church and others in the South. Claypool took to the assignment with vigor. He preached locally and across the state of the immorality of Jim Crow and racism. And he joined as a panelist on the weekly radio show *The Moral Side of the News.* He met and befriended a young black minister named Martin Luther King Jr. In April of 1961 they were pictured on the front page of the *Louisville Courier-Journal* having a cup of coffee at a diner. This did not endear Reverend Claypool to some of his parishioners, but he didn't care. Later in his career, he fought for equality for women too.

But it was not even his civil rights efforts that came to ultimately define his career. In 1968, when Laura Lue was eight, she was diagnosed with leukemia. She died a year and a half later.

The death of his child threw Reverend Claypool into a spiritual quest to understand—as so many of us long to—how God can allow innocent and morally centered people to suffer.

He continued to explore grief and faith in writings and sermons delivered at churches all over the country. In doing so, he developed a philosophy about the role that gratitude can play in grief. "One day, he just realized that he had a choice," his wife, Ann, told me. "He could either feel entitled—that he shouldn't have lost a child. Or he could take the road of gratitude—that he should be grateful that he had this child for even a day. That choice between entitlement and gratitude made all the difference for him."

On these principles, he built a nationwide ministry for bereaved parents. "He heard from thousands of people," Ann said. "When someone lost a child, their clergy told them, 'Call John Claypool.' "

It became Dessey's dream to meet Reverend Claypool in person. In late 2001, a friend of Dessey's who also knew the priest said that he had recently mentioned that he had never been to a golf tournament. "I can fix that!" Dessey thought. He tracked down Reverend Claypool's address and wrote him a letter. He thanked him for all the solace his sermons had given to him over the years and invited him to the next Masters tournament.

Reverend Claypool accepted, and alongside their wives, Dessey and John watched Tiger Woods win his third Masters trophy.

During the tournament weekend, the Kuhlkes hosted a dinner party for the Claypools, attended by some of the Kuhlkes' best friends. Mostly, the group listened to Claypool talk. "We sat there for four and a half hours," Dessey said. "We could not get up. It was incredible."

A few months later, Dessey and Barbara's oldest child became critically ill. Reverend Claypool was in regular touch with the Kuhlkes throughout David's illness and after his death. Again, Dessey found strength in Reverend Claypool's words.

Of Reverend Claypool, Dessey said, "He was the kind of person who put into words the kind of things you were thinking but could not express." Reverend Claypool's son explained it to me this way: "My father gave grief a coherence that people could latch on to."

Reverend Claypool died of complications after being treated for a cancer of the bone marrow in September of 2005—just a few months before Dessey hosted Bob at Augusta. He was seventy-four.

As I sank into writing about Mom's life and death, and the people who impacted her and us along the way, I began to think more about Dessey. Earlier in our relationship—when Mom was sick, and in the first year after she died—I was desperate for comfort, and I accepted Dessey's without question. But after some time I had a little perspective and was able to grasp how truly unusual it was for a stranger to extend himself so generously.

I now see that Dessey didn't just take my family and me under his wing because he's a nice guy. It was a necessity for him. He was soothing his own wounds by reaching out to others. Paying it forward, as it were, was part of a coping mechanism taught by Reverend Claypool. He had created a legacy of counseling people to nurture themselves by nurturing others. Even strangers. Or, perhaps, especially strangers.

After Mom died, Dessey sent me a few of Reverend Claypool's books. He called me to make sure I had received them, but it was a soft sell. He didn't probe me as to whether I would read them.

And for a long time, I didn't. Initially, I had been reluctant to read Reverend Claypool's writings because I assumed my Jewishness would preclude me from connecting with his teachings. But one day, I spent a few hours reading one of his books, *Tracks of a Fellow Struggler*, a compilation of sermons he delivered during the period of his daughter's illness and death. As I read, I started to grapple with the enormity of the Claypools' and the Kuhlkes' losses. I might have chided myself for self-indulgence, considering that my grief paled, by orders of magnitude. Instead, I let myself feel inspired by their commitment to survival. And I let myself feel grateful for having had for thirty-three years a mom who loved me. I found the gratitude so much easier to live with than the anger and sadness. So it was yet another gift from Dessey, one that he had passed on to me from Reverend Claypool.

I CALLED ROWAN Claypool to learn more about his father as it related to Dessey Kuhlke. But I found that Rowan and I were more connected that I would have expected a Yankee Jew and a southern Baptist to be. We are both children trying to make sense of what our parents left behind.

His father's funeral service was held at St. Luke's in Birmingham, Alabama, where Reverend Claypool had served for fourteen years as rector. The pews overflowed with congregants, family, and the elite of the Episcopal Church. The dean of the National Cathedral in Washington, D.C., led the service. It was a celebration of Reverend Claypool's career and his impact as a priest.

But Rowan felt a need to further honor his dad. Rowan planned a service to take place three weeks later at Crescent Hill Baptist Church, where his father first began his career. The church is in Louisville, where Laura Lue lived and died.

Rowan reached out to friends and family to let them know about the upcoming service, and to make a special request. He asked that people mail him dirt—yes, dirt—from sites that might have had meaning to his father.

He then asked two of his closest friends, former seminary students who had been influenced by his father, to join him on a one-day pilgrimage through Kentucky. They stopped at the family farm in rural Kentucky, where five generations of relatives had lived; at the tree where the reverend's great-grandfather had been buried after being killed in the Civil War; at the hospital where Rowan and Laura Lue were born; at the church where his dad had been ordained; at every home in Louisville where Reverend Claypool had lived. At each location, Rowan took a shovel, dug up some earth, and scooped it into a baggie while one of his friends took photographs and the other friend—a burly guy dressed in black and wearing shades—sat in the driver's seat of the rented black Lincoln Town Car. "I was surprised we didn't get arrested," Rowan said.

After the Crescent Hill service in Louisville, about sixty people gathered around a hole that had been dug in the church lawn. Rowan put into the hole a small red-leafed maple. The baggies of dirt—representing more than a dozen locations—were emptied in the hole. As each baggie was emptied, a person who knew of Reverend Claypool's connection to that particular site spoke of his experiences there. Then Rowan's son, John R. Claypool VI, scattered in some of his grandad's ashes.

The tree has taken root.

I DON'T THINK that my mom brought up Bob's dream of playing Augusta because she had some cosmic sense that she might set me on a path leading to people like the Claypools and the Kuhl-kes. Yet I believe that the universe has a way of taking you where you need to go, and that if you're open to letting new people into your life, you might find solace from strangers. Ann Claypool and I had an exuberant conversation about the afterlife from which I drew a lot of comfort. Rowan's story about his dirt odyssey and the tree that is connected to his dad's history shows me that there are many journeys that can lead us back to our parents. Whereas Rowan collected dirt, I collected stories: this book is my maple tree.

I'm not sure if my mom or God or fate drew me to Dessey Kuhlke. However it happened, though, I am grateful that it did. As instrumental as Reverend Claypool was in Dessey's healing, Dessey is as important to mine. He helped me address the reality of my mom's illness at a time when my mom would not. And he reminded me that life is for the living. He did this even though he was nearly twice my age and from a different walk of life. He is one of the best men I know.

The night before Bob was flying off for his stay at Augusta National, Dessey and I spent an hour and a half on the phone.

I told him that in the days leading up to the trip, my sister and stepsiblings and I heard the first notes of excitement and optimism in Bob's voice since my mom became ill. I told Dessey that he had given all of us a bigger gift than we could have ever imagined.

"This experience has meant more to me than it has to you," he replied.

Impossible.

Chapter Eight

The Pilates Proselytizer

In one of my favorite photographs of my mom, she appears to be gritting her teeth.

Hair pulled back into a ponytail and dressed in a tight tank top and exercise pants, Mom is captured in the picture working out in the Pilates studio that is adjacent to the house in Tucson. The studio is open and airy. Its huge windows put you so close to nature that you feel like a cactus might scratch you.

In the picture, Mom is on the reformer, an apparatus conceived of by Joseph Pilates sometime around World War I. It looks like a low-to-the-ground wooden table with a flat carriage on the top that slides along the length. There are leather straps attached at one end and a foot bar at the other. You move the carriage by sitting or lying across it and either pulling the straps or pressing against the foot bar.

Mom is doing an exercise often referred to as Shaving with Teaser. This exercise is, if you'll forgive the technical lingo, fucking impossible.

To start, you do a Teaser: You begin by lying down on your back. Then you simultaneously raise your straightened legs and your torso until you are balanced on your bottom in a 45-degree angle.

Then you add "shaving": while balanced in your Teaser, you pull the reformer's straps from behind your head toward the ceiling, grazing the back of your head and, in the process, moving the carriage of the reformer upon which you are oh-so-tenuously balanced. Then you carefully release the tension from the straps so your hands are again behind your head. Then repeat, if you can.

The black-and-white photograph captures Mom in motion: she is in near perfect Teaser formation, and as she tries to fully extend the straps overhead, her eyes are squeezed shut, her nose is scrunched, her jaw is clenched.

Mom was doing an advanced workout at a seminar taught by her idol, Romana Kryzanowska, who was, by then, well into her eighties. Though a controversial figure, Romana is a legend in the world of Pilates. It was Mom's dream to bring Romana to Tucson to teach a seminar at her studio. She once had been scheduled to come, but that plan was thwarted by Mom's unexpected and prolonged coma. Romana agreed to reschedule when Mom was physically strong enough, and they settled upon May 2004.

From around the Southwest, other Pilates instructors traveled to Tucson to attend the all-day session. One of them can be seen in the background of this photo. He is sitting on a reformer next to Mom's and is watching her with palpable awe. Despite her obvious struggle to execute the exercise fully, the corners of her mouth are curled upward. She is enjoying the challenge.

What the picture doesn't show are the dozen (perhaps dozens of) malignant tumors that were, at that very moment, lurking in her lungs, and in the bones of her hips, sacrum, and spine.

I was the photographer.

I take a lot of pictures, at times documenting moments at the expense of experiencing them. But in this case, I am so thankful I was snapping away. Because the picture reminds me of my mom's strength and grace in the face of cancer.

DOING PILATES GAVE Mom physical stamina and spiritual joy. Teaching it gave her a sense of purpose. Aside from family, Pilates was the abiding passion of the last dozen years of her life. Yet until she got sick, I belittled the central role it played.

It's not that I didn't love doing Pilates. I did, and I do. But I was dismissive of Mom's passion because it entailed a guru-worship of Romana—and all sorts of attendant drama. I didn't understand why Mom wanted to be a part of something so cliquish. I didn't understand why she bothered with all the politics and insularity that seemed to me to encapsulate the Pilates community.

I also came to find the whole thing irritating and irksome because much of the drama that Mom fretted over involved Jerome Weinberg. Jerome was the guy who danced with Mom at her fiftieth birthday. And during the course of their long relationship, he evolved into a spiritual guru who held powerful sway over Mom as he moved in and out of her life over the years. He had the ability to hurt her feelings, and whether intentionally or not, he made her feel insecure on occasion. Lizzie and I harbored a lot of anger at him for that, but as I set out to dig into Mom's Pilates obsession, I knew I was going to have to confront Jerome, and my own complicated relationship with him.

You'd think Pilates was just a method of exercise—and that all the people who practiced it and taught it did so in the spirit of good health and goodwill. To the casual participant, it is merely a wonderful method to slim down, strengthen up, and rehabilitate. But today, for those who become instructors or even think about becoming instructors, Pilates is about much more. It's about an entire infrastructure of trade groups, guilds, training programs, certification centers, politics, infighting, and the mad dash for market share. It's also about the worship of the grand doyenne Romana Kryzanowska, who is synonymous with modern Pilates.

Romana began studying Joseph Pilates's method around 1940. She was a George Balanchine dancer who was searching for relief from an ankle injury. Joe Pilates—a German who is said to have worked on his method while being interned in a work camp in England during World War I—was teaching a system of exercise he called Contrology out of a studio on Eighth Avenue on Manhattan's West Side. When Pilates died in 1967, his wife and close confidants bandied about the names of several people who might maintain the studio's practice. Romana was among them, and the first to accept the job. Over a few decades, the actual assets of the practice—archival photos of Pilates demonstrating his method and other memorabilia, plus the right to say you owned Joe Pilates's business—passed from one owner to the next. But Romana was a constant, and she stayed focused on the teaching of Joe Pilates's techniques.

For many years, the Pilates method was obscure and had relatively few followers. This changed in the 1990s, when Hollywood starlets adopted Pilates as the newest and best way to sculpt their bodies. Pilates studios began opening across the country. A struggle over who owned the rights to use the name "Pilates" ensued.

At the time that the popularity took off, many of Joe Pilates's assets belonged to a physical therapist named Sean Gallagher. Among the assets Gallagher purchased were the Pilates and Pilates Studio trademarks. With Romana's support, Gallagher began sending letters threatening legal action to anyone using "Pilates" in their business name or marketing materials. The threats resulted in a protracted lawsuit between Gallagher and a longtime manufacturer of Pilates equipment. The case went to trial. Romana's position was that she alone was qualified to decide who could teach Pilates under the Pilates name, as a representative of Joseph Pilates's method. This drew the scorn of many in the Pilates diaspora (including several other Pilates elders who, like Romana, had trained at the knee of Joseph Pilates). Finally, a federal judge ruled in 2000 that the term *Pilates* had become generic, meaning that since the trademark had not been enforced by its previous owners, the term—in a legal sense—had entered the lexicon of generic terms like *aerobics* and *yoga*. This was not just a defeat for Gallagher. It was a rebuke to Romana. But she and her acolytes—my mom among them—didn't retreat in response. Instead, as the method continued to proliferate, they became more entrenched in the belief that only Romana and those she trained could teach "authentic" Pilates. (To give you a taste of how subtly Romana's students distinguished themselves, consider the title of a book one of her students published in 2009: *Discovering Pure Classical Pilates: Theory and Practice as Joseph Pilates Intended—The Traditional Method vs. the Lies for Sale.*)

Anyway, in the aftermath of the failed lawsuit, the Romana-ites (the Romans?) regrouped. With her daughter Sari Mejia Santo and her granddaughter Daria Pace, Romana created an organization called Romana's Pilates (trademark!). Romana's Pilates provides a comprehensive Pilates teacher certification program, perhaps the most thorough and demanding of the many certification programs that have sprung up in the last couple of years. So even though the law says that anyone can call themselves a Pilates instructor, only an exclusive clique of instructors can say they've been certified to teach the methodology by the one and only Romana (and those she has deputized).

My mom took this *so* seriously. It drove me crazy.

Mom was much more than just an instructor certified by Romana. She was one of a handful of teachers tapped by Romana, Sari, and Daria to help teach would-be teachers.

Mom got the gig because she was both an incredible practitioner of Pilates and a truly marvelous instructor—a stickler for perfect form but a motivator, too. With a huge smile on her face and a high pitch in her voice, she'd say, "Reach! Reach! Reach!" and when you felt like you could reach no farther, she'd get you to reach a little bit more. Then she'd say, "Am I ever proud of you!" in her earnest, excitable way.

But maybe just as valued as her teaching abilities was Mom's loyalty. Being allowed into Romana's orbit required devotion to her way of practicing the Pilates method. Romana was said to teach the purest form of Pilates because she explained each exercise exactly as Pilates himself had explained it. Any deviation from Romana's way was (and still is) considered by some as heresy. I use that word intentionally. Mom and other Romana followers often spoke of their leader in biblical terms: "She is a direct disciple of Joseph Pilates," Mom would say.

Mom was faithful. Once, she told me that she was considering cutting loose a certain student because she had taken a class at another studio that was taught by two instructors known to teach a series of movements whereby students hold a ball (in their hands or squeezed between their legs) as they execute an exercise. As far as Mom knew, Joseph Pilates never integrated into his method use of such a ball.

"So what?" I said, rolling my eyes.

"I'll tell you 'so what,' " Mom shot back, furious. "Pilates with a ball is *not* Pilates."

Mom wasn't alone in her worship of Romana. When Mom came to New York to work out with Romana, Sari, and Daria, I would sometimes come for a session in the studio they taught from—a big open room where dozens of people might be taking private lessons. Once, while I was taking a one-on-one lesson from a young woman, Romana began to do a series of exercises that involved hanging from suspended rings like a gymnast, pulling herself up and maneuvering all sorts of flips. My instructor kept watching Romana and joining in the chorus of others from around the studio who were calling, "Romana, you are *amazing.*" Romana was in her seventies—approaching eighty, even—and this was, in fact, quite an impressive showing. Yet I was paying about $60 for this lesson, and my instructor was barely paying attention to me.

I finally said, "Look, could you please focus on me?"

"I'm sorry," she grumbled, embarrassed. But within minutes her glance was diverted again in Romana's direction. During another lesson, I was doing the exercise known as Pulling Straps, in which you lay your belly on a block that has been placed upon the carriage of the reformer and you move the carriage to and fro by (you guessed it) pulling leather straps.

When I performed this exercise, the metal handles at the end of the leather straps would bang noisily along the perimeter of the reformer and even get stuck in the track of the moving carriage. "Can I grab hold of the handle so it doesn't make that noise?" I once asked an instructor.

"That's not done," she said.

Just then, Romana walked by my reformer. She heard the banging of the handle.

"Here," she said, "try holding the handle as well as the strap."

"Romana," my instructor said, "that is *genius*."

Romana deserves a huge amount of respect. She is a transcendent figure whose influence on Pilates is immeasurable. She is beloved by many and feared by not a few, her physical talents outmatched only by her abilities as a teacher to truly inspire students. But I just didn't get why Romana—and the community she stood at the front of—played such an important role in Mom's life. Nor did I see how grabbing a handle was a sign of genius.

It's not that Mom didn't try to explain the lure to me. Beginning when I went away to college, I spoke to Mom on the phone every day—at least once a day, but often several times. (As did Lizzie; as do Lizzie and I still.) During these conversations, Mom told me about the students she was working with and about the daily dramas of those she was helping to get certified by Romana. But I paid far less attention to the content than to the fact that it annoyed me. I was a snotty, self-important daughter, far too wrapped up in my own life to take seriously my mother's silly [air quotes] career.

To come to terms with my dismissive and disrespectful behavior, I thoroughly researched Mom's Pilates world after her death. I flew to Tucson and Arlington, Texas, to conduct interviews. I called eighteen former students. I took lessons from instructors Mom had herself learned from, as well as from those she taught. I traveled across Manhattan to meet with people who had studied under Joseph Pilates in the 1940s, '50s, and '60s.

I devoted this kind of attention to Pilates for a few reasons. First, I wanted to pay homage to this important part of Mom's final years. I also had grown sufficiently curious—the journalist in me wanted to know more about this subculture that, politely, can be called quirky. Beyond all that, I believed that Pilates might be the lens that could reveal a lot about what Mom was thinking at the end of her life.

THE ROAD TO enlightenment started at the letter P in Mom's green Filofax. There were about six pages of poorly labeled listings. One by one, I started making phone calls.

I reached a number of answering machines and left rambling messages.

"This is Katie Rosman. I'm the daughter of Suzy Rosin, who I think may have been your Pilates teacher . . ."

One person I found this way was Theresa Levy. She hadn't known that Mom had died. "I am so sad," she repeated more than once.

Theresa is a married mother of two. She had taken lessons from Mom for two years, beginning in 1996—about nine years before Mom died. She had happened upon a group class that Mom taught at the local racquet club. Theresa loved Pilates, and Mom. Soon she was taking Mom's classes several times a week, eventually signing up for private lessons at Mom's studio. "The workouts were always intense and hard," Theresa remembers. "Your mom made really subtle but incisive critiques. She made you just try so hard. I've taken lessons with other people since, so I know the difference. She was an incredible teacher."

Theresa really solidified a sense that however much Mom loved to look good, that was less a motivating factor than, perhaps, it might once have been. "Your mom had the body of a nineteen-year-old," Theresa told me. "She looked amazing and was in fantastic shape. But she saw the use of being healthy. It wasn't about being strong just for the sake of being strong, or to look good. For her it was about being strong so she could dance and have fun and celebrate."

I worked my way through the list of names, calling those whom I knew, those whose names were a little familiar, and those who, to me, were complete strangers. Not everyone I spoke to raved about Mom. One woman said she was a client of Mom's for just a short time. "She and I didn't really get along," the woman said, adding that her husband was an astronomer. I didn't press her for a detailed account because I could sort of imagine it: Mom probably bragged about the accomplishments of her father, the astronomer, a bit too much, perhaps implicitly suggesting that this woman's husband didn't measure up. Other people I reached spoke of Mom kindly—a nice person and a good instructor—if not as someone who had a tremendous impact upon them.

But then there were people like Anna Landau and her mother, Katya Peterson.

I got to the name "Anna" and called the adjacent number. A woman answered. In my full nasal Michigan accent I said, "May I please speak to ANN-a?"

"No, AHN-a isn't available," she told me. "This is her mother, Katya. Can I help you?"

Ah, *AHN-a* and Katya! Those names resonated instantly. I recalled that Anna had been a young girl with scoliosis, and Katya was her mother. I guess I had listened to Mom, at least occasionally.

I explained to Katya that I was the daughter of Suzy Rosin, and that I wanted to talk to her and Anna about my mom's role as a Pilates instructor. "I am so glad you called," Katya said. "We just heard last year that your Mom died, and we were devastated." Katya gave me her and Anna's e-mail addresses, and we arranged a time for the three of us to talk together.

Mom began working with Anna in 1995. An active kid and an avid dancer, Anna was eleven and recently had been diagnosed with scoliosis. With two 50-degree S-curves in her spine and a 19-degree curve in her neck, Anna was told by doctors that she needed to wear a brace twenty-three hours per day, for five years. It was a heavily padded, corsetlike plastic brace that extended from her armpits to her hips. "It felt like the end of the world," Katya told me.

Katya instantly began to consider the implications for Anna's overall physical development of wearing a brace during such an important time of growth. She was worried about inactivity and muscle atrophy. She shared her concerns with a friend—a former dancer who lived in New York City and who had become a Pilates instructor. The friend told Katya that Anna should try Pilates. But she urged her to make sure that Anna worked out only with an instructor who had been Romana-trained.

It was the mid-1990s, and Pilates was still relatively obscure outside of Los Angeles and New York. Katya thought, "I'm in Tucson, Arizona. How am I going to find someone who has been trained by Romana in New York City?"

But she found my mom. For three and a half years, two days a week, Katya picked up Anna and her younger sister Sonya from school and made the drive to my mom's studio.

While the three of us were on the phone, Anna and Katya argued back and forth about the length of time it took to get from Anna's school to Mom's house.

K: "It was forty-five minutes."
A: "No, it wasn't that long."
K: "Anna! Yes, it was! It was forty-five minutes each way, and it was a big deal!"

Hearing a mother and daughter fight about a trivial matter made me ache for the opportunity to fight with my mom!

However long the car ride, Anna took three lessons a week from Mom, including a Saturday-morning group class. Anna and Katya had different agendas, as mothers and daughters most often do. Yet Mom managed to earn the confidence of both. Katya felt reassured by Mom's understanding that the stakes were high, that she was working with a child with a disease that brought with it complicated physical and emotional realities. "Suzy totally understood the implications," Katya said. Yet Mom didn't infantilize Anna. "She didn't treat me like a punk kid," Anna said. "She treated me like she would any client, like an adult. That was a big deal."

There were a lot of physical gains from Anna's Pilates lessons—even Anna's skeptical doctors admitted that. But there were significant emotional benefits too. Wearing a brace at school made Anna feel *other* in that dreaded adolescent sense. But her time with Mom helped her combat insecurity. "Suzy gave me a sense of confidence in myself," Anna told me. "Everything I did, it was always affirming. 'You are doing amazingly well!' she would say. She was reaffirming that I was in control of my body. 'You really understand what's going on here, you really get it,' she would say, and, 'You are exceptional among my students.' You can't help but feel good, whether it's true or not. It instilled in me a sense that *I can do this. I can do anything.* It was a very empowering relationship."

Of all the things that came from my conversation with Katya and Anna, it was a side remark that has stuck with me the most. Katya was telling me about the group classes Mom taught at the racquet club. She said the classes would be packed with between thirty and forty people. Mom would go around the room toward the end of the class and show each person a stretch personalized to their specific needs. "She just had a golden understanding of how to help each person," Katya said.

Then—and just sort of as an aside—Katya said something that I was unable to stop thinking about for days: "It's funny," she said, "because when I think of Suzy's hands, if you really looked at them, they didn't look like how you would expect a healer's hands to look."

I felt so proud of my mom. She was a healer.

I HAVEN'T BEEN able to pin down when my mom first began doing Pilates. I'm able to track down people she hadn't spoken to in years, people she only knew for brief periods of time. But I'm unable to verify for certain when she first tasted something that became an obsession and remained so until her dying day. It's a reminder to me of the limitations of reporting on a person who was never famous and is now, if you'll forgive me, dead.

In any case, I do know that by 1992, Mom was taking regular lessons.

I had graduated from high school a few years earlier and was ensconced in college life in Ann Arbor. Lizzie was living and working in Washington, D.C. By then Mom had moved from the house in which I was raised in suburban Detroit to a two-bedroom condo in Tucson. Bob's business remained in Michigan, so he traveled between the Midwest and the Southwest.

They knew the next phase of their lives was going to be based in Tucson. But at first they weren't sure what kind of life they would want to live. As they figured it out, Bob bought two plots of land. One was tucked in the foothills, a somewhat secluded spot above a country club and golf course. The other was a small parcel on the grounds of Canyon Ranch, which at the time was among the most ballyhooed spa destinations in the world. Owning land there entitled our family to use the facilities of Canyon Ranch. It was a privilege of which my mom took full advantage (much to the apparent irritation of the spa's owners and executive overseers, who treated my omnipresent mom with barely veiled contempt). She used it like a day camp.

As Mom and Bob were getting a feel for Tucson, the Ranch hired John White, a man newly transplanted from New York, to spearhead a program in the still fairly unknown method of Pilates. It was under his tutelage that Mom first fell in love with the method. John is super tall, lithe, my-oh-my handsome, and imbued with a palpable, joyful energy that is irresistible. Mom adored him from the outset, and they remained close throughout the remainder of her life. The night she died, he was among those who came to our house to hold her hand for a last time.

John himself was first introduced to Pilates when he was eighteen, in the late 1970s. A theater arts major at UCLA, he decided he wanted to become a professional dancer, but he lacked the requisite strength. He was told by a professor to start Pilates lessons at the studio of Ron Fletcher, someone who had been trained directly by Joseph Pilates. The Pilates work gave him the strength and flexibility needed to study dance. Within a handful of years he was dancing professionally, eventually joining the Martha Graham Dance Company for two years. He remained with the company until 1991.

Around the time that he left Martha Graham, John met a dashing young man (actually, my mom's great friend Joe Asciutto) who was visiting New York from Tucson. John decided to join him there. Soon after he arrived, John got a call from Canyon Ranch. Almost immediately after he was hired, Mom started taking lessons from him. She was so eager to learn—and John was so excited to teach someone in such kick-ass shape—

that they would work out at dawn or at night to accommodate John's packed schedule.

"She loved the movement," John told me after giving me one of the best lessons I've ever had. "We went through everything I knew in basically just a few years. She would just try anything and everything—fearless, absolutely fearless. There was certainly no one else that I taught that was anywhere near Suzy's level of fitness or ability. She was tiny, but she was very strong. She could do things that big guys couldn't do, and she loved that."

As Mom grew more and more enthralled, she told John she wanted to become a Pilates instructor. John told her about Romana, this woman in New York who had learned the method directly from Joseph Pilates, and who focused on teaching it exactly as it had been taught to her. It wasn't long before Mom was traveling every several months to New York to take lessons.

By this time, I had graduated from college and moved to New York. In 1995, I had taken a job as a coffee-fetching administrative assistant at *Elle* magazine. I know that when Mom came to New York, visiting me was a part of her motivation. But there were plenty of occasions when I had the right to question if I was the main draw. She spent as much time as possible at Drago's, the studio at which Romana taught.

Located on the sixth floor of an unremarkable building on West Fifty-seventh Street west of Fifth Avenue, Drago's was a throwback to a bygone era. Thin, fit women dressed in leotards, tights, and leg warmers (at least fifteen years post–Jane Fonda/ Olivia Newton-John's "Let's Get Physical") lay on mats doing leg lifts while men wearing wife-beaters, too-short shorts, and pulled-to-mid-shin tube socks hoisted in the air heavy medicine balls and swung from rings suspended from the ceiling. These people would mix in with the people like my mom, who were dressed in more contemporary workout gear (tight black exercise pants and body-hugging tank tops). The Pilates students cruised through dramatic and rigorous regimens on reformers and other pieces of hulking wood and vinyl Pilates apparatuses like the "Cadillac" and the "chair." The framed photos of Joe Pilates, in his barrel-chested octogenarian glory, only partially masked the degree to which the paint was chipping from the walls. The women's locker room had one grimy shower, toilet, and sink. The dressing area was dingy, free of amenities, and consisted of wooden benches where women sat uncomfortably while wrangling themselves into their work clothes.

Along the perimeter of the main room hovered young women and men, fresh-faced and fresh from small towns around the country. They were the apprentices, who were, in accordance with their teacher certification training, observing the sessions going on around the studio. When an apprentice had observed for a few hundred hours, he or she would get called on to give instruction to clients of the studio. The apprentices worked for free (after paying several thousands of dollars in tuition), and clients paid the studio to take lessons from the apprentices.

My mom never had to suffer through an apprenticeship because in the mid-1990s, people like my mom who were already exceedingly proficient in Pilates were exempt from the hundreds of hours apprentices were supposed to devote to observation and student teaching. Instead, they would become certified by taking a practical exam during which Romana evaluated their form and teaching technique. That was followed by a written test that included sections on anatomy and kinesiology.

Mom aced the practical evaluation. For the written portion,

she studied like a madwoman, immersing herself in anatomy texts, Pilates manuals, and flashcards that quizzed her knowledge of complex, dynamic exercises with names like Snake, Swan, and Side Splits. She failed.

This, I remember. As does John: "She was wrecked," he said.

When Mom was finally able to see the marks on her graded exam, she contested her score to Sari, arguing that the wording of some questions had been vague and misleading. It was decided that Mom should retake the test. She did so, and passed. She opened for business in the Pilates studio at her house, calling it Suzy's Pilates.

Even though Mom moved on quickly, I couldn't. When Mom was told she failed, she wasn't just distraught. She was totally mortified. "I worked so hard, but I'm no good," she said to me on the phone. Maybe my eye-rolling at the mention of Romana's Pilates was my way of trying to protect Mom. If an institution is not to be taken seriously, then who cares how it judges you? (When I discussed this with Sari years later, she noted that sometimes failing is a part of learning.)

Most nights, when Mom was in New York to visit Lizzie and me (before Lizzie moved to Los Angeles) and to work out with Romana, we would meet for dinner at Café Fiorello, a restaurant near Lincoln Center. However sophisticated Mom may have been in some ways, it didn't extend to her palate. She liked very plain food, and required little variety. It didn't matter that we were in a city with thousands of wonderful restaurants. Mom liked the restaurant's spaghetti marinara and paper-thin-crust pizza. "Let's eat at Fiorello," she would say again and again, and we would.

Nursing a San Pellegrino (no ice, no lime) as Lizzie and I relaxed with the house red, Mom would tell us about her day at the Pilates studio. But she didn't have to, because she wore it on her face. If she had a good day—a day of exhausting, challenging workouts in which she succeeded in trying something new and earned kudos from Romana—she would smile so organically and so broadly that the veins in her neck would protrude. But if Sari had spoken harshly to Mom, or worse, if Romana had been uninterested in Mom's presence at the studio, Mom would show up at the restaurant with her cheeks sagging, her shoulders drooping, and her eyes devoid of animation. It was hard for me to see her so vulnerable.

THE MORE I interviewed people, the more I could see the bifurcation of Mom's Pilates world. There was the hierarchy, bureaucracy, and politics of the Romana's Pilates establishment. And then there were the relationships she had with her own students.

Atasha Jaffe and Mom met in 1997 when Atasha was in her senior year at the University of Arizona. A modern dance major, Atasha had to undergo surgery on her knee and was looking for a way to rehabilitate it. Her family had a membership at the Tucson Racquet Club. There, she happened upon Pilates and Mom. She began attending class once a week, then three times a week, then five times. The effects on her rehab were great—she began dancing again, free of her knee brace. But Pilates connected with her on a deeper level too. "I really enjoyed sculpture, dance, and biology, and I felt like Pilates brought them all together," Atasha told me.

When Atasha decided that she wanted to get certified as a Pilates instructor, Mom told her she would help her get through the program. At the time, Romana insisted that people applying to go through the program first take seventy-five private lessons from an instructor whom Romana had already certified. Mom's rates were $50 for a private lesson. In exchange for Atasha's assistance at Mom's increasingly oversubscribed classes at the racquet club, Mom gave Atasha a 50 percent discount on private lessons. "It gave me total dignity," Atasha said. "The relationship was really balanced. She helped me, and I helped her."

The camaraderie developed outside the studio as well. Atasha was close with her own parents, but they were going through a difficult divorce that occupied them. Meanwhile, Mom was facing her own isolation: her children were living in distant cities, and her husband was frequently traveling to see to his business in Detroit. Mom would sometimes call Atasha and ask her if she wanted to take a Pilates lesson, eat a home-cooked meal, and spend the night in my or Lizzie's bedroom. "I get scared up here at night by myself," she would tell Atasha.

When they were out in public together, people would often mistake Mom and Atasha for mother and daughter. Atasha bears more than a passing resemblance to me. She too has blondish curly hair, bright eyes, and a bubbly mien. Mom would wrap her arm around Atasha's shoulder and say, "She's my third daughter!"

Atasha told me, "I used to worry, 'Would this be weird for Lizzie and Katie?' I had the sense that you knew that, coming from someone as openhearted as your Mom, there was enough love for so many people. The truth is, she missed you and Lizzie so much. She told me that over and over again. Her whole face and body would light up when she talked about you. 'You should hear what Lizzie did!' and 'You've got to read the article Katie wrote!' It was very powerful and very beautiful to see that kind of love that a mother had for her daughters."

I never was jealous of Mom's closeness with Atasha, though I didn't fully appreciate its depth until I interviewed Atasha recently. I'm not exactly sure why I wasn't threatened by Mom's closeness with other young women. I think there is something to what Atasha says—that Mom's love was so clearly an infinite resource, I never had to worry that attention paid to someone else would come at a cost to me. And considering how often my mom called me, I think I was happy to have someone deflect the attention.

I only came to get some insight on Mom's motivations unexpectedly—and from a woman who never knew my mother.

Struggling one day to write about Mom's relationship to Pilates, to Romana, and to the young people in whose lives she got so involved, I broke away from the computer to take a walk with a writer I know of my mom's generation. I shared with her the issues I, as a writer and a daughter, was working through. "I think I do the same thing your mom did," she said. "I take young women under my wing."

Why do you think you do it? I asked.

"It lets me redo some of the things I did wrong with my own daughter," she said. "It lets me have a mother-daughter relationship that is stripped of all the complications."

AFTER ATASHA EARNED her Pilates certification, Mom told her she needed to buy a reformer so that she could give private lessons. The cost of a reformer at the time was $3,200—a sum that was totally out of Atasha's reach. So Mom lent her the money, and

Atasha worked like a dog to pay her back within three months. "She gave me the ability, the foothold to start having a career to support myself," Atasha said. "She took an interest in young women trying to start their lives."

Mom's desire to help people, though, left her vulnerable. Just before she began working with Atasha, Mom also took on another student. Janet was really overweight, and Mom tried to motivate her to lose weight by giving her tons of lessons at a huge discount. Janet lost a lot of weight, like seventy-five pounds, and Mom was so proud of her—and of her own role in helping her student achieve such a weight loss. One day, Janet told Mom that her boyfriend had proposed marriage. Mom said, "That is so exciting! Is there anything I can do?"

"Well, you could throw a shower for me," Janet replied.

Atasha was at Mom's studio, helping out as she tried to rack up her apprenticeship hours. "Your mom was like, 'What?! Well, okay,'" Atasha said.

On a weekend afternoon, Mom's house filled up with friends and relatives of Janet's, none of whom Mom had ever met. Mom asked Atasha to help with serving the food Mom had prepared and cleaning up afterward. I had forgotten about the shower, but as Atasha described it to me, I began to recall my mom's discomfort with the situation. The shower had been foisted upon her in a way that made her feel a bit like the unhired help.

Then Janet asked Mom to serve as a bridesmaid at her wedding. It's bad enough when you are in your twenties to be asked to participate in a wedding between people to whom you aren't particularly close. Dressing up in an ugly, unflattering bridesmaid dress and arriving at a church three hours before the ceremony and then standing on dyed silk high heels for bridal party photos is a rite of passage suffered by young single women who soldier through by getting drunk on free champagne and keeping an eye out for a cute groomsman. But for a teetotaling, long-married woman in her fifties who was not in the habit of wearing much taffeta . . . well, Lizzie and I derived endless pleasure from imagining the scene.

Poor Mom was dreading the wedding, but when Lizzie and I teased her about it, she would righteously defend Janet. "She wants to honor me for the wonderful thing I helped her accomplish," Mom would say, a little wounded.

Mom always found a way to focus on people's best intentions. But she was sometimes naive in doing so.

Just as Mom lent money to Atasha to buy a reformer, she wanted to help Janet get one too. So she offered to sell her one of hers. The deal (as Bob, Lizzie, Atasha, and I recall it) was that Janet would take the reformer and pay Mom back in interest-free installments at her leisure.

Pretty much as soon as Janet took possession of the reformer, Mom never heard from her again. Though she was stunned by the betrayal, the incident didn't shake Mom as much as it did Lizzie and me. We were irate—not just because of what Janet had done, but by Mom's easy-come-easy-go reaction. "Why do you let people walk all over you?" I would ask.

It all seems so obvious at this moment—as obvious now as it was opaque then: Mom, by this point in her life, understood the calculus of relationships. She made herself vulnerable to avail herself of the possibility of making a meaningful connection with someone. She didn't need every relationship to work out in the conventional sense. She could see people for the good in them, even as the bad was impossible to ignore. She had arrived at a place where she was willing to abide by the Janets because without exposing herself to those who might hurt her, she would never taste the sweetness of the Atashas and the Cates.

In 1999, Cate Noble was a nineteen-year-old student at the University of Arizona who was working her way through college, first at a day spa and then at a clothing boutique. At the spa, she met a client of Mom's, who told her about Pilates. Soon my mom, the Pilates proselytizer, convinced Cate to work toward getting certified by Romana. She too needed to take seventy-five lessons. Mom wouldn't let her pay a dime. "I just want you to get through the program," Mom said. Still, she expected Cate to take her training seriously. "Suzy was really encouraging, but she was very demanding, too. When you did something that she didn't think was great, she'd just shrug her shoulders and move on. You so wanted to get that big smile out of her that you'd try harder and harder. I have never been as sore as when I was working out with your mom."

When Cate had to travel to Los Angeles to another Romana's Pilates-sanctioned studio to take her beginner and intermediate tests, Mom went with her. When Cate was to meet Romana for the first time, in New York, Mom flew in with her and introduced them. "Your mom was a very big part of my life," Cate said to me. "I thought of Suzy as my Tucson Mom."

When Mom became sick, her relationship with Cate intensified. While many college students were blowing off class and getting drunk, Cate was studying, working, getting certification as a Pilates instructor—and helping to care for a woman with cancer.

She would sit by Mom's bedside, she would run errands, she once even rushed Mom to the hospital when Bob was out of town and Mom unexpectedly got sick. Cate spent hours and hours over the course of Mom's illness keeping her company, holding her hand. They talked Pilates a lot. When Cate earned her certification, Mom urged her to open a studio of her own. Bob helped her negotiate the lease. Today, more than four years later, Cate's studio is doing well.

When Cate got married, a little more than a year after Mom had died, Lizzie and I flew to Tucson to attend the wedding with Bob. Knowing it would please Mom, we lent to Cate Mom's dangling mother-of-pearl earrings, which both Lizzie and I had worn at our own weddings. In a photograph from Cate's wedding, Lizzie and I are standing on either side of the beautiful bride. Mom's earrings, hanging from Cate's lobes, are prominently visible. From the right earring, a tiny iridescent blue sparkle is captured by the photo. "Of the hundreds of pictures from the wedding," Cate told me afterward, "the one with you, Lizzie, and me is the only one where the earrings give off that blue light."

ONE OF THE teachers at Cate's studio is a mother just a few years older than I am. Her name is Lori Jernigan. Lori was the last person Mom trained.

Lori found Mom through an advertisement Mom had placed in a local paper for Romana's Pilates training. Mom had already been diagnosed with cancer, "but I don't think anyone in the Pilates world knew at that point how sick Suzy was," Lori told me, "and I don't think Suzy admitted to herself what was going on."

Lori's recollection of Mom as a teacher contrasts with those of so many other clients and students I interviewed. "Suzy wasn't high energy," she told me. "She couldn't be physically involved in our lessons. She taught me by voice, just watching me and telling me what to do. Even then, she would sometimes say, 'I need to catch my breath.' She would be demanding. The compliments were not steadily flowing. But if you did something she liked, she would let you know. She would want more and more, and I would try to give it to her. She knew that about me, and that's what I liked about her. She knew how to get me to give it my all."

Lori did much of her training with Cate. But before Lori would fly off to New York for various tests and evaluations, my mom would ask Lori to come to her studio so Mom could be certain of her readiness. In the safety of her adored studio, and in the company of one of the people she knew least, Mom would share the emotions she kept hidden from us.

Once, Mom was giving Lori a lesson on the Pilates apparatus known as the Cadillac. It was after Mom had recuperated from the Sloan-Kettering operation but before we knew how rapidly time was marching on. Though Lori knew all about Mom's condition—Cate kept her apprised—she and Mom had never discussed it. And then, mid-lesson, apropos of nothing, Mom said, "I'm having trouble with my voice. I'm worried the cancer is coming back, and I don't know what to tell my daughters."

Months later, when Mom was really sick and Bob had to travel to Michigan, Lori took a shift (as so many of Mom's Pilates students did) keeping Mom company until a night nurse arrived.

"She just blurted out, 'I'm dying, and I'm scared,' " Lori said. Mom started to cry. "What if this is all that there is?" she said. "What if there is nothing after?" Then just as quickly as my mom broke down, she pulled herself together.

I sobbed as Lori told me this. After we hung up, I called Lizzie.

Why, I asked her, was Mom sharing with other people—virtual strangers—the sort of thing I had been desperate for her to share with us?

Lizzie grew silent for a minute and then answered. "You know, maybe by not talking to us about any of this, Mom thought she was protecting us. Maybe having people like Lori, people Mom didn't know well, to unload this stuff on, allowed her to shield us," Lizzie said. "Maybe it made her feel good, because she could still be the protective Mom."

This, I had never considered: that Mom might have been closed off emotionally to us not merely because she was afraid but because she wanted to shelter us from her fear. I hope that this is even a little bit true. The idea of her asserting herself as a mother—rather than suffering emotionally without the comfort from we who loved her so—is much easier for me to live with.

In the last months that Mom was still able to get out of bed, she would call Lori and tell her to come over for a lesson. Lori would arrive at Mom's, and instead of going straight into the studio, she would knock on the door to the house. Once inside, she would help Mom collect her walker and portable oxygen tank and inch her way across the driveway to the studio.

Lori told me, "There came a point, where I would think to myself, 'What am I doing?' And I would say, 'Suzy, please. We don't have to do this.' "

Mom would stop, lean on her walker, and take a deep breath. "Lori," she would say, "this is what I've been waiting for all day."

RECENTLY, I VENTURED back to Drago's—now called True Pilates—for the first time since my mom died. It was not without anxiety.

Since Mom died, when I pass 50 West Fifty-seventh Street— no matter how hurried or preoccupied—I feel my shoulders slump in sadness. There was no place where Mom seemed more vital and more a part of a community (for better or worse) than she did at Drago's. I imagine her in her cute exercise gear, bopping down the street, stopping by Mangia for a piece of fruit and a cup of coffee before heading up to a place where she was so proud to be known. On her behalf, I feel the crush of all that she wanted but didn't have time to experience.

On this particular occasion, the nervousness was intensified because I wasn't merely passing by but venturing into what my mom saw as a temple.

I was there to take a lesson from Jerome, who had become known among the international community of Pilates aficionados as a superstar, a Romana protégé of the highest order. But before he was Romana's protégé, he was Mom's student.

He was also one of her very best friends. As opposed to how we have felt about people like Atasha and Cate (and Cheryl and Jan and Lori and . . .), Lizzie and I had complex feelings about Mom's relationship with Jerome. We didn't hide those feelings from Mom, or from Jerome for that matter. "He takes you for granted," we'd say. "He can be too competitive with you," we'd point out. And at times, we were right. But we weren't honest about the fact that we were jealous of the time Mom devoted to Jerome.

Jerome had moved to New York from Tucson several years ago to work closely with Romana. Although we live in the same area, Jerome and I had not seen each other since Mom died, except for at her Tucson memorial service.

Once, months after Mom's memorial service, I saw Jerome on Fifty-seventh Street. I whizzed by him, hoping he wouldn't notice me—or wouldn't acknowledge me if he did.

I shouldn't have worried: as I was setting up all these interviews to learn about Mom's Pilates world, Jerome dodged my calls for about six weeks.

One such interchange, similar to others, went like this:

I called the studio and asked for Jerome. The guy who answered the phone told me Jerome was teaching until noon. I should try to call at about 12:05, he told me.

12:05

GUY: "True Pilates . . ."
ME: "Hi, is Jerome available?"
GUY [*shouting away from the phone*]: "Hey Jerome, phone!"
[*grumbling*]
GUY: "Who's calling?"
ME: "This is Katie Rosman, Suzy Rosin's daughter."
[*more grumbling*]
GUY: "Uh, sorry, but Jerome actually just ran out to lunch."

A few days later, I reached the same receptionist. When I identified myself, the guy realized that Jerome had actually just gone into the locker room to take a shower.

This happened repeatedly: Jerome would suddenly go missing when I identified myself. So, one day—after six weeks of trying—I got obnoxious and said this to the receptionist: "Please tell Jerome that Katie Rosman called, and tell him that out of respect for my dead mother, I expect him to return this call."

This is not exactly the tone I usually take to build a reporter-source relationship, but my tactic worked: Jerome called me back minutes later. I was very friendly, and neither of us acknowledged the tension. We decided I would come to the studio, take a lesson from him, and then we'd sit down to talk.

Jerome looked the same, but older. Brown bangs grown long and pushed off his face. High cheekbones jutting out beneath bright brown eyes. A goofy sort of smile. We hugged awkwardly, and hurried off to start the lesson. I lay down on the reformer and began to do my workout.

"If your mom could see us together now," he said.

Yes, the sight would have shocked the hell out of her. But I was exactly where I had to be.

Soon after Mom and Jerome had met when Jerome was working as a fitness instructor at Canyon Ranch, Mom began arranging private funk dance lessons with him. They would meet in the Ranch's racquetball courts, where they could take advantage of the slick wood floors. Mom loved people who could express joy and beauty through movement, and she was drawn to Jerome for this reason.

When Mom and Bob opted to build a house in the foothills—to leave behind the life of Canyon Ranch, which to Bob felt too insular—they built a dance studio off the master bedroom, with big windows that looked up the mountain. There, Jerome continued to teach Mom dance. Over the years, they added meditation and yoga to the menu of spiritual and physical disciplines that Mom turned to Jerome to experience.

Jerome was unlike most people my mom had been exposed to in her previous life as a suburban Detroit mother and wife. Born in 1954 in Okinawa, he was the son of a Japanese woman and a Jewish American father who was stationed in Okinawa by the U.S. military. The Weinberg family moved to Tucson in 1965, and Jerome came of age during the turbulence of the Vietnam War era. Jerome couldn't make sense of his father's support of the war, so he left home after high school, moving to an ashram in Tucson. After steeping himself in the study of yoga, he relocated to Hawaii before cofounding an ashram in Japan. After ten years of such yoga-fueled, meditative living, Jerome decided to move back to Tucson. "I knew I needed to learn how to grow in other ways," he said. He was hired by Canyon Ranch to teach yoga and dance, and to lead hikes. He met an exercise teacher there. They married, moved to India to study yoga, returned to Tucson and the Ranch, and eventually divorced.

Around this time, Jerome met Mom. "We were kindred spirits," Jerome said to me when I interviewed him after the Pilates lesson. "We saw things alike. We liked a life filled with dancing and laughing."

In the late 1990s, Mom convinced Jerome to try Pilates. In doing so, she changed his life. She trained him—for free—and helped him become certified by Romana. Then she helped him move to New York—literally, she came to the city with him and helped him get settled into the foreign ways of big-city culture.

One of the main issues Lizzie and I have had with Jerome is

our sense that he hasn't given Mom enough credit for the role she played in shaping the life he now enjoys. It's as though he could handle his and Mom's dynamic when she existed as his student, eager to soak up his spiritual lessons. But when it came to Pilates, something Mom excelled at as well, he could be dismissive of her talents, and even competitive.

When I sat down with him at True Pilates, Jerome didn't much assuage that feeling. When I brought up that Mom had been his first teacher, he said, "She *was* my first teacher," as if he had forgotten such an incidental detail. "One day she talked to me about Romana and about how exciting it was to be with Romana. I thought, 'I have to meet this woman.' So Suzy taught me the basics." What I heard was that in Jerome's view, Mom's singular contribution was whetting his curiosity about Romana and doing a good job of mindlessly passing along the primary lessons. In fairness to Jerome: the dominant principle of Romana's Pilates is that she and only she can impart the Pilates method as Joseph Pilates intended it to be taught. So that Mom did not deviate from Romana's instruction is, in that world, a testament to her skill. And I understand that a mathematician who learns the intricacies of quantum theory from an MIT professor doesn't spend a lot of time praising his high school algebra teacher. But there was something ungracious about how quickly Jerome dismissed Mom's contributions.

What had made Lizzie and me most uncomfortable was the financial aspect of their relationship. Mom took on the role of benefactor, often paying Jerome for the time they spent dancing or meditating together. But as their relationship changed—from teacher/student to friends—the fundamentals of the financial arrangement stayed in place. Mom helped him in myriad ways: storing his belongings in my bedroom in the house in Tucson, letting him keep his car in her garage when he was shuttling between New York and Tucson, giving him free access to her Pilates studio to teach clients without asking him to share any proceeds, flying to New York to help him get settled in an apartment when he decided to make the move. I don't think Mom ever asked him to pay for a lesson when he was learning Pilates from her.

Bob used to gently tease Mom about Jerome's dependence on them, but Uncle Eddie wasn't so delicate. He calls Jerome "Kato"—as in Kato Kaelin, O. J. Simpson's onetime, longtime houseguest. Lizzie and I didn't respond to Mom's friendship with humor or sarcasm. "Why do you let him take advantage of you like this?" we would ask, exasperated.

"You can't be taken advantage of when you are aware of what's going on," she would say. She wasn't being snowed, she would assure us again and again, because she got a lot of satisfaction from being with Jerome. "He's got to pay his bills," she said, "and I'm asking him to spend time meditating and dancing with me." When she liked someone's energy, she took pleasure in helping that person in ways that would have no impact on her and Bob's life. ("Maybe this explains why Bob is such a Republican," Joe would say to me. "He's married to a Marxist who redistributes his wealth.")

I asked Jerome about the ways Mom had set him up financially. He didn't betray a hint of embarrassment. "She helped me, and I helped her. In our relationship, it always equaled out." Later, we returned to the topic. He said, "Your mom did a lot for me, and she helped me a lot with money. I'm not denying that. I was asked by Romana to travel around the world with her and while I did, she taught me things she taught to very few people. And then I would come back and share all of that knowledge with your mom. It meant something to her." I think Jerome made a really fair point: there are different kinds of currency.

While the young women mentored by Mom relied on her for encouragement as they sought to build their own lives, Jerome seemed to turn to Mom for help in navigating the world outside the dance/yoga/Pilates studio in some fundamental ways.

One of the last times I saw Jerome during Mom's lifetime was in Tucson. He had already moved to New York but was back for a visit. Joe and I happened to be in town too. Some of the Tucson Pilates crew went out to dinner, to a beautiful restaurant located in a former Spanish hacienda. The waiter came to take our order.

"For you, sir?" he said to Jerome. Jerome's eyes widened; his neck tensed. He turned and gave my mom a terrified, pleading look.

"He'll have plain noodles, and can you put just a little marinara sauce on them?" my mom said to the waiter.

At the time, I kicked my husband's shin under the table and ordered another drink. But now I see that Jerome really leaned on my mom. She was his ambassador, his spokeswoman. It must have been terrifying for him to consider navigating the world without the safety net she provided.

As Mom got sicker, we were confronted with the good and the bad of Jerome's innocent, simplistic worldview. When the financial logistics of his taking time off from his job at Drago's could be worked out by Mom and Bob, Jerome would come spend weeks at a time with Mom in Tucson, practicing meditation and Pilates. I think these were among the most serene times Mom experienced at the end of her life. "We would meditate," Jerome said, "and I would tell her, 'You are the light. You are much greater than your physical life.' I taught her in meditation that such a light could never die."

But when meditation failed to ameliorate the agonies of cancer, Jerome's innocence came across as childish. In the last few weeks of Mom's life, when Jerome visited, he sat by her bedside for hours as she spoke—in denial and on drugs—about how one day she was going to get stronger. She told Jerome he could move back to Tucson, and together they would revive her Pilates studio.

At one point, Jerome left Mom's room and went to find Lizzie, who was also in town. "Lizzie," he asked, "when do you think your mom is going to be better? Because if I'm going to start working at her studio again, I'll need some time to plan."

Lizzie called me immediately after. She was *enraged* that (a) Jerome interrupted her while she watched the finale of *The Bachelor*, and (b) on top of all else she had to deal with as her mother was dying, she was expected to explain to Jerome realities that would be obvious to anyone else in the world.

But maybe this was at the core of what Mom loved about Jerome—their shared belief that all obstacles could be overcome, that there was always hope that good could prevail, that artificial norms imposed by society didn't have to be obeyed.

"She was a deeply spiritual person," Jerome said of my mom. "She stood for the truth. She was a symbol of integrity. She had her values. She knew what was right and wrong. She had an incredible amount of tolerance for people who were different from her." Jerome didn't say this pointedly, but if he had, I wouldn't have faulted him.

I called Lizzie after and relayed the conversation. "Mom really was, like, the least judgmental person," I said.

"Well," she said, "that trait sure skipped a generation."

JUST BEFORE ROMANA came to Tucson to give the seminar at Mom's studio, Mom was asked by a newspaper reporter about the allure of Romana. Mom responded, "She teaches with love and energy. Just being in her presence is so exhilarating and exciting. I absolutely worship her."

I knew it was essential that I understand the hold Romana had over my mom. First, I tried to get a sense of Romana through old-fashioned reporting. I sought out people who knew her as a teacher and a mentor. People spoke of her exuberance, her energy, her toughness. Mari Winsor—who, with her infomercials is probably more responsible than anyone for the mass awareness of Pilates—told me, "There is one word that captures Romana and what she gives off when she is teaching: joy."

But I knew it was important to go directly to the oracle. A few years before Mom died, Romana had moved to Fort Worth, Texas, where her son lives. So I flew there to meet with her.

Metroplex Pilates, where Romana now teaches, is situated in the back of a ballet studio, on a gloomy street off the highway in Arlington, just outside of Forth Worth. In every possible way, Arlington is a long way from New York City. It's the home of a Six Flags amusement park, of the stadium where the Texas Rangers play, and of another stadium built for the Dallas Cowboys. There are a lot of strip malls. Frankly, it's not the type of place you dream of visiting. Yet on a hot summer morning, as I drove to meet Romana, I felt a pang of melancholy: this was a trip Mom should have been taking. I felt as though I was completing a pilgrimage in my mother's stead.

At the time of my visit, the studio was headed up by Cha Cha Guerrero—a senior-level Pilates instructor—and her boyfriend Roberto, who doesn't do Pilates but explained his job to me: "I'm Romana's confidant."

"We all run the studio together, but of course nothing happens without Romana's final say-so," Cha Cha told me.

At the time of my visit, the studio didn't have much of a local clientele. Instead, it was operating as a teacher-training center and continuing-education facility. To get certified and to maintain good standing as a Romana's Pilates instructor, apprentices and continuing-education students are not required to study with Romana directly. In fact, doing so would be logistically impossible as Romana's teaching schedule has been scaled back in the last several years. Her daughter and granddaughter have designated a handful of studios around the country as training centers. Yet for many, the reason to get certified by and remain affiliated with Romana's Pilates (as opposed to another certification program) is (at least in part) to have some access (however limited and expensive) to Romana. Plenty of students have taken on the expense of flying to Texas (or New York or Florida, where she also has taught in recent years) to get some instruction from this Pilates legend herself. Without Romana's involvement, I don't think Romana's Pilates has nearly the same sheen. I hate to be crass, but Romana is the golden goose, and perhaps this is why a certain amount of territorialism and drama follows her. (To boot: between the time of my visit to Texas and the time I've spent writing and editing this book, there has been some sort of split between Cha Cha and Roberto, and Romana's daughter and granddaughter. Now, when Romana's Pilates students want to take accredited private lessons and seminars from Romana, they need to do so when she visits Florida and New York.)

But a big part of the reason I traveled to Texas was to try to get a glimpse past the politics—to get a sense the woman my mother so revered.

When I arrived there, Romana and Cha Cha greeted me. Romana looked pretty darn good for a woman of her age, which she put at eighty-five. Her light brown, thinning hair draped to her chin. She was dressed like a dental hygienist: white pants with an elastic waistband, brightly flowered V-neck shirt, and orthopedic shoes. She moved easily, elegantly toward the reception area where we would sit and talk. As we walked toward the chairs she hung back a step behind me. "Pull these things in and down," she said, correcting my posture as she traced my shoulder blades with her thumbs. It's just the sort of thing my mom used to do.

We sat down. I didn't really expect Romana to remember my mom for many reasons: because she was elderly, because my mom had been dead for a few years, and because there are dozens of people like my mom who studied under Romana, adored Romana, and vied for the attention of Romana. So I began with a general outline of my purpose: "I am writing a book about my mother and the major influences in her life, which very much includes Pilates and you."

Romana burst into tears. "My mother bought me a horse, and she taught me how to shoot," she said. "I was eleven or twelve. I remember that well." Her father, a Russian, had died when she was three, she then told me. Her mother remarried. They lived in Florida. "It was a wonderful place to live. I played piano, every day I had lessons. I had a pet goat. I became a dancer."

I was disarmed. I wasn't sure if my mention of my mother evoked her response, but it felt like a non sequitur. I didn't want to respond in any way that would make Romana feel self-conscious or embarrassed. I stammered, trying to direct the conversation and to keep Romana on topic. I kept thinking how odd it was that no one had warned me. No one said, "Romana is an old woman now, and she's not always with it." It all made me question if she was merely being propped up at the top of the organization to attract students from all over the world. Mostly, I wondered if Mom would have been upset by it all, as I was.

Suddenly, Romana stood up from her chair, kicked her leg high, and posed her arms like a ballerina. "I have always loved to see people move," she said, her arms affixed in an elegant halo over her head. There was joy and grace in her motion. She had an aura. And despite the fact that I realized I wasn't really going to get the interview I had flown across the country for, I got a sense of what so captivated my mother.

As we walked back toward the studio, Romana turned toward me, and I noted a change in her eyes, a cognizance I hadn't seen earlier. "I went to visit our friend at her house once," she said, and then she turned back and continued walking.

Intellectually, I knew that whether or not Romana remembered my mom had no bearing on Mom's value within the larger Pilates community. Yet when Romana said she had visited my mom at her house, which she in fact had done, I was struck by a sense of contentment, on my mom's behalf and my own, to know that in some recess of Romana's brain was Mom's imprint.

IT WAS IN May of 2004, about five months after Mom had returned home after her prolonged hospitalization in New York, that Romana flew to Tucson to lead a seminar. Mom was thrilled; it was her dream to have Romana see her gorgeous studio and to lead a class there. But I also think Romana's mere presence at Mom's studio conferred importance upon Mom, and that excited her too. I came to town to witness Mom's glory. "You're always flying in to deal with the terrible stuff," my husband said. "You should be there for a happy moment too."

I sat on the periphery of the studio and took lots of pictures. But I didn't feel cheery as I watched my mom. She looked to me to be physically uncomfortable, if not in pain. Her face was drawn, her eyes sad, her wrinkles more prominent than usual.

As far as the state of Mom's health at that moment, we were all a bit unsure. At Sloan-Kettering, the surgeon had removed the tumor in her lungs, but pathology reports noted "microscopic" cancer in her lymph nodes. None of us knew if that meant with certainty that the cancer would return or metastasize. Mom, in her optimism and denial, took the position that she was on the mend.

We knew we would have more information soon. Mom was scheduled to get a scan a few days later—it would be her first since leaving Sloan-Kettering and Helen Hayes. Dr. Brooks, her Tucson oncologist, suggested that she have a scan a few weeks before the seminar, but she insisted on waiting until after.

So, seeing her look flagging at this event that she had for years longed to host, well, I was crestfallen.

"You feel okay, Mom?" I asked her when she and I were in the kitchen during lunch.

"Fine," she snapped. She was a real bitch to me for the rest of the day.

Atasha, who had driven in from Phoenix to attend the seminar at the studio where Mom had years before trained her, incurred Mom's wrath too.

After a rigorous stretch of instruction, Romana called a water break. Atasha walked into the large bathroom in the studio to wash her hands. Mom was in there, taking a bunch of pills. And she was coughing.

The sound of the cough really upset Atasha. She had lost her stepmother to lung cancer. "I knew that cough," she said to me when we discussed the incident years later.

Atasha said to Mom, "Are you sure you're okay? Are you really completely better?"

"It's just allergies, they're doing construction up the street and it knocks a lot of dust around," Mom replied to Atasha. There was a defensive tone in her voice.

Atasha had always considered my mom as someone who radiated health. But in that moment, she looked at my mom, her mentor, and thought, She looks like she has cancer.

She did have cancer, everywhere. The results from the scan taken a few days after the seminar showed tumors in both lungs as well as in the bones of her hips, sacrum, and lower spine.

RECENTLY, I ASKED Mom's brother, Uncle Eddie, why he thought Mom was so transfixed by the aura of Romana and Romana's Pilates. I asked with trepidation because, as free-spirited, nutty, and open-minded as my mom could be, her baby brother is equally skeptical, cynical, and sarcastic. I didn't want to invite a conversation that could lead to "She was a bit of a flake!" jokes, even those told with love. But Eddie surprised me with his thoughtful perspective.

"Your mom had the instinct to nurture and have a family and be a wife and a mother, but she also had this need to have a professional identity because of her father and *his* professional identity," Eddie said. He was speaking, of course, about Grandpa Leo, one of the most prominent astronomers of his generation.

When Mom and Dad divorced, Grandpa Leo urged Mom to go to law school. He and Grandma Charlotte even offered to let her, Lizzie, and me live with them in Tucson, where she could study at the University of Arizona. Mom declined, and married Bob very shortly after her divorce was finalized.

As Eddie sees it, Romana offered Mom redemption from a sense that she had disappointed her father. "Your mom was able to say, 'I studied with the renowned Pilates instructor Romana,' just like Dad would say, 'I studied with Donald Menzel at Harvard.'

"I think she had something to prove," he went on. "She just wasn't going to be an exercise teacher. She was trying to take this to almost an academic level, as if she was getting her PhD from Romana. I think being involved in the intricacies of a political, hierarchal, educational system, well, it gave her the identity and legitimacy that, being Dad's daughter, she craved."

As a point of rebellion, I had for many years refused to take Pilates lessons—from Mom or anyone else. I changed my mind when, at twenty-eight years of age, I came to a startling realization: my fifty-five-year-old mom had an amazing body, and I wanted to look like her.

In the lead-up to our wedding, Joe and I took two lessons a week at Drago's. At the time, Mom was in New York all the time because three of her prized students were frequently in town to take tests and accumulate apprenticeship hours.

When Mom got sick, I came to treasure the occasions that I was in Tucson and she was well enough to give me a lesson. But before I had a sense of her mortality, I was far too petulant to take direction from her. I hated her telling me what to do, which is exactly what an instructor does during a lesson. So Mom knew better than to offer herself up as my teacher on those mornings when we were all at Drago's together.

But with Joe, her future son-in-law, she had no such compunction.

"I'm going to be teaching you," she said to him one morning when we showed up for our private lessons.

I saw a look of uncertainty on Joe's face, and Mom must have seen it too. "Don't worry," I heard her say as she led Joe toward a reformer. "I'm going to kick your butt."

An hour later, I saw Joe heading toward the men's locker room, cheeks red and brow sopping. "Your mom *kicked my butt*," he said, bemused and winded.

Vanity may have brought me to Pilates. But in the aftermath of my mom's illness and death, I have clung to Pilates because I believe it connects me to her spiritually. Dragging myself out of bed and toward the subway to make it downtown for my prework lessons on early Wednesday mornings, I have heard myself saying aloud: "I'm going to Pilates for you, Mom."

On days that I want to feel close to Mom—her birthday, my birthday, Mother's Day—I schedule a special private lesson at one of the studios I frequent.

On the second anniversary of her death, my teacher Matt Devlin came to work on his day off to give me a special lesson. Because Matt had himself studied under Romana, I had shared with him copies of a bunch of photos that I had taken of Mom working out during the seminar Romana held at Mom's studio. Matt brought the photos to the lesson. "You're going to do the workout your Mom did," he said.

And so I did, or at least, I tried. With a body filled with tumors, Mom, at fifty-nine, was stronger and more agile than I, a healthy thirty-five-year-old woman. When it came time to do Shaving with Teaser, I closed my eyes and imagined the look of determination on Mom's face in that wonderful picture. I could only partially do the exercise; Matt had to hold my feet up for me.

The next morning I woke up with every muscle in my body aching—*aching*. Somehow, I threw my legs over the side of the bed with a groan, then I hoisted myself into a sitting position.

"What's wrong" Joe asked.

"It was yesterday's Pilates lesson," I managed. "My mom kicked my butt."

Chapter Nine

Vintage Glass, Fragile and Resilient. Like Mom

Around the time that Mom started to look for the cause of her angry cough, she began collecting Venetian, Steuben, and Depression-era glass art and tableware bought at auction online. She had always loved going to flea markets in search of treasures to add to her green glass canister collection or her portfolio of funky serving plates and baskets. But her zeal to amass "art glass" (as it is known by those in the know) surpassed any side interest in flea-market antiques.

Lounging on her couch in the den with her white Apple iBook nestled beside her and eyeglasses perched on the tip of her nose, she'd troll eBay for Steuben *verre de soie* ("glass of silk") dessert plates, hand-etched wine and port glasses from the 1920s, and delicate *vetro a filigrano* vases in purples and reds made by Venetian artisans.

Occasionally, she'd say she was buying all this stuff as an investment. She called it "my business."

"Your mom's an arbitrageur who forgets to sell," Joe would say.

When Mom won an auction, she paid her bills quickly and was rewarded with glowing buyer ratings on her eBay home page from various glass dealers. "Great buyer . . . smooth transaction . . . A++++++," said one. "suzyrosin is the best of the best," raved another. She was proud of her high rating, and she nurtured it carefully.

In the days before her surgery at Sloan-Kettering, Mom spent a lot of time scouting eBay, so she had a sense of what would be in the e-marketplace while she was laid up. I helped her get set up on eSnipe—a service I had written about in an article about sorority and fraternity pin collectors. Users tell eSnipe the maximum amount they are willing to spend on an item, and then the service makes a "snipe" bid on the user's behalf in the last second of an auction.

Since she recovered so quickly from her first surgery, Mom expected that she'd be out of eBay commission for only a few days following the operation. But as she was moved into the ICU, and discussions about inducing her into a coma began, Mom knew this was not to be.

So as her lungs filled with fluid due to postoperative pneumonia, her mind filled with thoughts of the auctions she might win while lying unconscious, the bills that would go unpaid, and the ensuing negative feedback from sellers that would tarnish her superstar status.

Again and again, I have replayed in my mind those last moments in the ICU before Mom went unconscious. The beeping machines. The manic bustle of nurses. Doctors spouting terms like *abnormal blood-oxygen level* and *lung failure*. My mom's terror.

Just as nurses were ushering us away from Mom's bedside and into the waiting room, Mom summoned all of her energy and whatever oxygen she could to make a last request.

"Take care of my eBay," she said.

MOM DID NOTHING in moderation. She was about all or nothing, black and white. When she quit smoking, she also quit booze, wine, and all processed food. When she developed a recipe for organic, fat/white sugar/taste-free muffins, she opened a catering business that she operated out of our home before opening an actual bakery at a neighborhood mall. When she focused on hiking, she did so completely. She dragged Lizzie and me up to mountaintops at five a.m. She lobbied Canyon Ranch to hire her as a trail guide. She got competitive about how far and high she could go.

She was also ritualistic, a developer of The Right Way to Do Things who let nothing keep her from strict adherence of her selected methods.

For instance, she liked to check on auctions repeatedly in order to monitor the competition as the conclusion approached. These were the days before BlackBerrys were ubiquitous and before iPhones had been introduced. But Mom didn't let any distance between her and a computer thwart her habits.

From the chemo chair at the doctor's office or the colorist's chair at the hair salon, she would call Lizzie and me—sometimes several times a day. "Can you check my eBay real quick?" she'd ask, refusing to acknowledge the inconvenience she might be causing Lizzie (then a mother of two babies) or me (a full-time reporter for the *Wall Street Journal*). I could type her password as quickly and as mindlessly as my own. It was "SaTaNaMa," which, I later learned from Google, is a yoga chant.

"The auction has five hours and 22 minutes to go, and glassy-girl has the high bid of $450," I might report to her, hurriedly. For sure I'd be rolling my eyes.

"Uh-oh," Mom'd reply, unhurried and impervious to my irritation. "I'm not going to let myself lose to glassygirl again. You'd better increase my high bid to $600. Just in case. This is a *very* important piece."

When packages were delivered—and packages were delivered pretty much every single day for at least a few years—they had to be opened promptly (lest their multitudes clutter the entryway of the house) and in a certain fashion. The packing tape was to be cut through carefully, gently, with a pair of scissors kept in the top right drawer of Mom's desk. (Knives and kitchen scissors: not permitted.) Plastic bubble wrap—in amounts that would make an environmentalist weep—was cut (carefully!) to reveal the glass item. The glass was set on the dining room table for careful inspection. The boxes then needed to be broken down, made flat. The Styrofoam peanuts were then transferred into a garbage bag. Great effort had to be taken to ensure that no errant peanut ended up on the floor. Then the flat box and peanut-filled bags would be dragged into the garage . . . and within twenty-four hours, they had to be driven to Mail Boxes Etc. for recycling. It was annoying enough to watch Mom go through these motions—a slave to her systems. But it was far worse when cancer fatigue forced her to delegate the tasks to Lizzie and me. She demanded that we open the boxes and discard the packing material exactly as she would. As she watched over me as I tried to follow her exacting instructions, I was often filled with anger that she allowed herself to be so clueless to the myriad ways I had put my own life on hold, and that she was so rigid in the face of my altruism. But a part of me was proud that I could connect her to the kind of routines that we all take for granted for the sense of normalcy they give us.

At night, every night, Mom and Bob would cozy up on the couch—Bob sitting properly with his shoes touching the floor, Mom, as if on a chaise longue, with her feet on Bob's lap. Bob would scroll through the DirecTV channel guide while he and Mom discussed the merits of each of the gazillion offerings before settling, inevitably, on *Law & Order.* As Bob rubbed Mom's feet, she'd drink her heated-up Mandarin Orange Arizona Iced Tea (diluted with water, warmed in a glass Pyrex measuring cup, and then transferred into a black porcelain coffee mug) and surf eBay.

There was something cute about how addicted to the computer she was (you know, Mom and her obsessions), until it wasn't cute anymore. As she got sicker, as her energy evaporated, she spent longer chunks of time hunched over her laptop. It was obvious to us she was in retreat from us, and—as much as cancer allowed—from reality.

Lizzie and I worried about how she was isolating herself. We had hand-wringing discussions in which we worked to remind each other and ourselves that we wanted to let Mom live the end of her life as she wished. But we agonized over her aloofness.

AT SOME POINT, we all have to confront and deal with the detritus of an ended life. The difficulty in doing so is greater than the sum of the stuff: after a death, every object can take on heart-breaking meaning. That's why I walk around in beautiful pants that happen to be too tight and too short—because they were Mom's. It's why Lizzie and I made photocopies of Mom's address book. And why Mom's glass has come to hold such power in my imagination. I am not a "things" person, but the things a person leaves behind become markers of a life once lived, like a Swiss Army knife inscription on a wooden rafter: Mom Was Here.

There are more than "things" left in the wake of someone's life. In today's world, there are often a lot of virtual threads— from e-mail accounts to blogs—to unwind as well. This certainly was the case with my e-addicted mom. Lizzie and I discontinued neither her e-mail nor her eBay accounts, and in fact have occasionally sent Mom e-mails on the assumption that if anyone can log on posthumously, it's she.

It was those electronic accounts that helped me understand better why Mom cared about her glass collection as she did. When she was dying, it gave her life.

I BEGAN THE process of uncovering all this in a municipal building in lower Manhattan. I was on jury duty, serving my civic duty by sitting in a mammoth room on an uncomfortable chair with dozens of others who similarly prayed not to hear their names called. There, I burrowed into printouts from my mom's e-mail and eBay accounts, snooping through her files. I was happy to see she had saved various e-mails of love, encouragement, and jokes from Lizzie and me. Luckily, she had saved electronic PayPal receipts of the payment she had sent to sellers. Most of these documents include information about the item itself, the amount of the winning bid, and, in some cases, contact information for the seller. On her e-mail, I found 106 discrete receipts detailing transactions ranging in value from $30.50 to $1,000. I don't know if these represent everything she bought. The earliest saved record is dated October 3, 2002—just as a persistent cough was causing the doctor to order CAT scans and bronchioscopes. The last purchase (a $180 Murano Venini dresser mirror tray) is from March 29, 2005, less than three months before she died. In total, she spent about $25,000 on glass.

Sifting through the receipts and e-mailed correspondence helped me grasp the scope of the collection and map out a timeline of her purchases. Instantly, I began noticing clusters of buying that I considered noteworthy. For example, in the month before her first surgery—when one medical test after another refused to rule out cancer as the source of a spot found on her right lung—there was a notable uptick in activity. In thirty days, she spent $3,078.93 to win sixteen pieces, including a 1930s Barovier E Toso clam bowl and a topaz Steuben compote dish.

A similar pattern occurred after she emerged from the coma to learn that the cancer had spread to her lymph nodes. She began to routinely spend larger chunks of money than she had previously. Gone were the cheap candlesticks. In the first purchase she made after learning that the cancer was in her lymph nodes, she spent $1,000 on eight Buzzi glasses. Then there was the $406 Salviati decanter and the $1,200 Paolo Venini charger plate.

Of all the receipts, only one showed any indication of what Mom intended to do with an item. It was a vase described on the receipt as "mezza filigrana Venini Murano Scarpa vase." She paid $36 for it. It was bought on February 24, 2003—the day she was officially diagnosed with cancer. In the subject line of the document, she had typed, "Katie's vase."

I had stashed this vase on the very top shelf of a kitchen cabinet since it arrived in the mail four and a half years ago. I had no clue that on the very day her life started to end, my mom bought me a light green bud vase.

FROM THE ONSET of my research, I knew there would be a few keys to opening this world. One of them is a man named Carl Bellavia. He is an avid collector of glass whom my mom met online. She spoke of him frequently as a sort of glass-world guru. "Carl told me this was a very important piece," she would say while liberating a recently purchased glass bauble from layers of bubble wrap.

She invoked him enough to make me include him among the recipients to whom I sent blast e-mails with updates on Mom's health. And I had a vague recollection of contacting him with the news of her death. I searched through my personal e-mail account, found his address, and sent him a note.

"Dear Carl," I wrote, "I'm hoping you'll remember me—or at least, remember my mom, Suzy."

"Of course I remember you," he replied, "and think of your mother often."

The next day, I called him. Initially, the conversation was awkward: he and my mom knew each other only for a few years and only in the context of collecting glass. Or so I thought. My unease quickly turned to shock when I realized that, in her own way, my mom had confided in this man. "She bought a lot of things that she wanted to leave for you guys," he said of Lizzie and me.

When we spoke, I was sitting at my desk at the *Wall Street Journal*. As the implications of what Carl was telling me settled in, the regular newsroom whirl blurred into visual white noise. To this stranger, my mom had admitted what we were forbidden to acknowledge: she was dying.

The disclosure stung. I immediately felt hurt that she was willing to share these intimacies with an e-mail friend but not me. But after a few deep breaths, I decided to be grateful for the bread crumbs she had left.

CARL LIVES IN Jersey City, New Jersey, just across the Hudson from downtown Manhattan. We first met at a restaurant in Greenwich Village several days after speaking on the phone. Again, I felt pulled between familiarity and strangeness. I wasn't sure if I should hug him or shake his hand. (We shook hands.)

In almost every way, Carl seems the opposite of my mom. He is a large man with a wild mess of gray curls and a shaggy beard. He chain-smokes Dunhill cigarettes. When we met for the first time, at four p.m., he settled in over a huge bowl of pasta.

He told me a bit about his life. He was born in 1953 and raised in Queens. An only child, he lived in the same home as his parents, aunts, and grandparents, who had emigrated from Italy.

Since his father gave him a camera when he was fourteen years old, Carl has lived, as he puts it, "on the fringe of the arts." He attended the School of Visual Arts and New York University's film school. He got heavily involved with drugs but has been sober since the mid-1980s. He maintains a successful freelance career as a commercial photographer and location scout for television commercials and films such as 2005's *King Kong*. When his aging parents were ill, he moved back to his childhood home for several years to care for them. After they died, he began collecting glass.

His large, bright apartment is littered with stacks of design magazines, Venetian glass, and other art objects. In the den off his bedroom, he spends hours on his Mac G4, combing through Venetian glass listings on eBay while smoking one cigarette after another.

It was sitting in this room that Carl "met" my mom. At that moment she most likely was perched on her couch in Tucson. It was late 2002, and they were bidding on the same item—a coffee-colored Venetian compote dish. Carl won the auction, but decided he didn't want the dish when it arrived by mail. He e-mailed the next highest bidder—my mom—and sold it to her. Within a few weeks, they were frequently discussing, via e-mail, Venetian items being auctioned on eBay. "We probably were in touch six days a week," he told me.

Not for the first time, there was a hierarchy in this friendship of Mom's: Carl was the guru, with my mom his eager student. If a piece came up for auction that they both coveted, my mom would bow out, he said. But she didn't completely defer to him: she frequently bought pieces despite Carl's explanations that they weren't important works. "I don't care if it's 'important,' " she would tell him. "It's pretty."

Mom told Carl about her illness soon after being diagnosed, he said. "Your mom was angry," Carl said. "She was surprised. She was devastated. She had been dealt a very bad hand. At the same time, she was adamant about beating it." My mom shared more with someone she had never actually met than she did with her family.

Buying vintage glass—fragile but resilient—was her escape from a life that quickly became defined by disease. The glass "gave her focus," Mr. Bellavia told me. "It was a release. Something she could do. Something that she had power over. She said that to me. She said that it gave her a sense of being normal."

Throughout the conversation, I was struck by Mom and Carl's relationship, with its juxtaposition of intimacy and unfamiliarity. For instance, I learned from listening to Carl refer to himself that his last name is pronounced Bell-a-VIA. Yet Mom called him Carl Buh-LAH-vee-uh. She was sharing her inner life with someone whose last name she wasn't pronouncing properly.

So I asked Carl if my mom's confiding in him made him uncomfortable. Was it surreal that some woman across the country whom he had never met was telling him about the emotional isolation brought by cancer? Was he burdened by her needs?

"I went to church and lit candles for her," he said. Then he grabbed my hand and sobbed.

AFTER LEARNING FROM Lori, Mom's Pilates student, and Carl too, that I shouldn't make any presumptions about who might be able to give me insight into my Mom's end-of-life psyche, I cast a pretty wide net in my investigative pursuits. I fixated on the idea that the UPS guy might have some funny story to share, considering the frequency with which he was delivering packages to Mom.

First, I called UPS's press relations department, and with a company representative, tried to navigate the maze of figuring out who, among thousands of employees, was Mom's delivery guy. No luck.

So the next time I was in Tucson, I kept watch for a big brown truck, hoping that a neighbor might get a package delivered, and I'd be able to race outside to chat with the driver.

At one point in the afternoon, I dashed out to Starbucks to grab a cup of coffee. As I pulled back into my mom's driveway, I saw a UPS delivery truck driving past her street, headed farther up the mountain. I threw Mom's car in reverse and floored it. I may have actually screeched the tires. It was all so very *Dukes of Hazzard*.

The drive up from my mom's house to the homes located higher on the mountain is perilous—the hill is incredibly steep, and the road zigs and zags. The UPS truck zoomed up; to keep it in eyeshot, I had to drive far faster than I was comfortable doing. When I finally got close enough, I started waving one hand out the window wildly and honking the horn with the other. Bewildered—if not a bit frightened by the crazy lady trailing him—the UPS driver pulled over. I popped out of the car and ran up to his window. He said he was new to the route and that the guy who likely delivered to my mom had left the company. (A for effort, right?)

I also tried to talk to a woman whom Lizzie and I first became aware of when Mom was in the coma at Sloan-Kettering. After a bad day that stood out even amid many really bad days, I had e-mailed an update to friends and family, including Carl Bellavia. Carl wrote back, thanking us for letting him know how Mom was doing. He added, "Uschi is devastated."

Lizzie was reading over my shoulder when I opened this e-mail. In unison, we said, "Who the fuck is Uschi?"

Uschi, it turned out, is a glass collector and dealer who lives in Germany. She was Carl's mentor, making her the guru's guru, and he e-introduced Uschi and Mom.

Poor Uschi and her utter devastation: she (and it) became the source of so much ICU gallows humor. When Dr. Daniels told us Mom would not make it through the night, Lizzie overcame her crying for long enough to ask, "How are we going to break it to Uschi?"

So Uschi, at least by name, held a special place in my heart, and I was eager to interview her. She was willing to be interviewed only via e-mail, however, and the language gap was sufficient to make the effort futile. She wrote that she was fond of Mom (who bought a number of pieces from Uschi at Carl's suggestion—so what's not to like?). She and Mom may have had involved interactions, but Uschi couldn't articulate them to me if they did.

I had better luck with Tina Oldknow, the curator of modern glass at the Corning Museum of Glass near Ithaca, New York. I e-mailed her photos of nearly all the glass pieces. Tina spent a few hours on the phone with me, looking at them item by item. Some pieces she couldn't see clearly enough to really remark on. When she identified something as likely "tourist glass," she was never disparaging or condescending, instead explaining what artist and period likely inspired the vase, the bowl, the candlesticks.

There was one piece we spoke about at length. Thick, sturdy, and standing nearly three feet tall, it's a massive chalice with a gold double-helix pattern swirling through the stem. On the bottom, "Steuben" is etched in neat cursive letters. "It was meant to be passed around," Ms. Oldknow told me.

I remember that I was in Tucson when the chalice arrived. It was right before Mom's surgery at Sloan-Kettering. Mom went through her box-opening ritual and could barely conceal her excitement as she combed through the packing material to reveal the goblet. "When I'm all better, I want you to use this to toast to my health," she said to Lizzie and me.

Months later, on her second night home after the long hospitalization and rehab at Helen Hayes, we had that small dinner party at Mom's house to celebrate her fifty-ninth birthday. Bob stood and proposed a toast to my mom. "L'chaim," we said, and then each one of us took a sip of wine from the big glass chalice.

HOWEVER MUCH MOM held back from expressing her fear to us, she was not as private with her anger. She vented plenty at us. And it found its way into her virtual glass community too.

For instance, she picked a fight with a seller from whom she bought a Venetian piece on August 11, 2003. It was a wine glass decorated by a swirl of red and blue piping that gives it a plaid look. After receiving the delicate glass by mail, Mom e-mailed the seller, saying that she believed the glass she was sent was a marriage of a vintage wine stem with a more modern cup.

My mom wrote to the seller: "There is no doubt that the stem may be old, but the cup is new. This was not what I intended to buy and plan to return it. Yes, there is no mention of an old glass, just stem, but this is not what was represented." (She saved this correspondence in a special e-mail file she labeled "Fakes.")

The seller replied that she would not accept a return. "It is really annoying to have you tell me this. . . . The bowl is not a 'newer style.' . . . That is just ludicrous Suzy."

Mom: "I will not be taken advantage of."

Seller: "IT IS JUST TERRIBLE THAT YOU IMPLY THAT I AM TRYING TO TAKE ADVANTAGE OF YOU. . . . I AM ALSO PUZZLED THAT YOU THOUGHT THE USE OF THE WORD 'STEM' (AS IN WINE STEM) REFERRED

ONLY TO THE STEM AND NOT THE ENTIRE PIECE.
CURIOUS CONCEPTS FROM AN ADVANCED COLLEC-
TOR LIKE YOURSELF."

Mom: "Your rudeness and interpretation of events are neither
accurate nor worthy of my time and energy." (I loved my mom's
sanctimony—when it was pointed at someone else.)

To me, the exchange reads as if my mom accused this woman
of purposefully misrepresenting a wine glass ("stem," or whatever I
should be calling it) without much justification. The seller then took
a catty swipe at my mom (who was asking for it, in my opinion).
Mom ended the imbroglio by pretending to be above it all. But she
was obviously very upset by the fight. She had forwarded the correspondence to Lizzie. Always the loyal daughter, Lizzie replied to
my mom, "What a huge bitch she is!!! Go Mom!" (I sent the seller
numerous e-mails to discuss the incident, but she never replied.)

Carl remembers the big smackdown as well. He says he was
surprised by my mom's venom—which, even at the time, he at-
tributed to misplaced cancer rage. Still, he was delighted to learn
that Mom had a feisty side. "She went *ballistic*," he told me. "I
thought it was hilarious."

A humorous coda to the story: When I was interviewing Ms.
Oldknow, she singled out the photo of the red-and-blue glass
without prompting. "This might be the most authentic piece in
your mom's entire collection," she said.

IN OCTOBER 2004, as the cancer coursed through the bones of
her hips, sacrum, and spine, my mom expanded her hobby into
a different realm: the live online auction. The mechanics of live
auctions are slightly different from those of the average auction,
and her experimentation proved to be a mistake.

Mom had forayed into a live auction site manned by a company in Indianapolis with the intent of buying two Murano vases. Inadvertently, she also bought a large, black wooden desk.

My sister and I remember well when my mom received an e-mail alerting her that she had "won" this table. Mom instantly told us that she was being billed for an item that she had not bid upon. Obviously, the dealer was in error, she told us angrily. She then reported to us that she had made this contention to the company itself, but the company insisted that she had, in fact, submitted the winning bid.

My mom was terribly upset. After days of cursing the dealer, she began to acknowledge that maybe the oxycodone she was taking to help dull the pain from the bone tumors had compromised her bidding precision.

She indicated to me that the table had been very expensive—about $4,000. She was worried my stepfather would be angry with her for spending so much money. We tried to explain to her that after thirty-one years of marriage and I-can't-even-imagine-how-much money, Bob wasn't going to be angry at her when she was drugged out and suffering from cancer. But Mom wouldn't hear it.

We suggested that she alert the antique dealer—if not eBay's administration—that her cancer medication had resulted in an accidentally placed bid. Mom adamantly rebuffed that idea. She insisted that eBay rules stipulated that such a disclosure would result in her privileges being rescinded. She was beside herself about this for weeks. Mom never told me how she resolved the table incident.

As I was diving into Mom's eBay second life, I knew I had

to find out what had happened with the table, though it pained me, even all these years later, to remember the anguish the incident caused her. I located one brief e-mail correspondence about it. The thread led me to Jeb Banner, a musician and Web developer who is about my age and lives in Indianapolis. He had been a co-owner of the live auction house from which my mom bought the table. Jeb remembered the incident: he said it was resolved when he sold the table on consignment and my mom made up the difference between what she had promised to pay and what a new buyer would offer. Remembering that my mom expressed to me tremendous irritation with the dealer, I asked Jeb if my mom had been surly or otherwise unpleasant (as we who love her know she could be). "She was very frustrated," he said, diplomatically.

I told him the backstory—about the glass collection, her attachment to eBay, her illness, the bone tumors, the oxycodone. He was shocked. "If she had told me about the cancer, I would have let her off the hook immediately," he said. I also contacted eBay: a spokeswoman said they mediate all sorts of disagreements between buyers and sellers. "We would not have revoked your mom's privileges," she told me.

The greatest shock came when Jeb unearthed, and forwarded to me, the listing for the table: my mom's winning bid was $300—a price not even close to the $4,000 cost she had mentioned to me.

Why would she lie? Why would she freak out about $300? She had wasted far more (I have to assume) in other auctions, bidding on pieces that upon arrival she decided she didn't like, pieces that summarily ended up stashed in a closet. How she tortured herself over the ordeal! I was so frustrated. I wanted to (posthumously) throttle her.

But once my exasperation abated, it didn't take me too long to realize that the whole matter about the stupid table was never about the money. The cancer had spread to her eBay world, and for my mom, the toll was incalculable. She suddenly was alienated from the one community where she wasn't Suzy with Lung Cancer. I don't know that I am better off knowing this. It's a little devastating, when you really think about it

Mom's buying significantly tapered off after the table ordeal, according to the archived receipts. She bought only three items in the seven months between this incident and her death.

To COMPLETE MY glass investigation, I flew to Tucson one hot June day. I asked Bob to allow me a day alone in the house with Mom's glass. I looked at the collection as I hadn't before. I spent an entire day examining each piece from every angle—admiring its design and feeling its fragility.

When I was curious to learn what I could about the dozens and dozens of wine glasses that are a part of Mom's collection, I contacted Rosemary Trietsch, a dealer who has written about glass identification for *Antique Week*. According to receipts I found, Mom had bought several pieces from her, including etched water goblets.

Rosemary remembered my mom by the pieces she bought. Mom was solely interested in pieces she could match with other pieces—she might have only wanted eight hand-etched red wineglasses made in the 1930s if they would look elegant on a table next to the port glasses made in the same era that she had bought after seeing Lizzie's husband order port after dinner one night. "She was putting sets together," Rosemary said. "She wanted to make sure she had enough to entertain."

I suppose Mom's motivation was to leave Lizzie and me a gift to use and enjoy while spending time with friends and family. Looking through the armoire in her bedroom, stacked with Steuben glassware, I could visualize what my mom might have been imagining: Lizzie and I as swells, serving our dinner guests an *amuse-bouche* in translucent, iridescent Art Deco sherbet glasses designed by Frederick Carder for Steuben in the 1920s.

I had for so long considered Mom's glass collecting as something she did to pass the time as she was dying. But now I see that to Mom it represented a joyful gift she could impart to Lizzie and me.

As I FLEW back to New York the next morning, I felt almost giddy. When I got home, I climbed onto the stepladder and fished a vase out of the cabinet. It was the little green vase my mom had found beauty in on the day she was told she had cancer. I wiped it clean of dust. I poured in some water. I put in five pink roses and set it in the family room.

Chapter Ten

The House That Mom Built

The happiest time in my mom's adult life began when she and Bob built their house in the foothills of the Santa Catalina Mountains in northwest Tucson. Technically, you couldn't call it her "dream house," because I don't think she'd ever imagined she'd live somewhere so beautiful.

It wasn't just the house's beauty that made Mom happy. The house came to represent so much of what she loved. Her life in Tucson and the house have become, at least in my mind, intertwined.

There is no hiding from the fact that my mom was materialistic, and the house was a repository of all of the wonderful things, expensive and not, that she had amassed over the years.

Sectioned off in a little nook by an antique wrought-iron gate found at a flea market was her bed and its prodigious display of her linens—Egyptian sheets with intricate embroidery; oversize needlepoint throw pillows, the fronts and back of which were joined at the seams by maroon velvet rope; jacquard bedspreads in cotton.

The airy kitchen is brightened by wide windows that span the length between the terra-cotta floors and the plaster ceiling—windows through which you can look up the mountain at nothing but blooming cacti, spare bushes, and jagged rocks. Against the windows are shelves and cabinets of maple wood and glass that are carefully filled with Mom's eclectic stuff: oversize Italian ceramic dinnerware—each piece bearing a different whimsical animal—and the twenty-seven Depression-era green glass canisters that sit along the top of the cabinets with the sunlight reflecting off the silver plates that label them SUGAR, FLOUR, and COOKIES.

Throughout the house, she displayed her art collection, largely made up from work by southwestern artists and their colorful, mystical depictions of hovering angels and of matriarchs tending to cooking and babies. Outside, clinging to the exterior stucco walls, grew climbing ivy and the rose and peony bushes that she planted, nurtured, and pruned herself. From vases and glass bowls wafted the fragrance of flowers she snipped with her big garden shears and arranged in the tousled, elegant style that was her hallmark.

But the house is—and my mom was—about so much more than things. It's about the dance studio built right off her bedroom where she grooved with Jerome, where she "flowed" with Chris, where she tangoed with Bryan, another dance instructor. It's about the stand-alone Pilates studio built right next to the house where Mom hosted her idol, Romana, and where she gave free lessons and a mother's love to Atasha and Cate and so many others, like Jan and Cheryl. It's about the open design, where the kitchen spills into the living room and overlooks the freshwater swimming pool. It's about the dark, cozy den with the massive armoire filled with toys for the grandchildren she imagined she would watch grow up.

MY MOM'S PARENTS, Leo and Charlotte, moved to Tucson in 1971 after Grandpa Leo had retired from his position as chairman of the astronomy department at Harvard and accepted a job running Kitt Peak National Observatory in Tucson. From the time Lizzie and I were about nine and six, respectively, we would make the pilgrimage to our grandparents' at least once a year. Mom would pack a tin lunch box with fried chicken and apple slices and hand us over at the airport to the stewardesses (they were stewardesses then), who would affix wing-shaped pins to our Izod shirts and watch over us as we made the trip across the country.

At the time, Tucson was, in the main, a desert with a big university, a smattering of residential communities, and a few Old West attractions for tourists. We didn't need much more: but for the one day per visit when we would go to Old Tucson (an homage to pioneer towns where—this is the part that thrilled Lizzie and me—Hubba Bubba ads and a few episodes of *Little House on the Prairie* had been filmed), Lizzie and I spent all day in Grandma's swimming pool. When the sun began to cool down after dinner, we'd play kickball in the yard. Lizzie and I were on opposing teams; Grandma Charlotte was all-time pitcher.

Grandma still lives in Tucson. As I write this, she is approaching her ninety-fifth birthday. She is an exceptional woman, and not just because she has lived so long and survived so much without losing her vim. She is a spitfire, a trailblazer, a salty gal. She went to college during the 1930s—a time when educating girls was seen as a frivolity. In the 1950s and '60s, she was a working mother—employed first as a phys ed teacher, then as a high school counselor. She became a travel agent when she was in her seventies. She quit in her early eighties, but got bored quickly and returned to work. She sent her clients a flier: "I'M BACK!" it began. "I couldn't STAND retirement!" Until she was in her late eighties, Grandma led groups (and I don't mean senior citizen groups) on rafting trips through Alaska and safaris in South Africa. She has traveled the world, visiting nearly every country on six continents. She hasn't made it to Antarctica, but she did boat down the Amur River in Siberia when she was eighty-five.

She is outspoken, describing herself and her experiences in declarative sentences. Of her abilities as a golfer—she rarely scored below 110—she would say, "I'm rotten!" She loves to be provocative, to blurt out things you wouldn't expect from a little old lady. Of the hoopla that surrounded President Clinton's oral dalliance with Monica Lewinsky, she said, "I don't see what the big deal is. When I was growing up, we called that necking!" She said this at Thanksgiving dinner, sitting at Mom's dining room table alongside a random group of Pilates students none of us knew well. In unison, Lizzie and I yelped *"GRANDMA!!!!"* with a mixture of horror and bemusement. Mom nearly choked on her turkey.

Grandma loves saying things for shock value. And we all love to be scandalized by her. But Mom didn't take all of Grandma's habits with good humor. Mom used to get furious when she would find a huge jug of Grant's Scotch underneath the kitchen sink in Grandma's apartment at the assisted living facility. "You could fall and break your hip, Mother!" my teetotaling Mom would say.

Eventually, when she was about eighty-eight, Grandma agreed that whisky might be a bit much for a woman of her age. So she switched to wine. "What's your favorite kind of wine?" I'll ask her before coming to the nursing home to hang out with her and her friends during happy hour. "The kind with a screw top!" is her standard answer.

That Mom didn't drink and that Grandma loves whisky is only a surface representation of their differences. Though my mom, like my grandma, was always an athlete, she also was always focused on fashion and concerned with her appearance. Grandma Charlotte has never been willing to give a lot of time to these matters. She was raised during the Depression, and the impact of poverty has long shaped her relationship with money. She is very frugal.

As I've mentioned, Mom was exceptionally close to her grandmother—Charlotte's mother, Rose Wyman. Great-Grandma Rose (who immigrated from Russia and called Mom "Suza" and Lizzie and me "Lizza and Kata") doted on my mom, indulging her girly and materialistic instincts. It's my sense that Rose may have favored Mom above her other grandchildren, and perhaps even above her own children. When I was younger, I wondered how that made Grandma feel, both as the mother of Suzy and the daughter of Rose. But as I got older, I could see the closeness between Mom and her mother, and I came to understand that it played out in ways that were subtle. I don't ever remember hearing them say "I love you" to one another—words that flew constantly among me, Mom, and Lizzie. Yet they had an undeniable closeness that is hard to explain fully and has helped me to understand that people express love and affection in ways different from my own. Mom loved Grandma's physical strength and her stubbornness. "You've got some strong woman genes," she would say to me. She loved to be outraged by Grandma's saltiness. "Wait until you hear what your Grandma said this time," Mom began many phone conversations with Lizzie and me.

However fundamentally different Grandma and Mom were, they had Lizzie and me in common. Grandma has always adored us. I think that seeing her mother smother her daughters with love and attention—in her all-time-kickball-pitcher sort of way—pleased Mom a lot and provided a source of redemption to what may have once been a difficult relationship. As we have grown older—and in the aftermath of Mom's illness—Lizzie and I have only become closer to Grandma.

Uncle Eddie and his wife Teresa have borne primary responsibility for Grandma since Mom died. (Uncle David, to whom Mom wasn't particularly close during her adult years, lives in Colorado. David and his wife, Margaret, are close to Grandma, too.) But Lizzie and I do what we can to stay connected to Grandma and to buoy her spirits.

Since Mom died, Lizzie flies to Tucson every year for Grandma's birthday. They often play mah-jongg. They always go to happy hour. There, Lizzie is encircled by men and women with walkers, wheelchairs, and plastic cups filled with cheap, almost undrinkable wine. They ask her a million questions and tell her about their grandchildren. Grandma looks at Lizzie proudly and tells her friend, "She flew all the way here *just* to see me."

LIZZIE AND I were never as close to Grandpa Leo. He was an exacting man with high expectations, and his grandchildren were not spared his toughness. Once, when Lizzie was maybe fourteen years old, she failed to send a thank-you note for a birthday gift Grandpa Leo sent her. She received a letter in the mail from him that read:

Dear Grandpa Leo,

__ *I did receive the gift.*
__ *I did not receive the gift.*

(Please check one.)
From, Lizzie

He also included, for Lizzie's convenience, a self-addressed stamped envelope.

During our visits to Tucson, Grandpa Leo wasn't around all that much, but when he was, his brilliance and his assumption that everyone cared a lot about stars and nebulae made him inaccessible as a grandfather. On the nights he ate dinner at home with us and Grandma, he would prepare slide shows about the planets for us to watch after kickball. It was during those slide shows that I started biting my nails—which resulted in my manicure obsession. So in that way, Grandpa Leo had a major impact on my life.

In the early days, Mom didn't go with us to Tucson, and I think that was because she and her dad were estranged. The reason why was never really explained to us. I now think it had to do with his lack of approval that Mom remarried so quickly after her divorce from Dad. Grandpa Leo saw Mom as perhaps his smartest child and didn't fully respect her decision to focus on being a mother and a wife.

However, they overcame their estrangement in the mid-1980s. I don't know how it happened. After years of Mom not caring that we weren't close to Grandpa Leo, she suddenly cared very much. She insisted that we write and call him frequently; she was adamant that we listen to her stories about him. It was quickly evident that she worshipped him. And I now imagine that their estrangement must have been devastating for her. For many years as a child, I thought Mom hated Grandpa Leo (which led to my lack of interest in knowing him better). Yet I have to believe that Grandpa Leo's disapproval of Mom tortured her. Once freed from the feeling that she had failed to meet his expectations, she rushed back into her daddy's arms.

It was the renaissance of the relationship with her father that hastened Mom's interest in spending more time in Tucson. Mom and Bob started accompanying Lizzie and me on our trips out west. Mom then started to go there by herself to hang out with Leo, Charlotte (by then my grandparents had divorced), and her brothers, who had moved to Tucson too.

Grandpa Leo died in 1987, a few months after being diagnosed with lung cancer. He was cremated, and his ashes were strewn on Mount Lemon. That intensified Mom's spiritual connection to Tucson.

IN THE EARLY 1990s, Mom and Bob decided to build a house on a beautiful mountainside. While it was being built, they lived in the small condo Mom had bought a few years earlier. They hadn't yet sold the plot of land at Canyon Ranch, so Mom was still spending much of her days there, hiking and dancing.

To maintain the grounds of its resort campus, the Ranch would use fertilizers and other solutions to keep the greenery green and the guest accommodations bug-free. Mom said that she could tell, just by the way that she felt, the days that the grounds had been sprayed with various chemicals.

Chemicals and pollutants of any sort drove her crazy. Like, totally bonkers. But even neurotic people are right some of the time.

In the early 1980s, when I was a little girl and we were all living in suburban Detroit, Mom began having grand mal seizures during her sleep, maybe once or twice a month. Bob witnessed them more than anyone, but sometimes she was stricken while napping in the afternoon, and, hearing a commotion, I would race in her room to find her flailing about. It was incredibly scary when it happened—both for those who saw her in the throes of a seizure and for my mother, who woke from them disoriented and exhausted. She went to see neurologists, who ordered all sorts of CAT scans and MRIs. But the legions of tests and examinations revealed no detectable physiological problem. The doctors told Mom she needed a shrink.

Well, obviously! The lady was a loon.

But her needing a shrink seemed completely separate from these scary seizures. So, long before it was in vogue, Mom began seeking guidance from alternative doctors and healers. The daughter of a genius, authoritative father, my mom loved her gurus.

By the mid-1980s, Mom found her way to an allergist in Ann Arbor who specialized in treating people with acute food allergies and chemical sensitivities. Mom had total faith (blind faith?) in this doctor, who told Mom she was allergic to, well, basically everything in the world. I think Mom was happy to have found a doctor who didn't dismiss her as a silly, hysterical woman, who didn't tell her she was full of it or that she was imagining her symptoms. Mom became increasingly focused on what she should or should not be exposed to, in food or the environment. Always a picky eater, Mom stopped consuming everything but fish and green vegetables. The doctor said she required allergy shots with such frequency that she taught my mom how to inject herself: every morning as I was getting ready for school, Mom could be found shooting up. She said her car was "making her sick," so she drove car pools with an air purifier sitting in the front seat. She took fistfuls of vitamins, perhaps hundreds a week. She submitted to odd treatments whereby the doctor had her sit in a sauna for hours while in a garbage bag—the intent was that Mom would sweat out the chemical impurities in her body.

Mom's adherence to this doctor's recommendations was a source of conflict in our relationship. I believed the seizures were serious; I saw them with my own eyes and knew Mom wasn't making anything up. Yet I was a smart-ass teenager, and I was highly skeptical of her doctor. Once, Mom made me have an appointment with The Quack (as I ungenerously referred to her), and she diagnosed me with a host of allergies. I said, "With all due respect, I think if I went to see a podiatrist, he'd tell me there was something wrong with my feet." Mom was mortified and furious. "How dare you insult her like that!" Mom said to me after the appointment. I wasn't sure if my transgression had been to compare Dr. Q to a foot doctor (and by the way, what's wrong with being a foot doctor?) or to imply that she was an allergist who believed every problem could be explained by allergies. Either way, Mom never again wanted to risk my shooting my mouth off, so there were no more trips to the allergist for me. Score one for the smart-ass.

WHEN MOM AND Bob were deciding where in Tucson they wanted to plant more permanent roots, they explored neighborhoods by checking out existing homes that were on the market. One of them, a new house in a district with some very cool haciendas, had polished cement floors. Mom loved it. She asked the realtor to connect her with the architect of the house. That's how Mom and Bob met Bil Taylor.

Bil was almost fifty and about fifteen years out of architecture school at the time. The house Mom and Bob had been so impressed by was the very first house Bil had designed on his own. Architecture is his second career. He grew up near Philadelphia, where he got a degree in history and worked as an elementary school teacher. He loved building things and had a sense of adventure. So in the early 1970s, when he was well into his thirties, he made his way to Arizona. Construction was starting to boom. He began working as a contractor and enrolled in architecture school at the University of Arizona.

I flew to Tucson to meet with Bil at Mom's house. He is quiet and tidy, and you get the sense that he's most comfortable when working with his hands. He's also plainspoken and honest. When we sat down in the living room, he said to me, "Your mom could be a pain in the butt." (Oh, Bil, you're telling me.)

Mom had very definite and quirky ideas of what she wanted. First and foremost, she wanted the house to be designed so that it did nothing to disturb the existing wild landscape. She wanted Bil to shape the house around all the saguaros and to figure out how the plans could incorporate the wash—a long trenchlike ditch, naturally formed by water running off the mountain.

Most houses built on the mountainside are oriented so that the views are primarily of the twinkling city sprawl below. Bil told Mom that was an important feature in terms of the house's value, should she and Bob decide one day to sell it. But in her house, Mom said she wanted the eye to be drawn to the back of the house, and up the mountain. "That made her very interesting to me—to totally disregard resale principles in favor of being able to look out at the mountains," Bil said.

Mom told Bil about her sensitivities and asked him to build her a house as free of chemicals as possible. Bil started to read up on the "healthy house movement," a trend in construction that was just budding. The gist isn't so much about a house being minimally invasive to the environment—though that's often a byproduct. Instead, a healthy house is one whose materials are as natural and chemical-free as possible. It's not about "green" as much as nontoxicity.

It was a challenge for Bil, and he took to it. He needed to rethink some of the fundamentals of building. Normally, when you build on a site, you treat the soil with various chemicals that help eradicate bugs and termites—a significant issue for a stucco-covered wooden house like Mom and Bob's would be. Bil and Mom went to a store in Tucson called the Ecology Shop to seek an alternative. A shop clerk recommended that they buy hundreds of millions of microbes and let them work through the soil until it was ready for building.

One of the biggest issues facing Bil was the actual material of the house. He chose wood, but wood naturally emits "off-gases" that can be harmful to people with acute allergies and sensitivities. So into the house's frame and insulation, he built layers of plastic that trapped the gases and expelled them through a ventilation system. The maple cabinetry was specially laminated to seal off the gases too. Instead of simply using drywall, Bil made the walls from cement-based plaster (though today, clay plaster is a more popular "healthy house" option because it's easier on the earth to mine and transport). Paint has tons of chemicals in it, so to color the walls, Mom and Bil sat over big vats of the plaster that he would be using to make the walls, and they added different minerals until the plaster turned a color Mom liked. The floors are made of polished concrete. Bil estimates that the "healthiness" of the house made it at most 5 percent more expensive to build than it might otherwise have been.

Bil's favorite part of the house is the swimming pool. It's carved into the mountain and is separated from the wild brush by a wrought-iron fence that runs along one side and is intended to keep the javelinas out. (Javelinas are wild animals that look like a cross between pigs, dogs, and porcupines. They're all over the mountain. They're scary.) The pool is filled with fresh water—with minimal chlorine—and there is a tiny waterfall that runs off the mountain and into the basin. "I think this might be the best pool ever," Bil said. "Suzy loved it as a transition from the natural to the man-made."

I knew Mom's house was free of toxins, but before interviewing Bil, that was the extent of my understanding. I was in college when this house was being built. Maybe Mom had told me about it all. She and I spent a lot of time on the phone together in those days, but I managed to tune out much of what she said. I'd sit on my mattress-on-the-floor while watching a *Brady Bunch* episode on mute or working a crossword puzzle in the *Michigan Daily* as Mom chattered on and on about whatever moms chatter on and on about.

As Bil and I toured the house, it occurred to me how wrong I had been to wonder if (worry that) I'd be frequently upset when revisiting my mom's life. The story wasn't entirely sad. I was getting a second chance to learn the things I had been far too hungover or too busy watching *Friends* reruns to pay attention to when I was young and Mom was healthy and we had nothing but blue skies in front of us.

MOM WAS A different person in Tucson than the one she had been in Detroit. The house played a role. The mountain air helped. The reconnection with family made her happier. But the evaporation of her depression resulted largely, I think, from something the DuPont company once referred to as "better living through chemistry."

I was Mom's guinea pig, sort of. In the mid-1990s, when I was working as a coffee fetcher at *Elle* magazine, I was suffering under the weight of intense self-criticism because I wasn't a size 0. Working at a fashion magazine can be a dangerous gig for someone prone to negative body imagery and eating disorders. I suffered sufficiently that I sought help from a shrink. The doctor suggested Prozac.

At the time, I was maybe twenty-four or twenty-five years old. I still identified more with being a grown child than an adult, and I agonized over whether my mom would approve of my taking an antidepressant. I assumed she'd see Prozac as a chemical and, therefore, part of something she would consider "the problem." But I was desperate to be released from the grip of this obsession with food and weight. I decided to go on Prozac without consulting Mom. To me, this was a huge departure from established family protocol. My decision felt illicit. It was a giant step toward autonomy and adulthood. That was scary.

But, boy, am I glad I did it. Prozac changed everything for me. Coupled with regular meetings with a therapist, it helped me to let go of my constant (*constant*) focus on what I then considered my physical imperfections (which included, but were not limited to, my weight).

A few months after starting on the medication, I went to visit Mom in Tucson. A couple days into the trip, Mom and I took an early-morning hike up toward Picture Rocks in Saguaro National Park, which is a few miles from Mom's house. On a break, we drank some water and caught our breath. As I nibbled the multigrain bread topped with homemade peanut butter that Mom had packed in our fanny bags, Mom gave me a serious look. "You seem different," she said. "Happier."

"I'm taking Prozac," I said, and then I took a deep breath and spoke to my mom like the adult I was trying to become. "If it's so powerful in helping me with depression, and we share the same blood and body chemistry, then maybe you should try it too."

She didn't say much. But I guess I had an impact, because a few weeks later, Mom went on Prozac too. The change in her moods and disposition was stunning. The sunny Suzy was not nearly as shaded by depression.

So, there she was in the place—geographically and emotion-ally—that she for so long yearned to be. The struggles were all in the past. Everything in her life had come together.

My bedroom and Lizzie's bedroom—with a bathroom sand-wiched between them—are the only rooms on the second floor of the Tucson house. When you go up the stairs from the den, Lizzie's room is on the left and mine is on the right. There is a balcony off of each room. From my balcony, you look over the courtyard in front of the house and its entryway. A fountain was erected in the center of the small, sweet courtyard, around which stood a few wrought-iron sculptures. Mom told me once that she had always envisioned Lizzie or me standing on the balcony with a man serenading us from next to the fountain, "a Romeo-and-Juliet moment," she once told me.

So Mom imagined romance when she pictured my bedroom. But by 2004, there wasn't much of that in our lives. Lizzie and I were miserably unhappy—always operating in a bubble of fre-netic stress, jumping from crisis to crisis, treatment to treatment, coast to coast.

I was exhausted because I was trying to build my life at the same time that I was trying to help my mom save hers. Freelanc-ing is a hustle. You have to scrounge for stories, as any reporter does, but then you have to be scrappier than a staff reporter might. First you need to convince your sources to give you an exclusive, even though you are an unattached reporter who has no idea if a magazine or newspaper will actually be interested in the story. Then you have to figure out which publication and which editor would be best to pitch to and get that editor to take your calls or read your e-mails. Only then—if you get the assignment—do you start actually reporting and writing the article. Once the article is turned in and edited, you have to fight—even though you are an outsider and mostly powerless—to get the story run in a timely fashion. I did this for the first half of my mom's illness—and then endeavored to prove myself worthy of my new job at one of the world's best newspapers for the second half. It was stressful.

That was just the career stuff.

I was also trying to get pregnant, which, I found out, is not always as easy to do as they tell you in high school health class. Turns out you need to have sex exactly at the right time, which is difficult when you are traveling constantly, exhausted, depressed, and not in the mood for love.

My mom showed little sympathy. Cancer didn't curb her Jewish-mother tendency to manipulate. If anything, it exacerbated it. "It'd be very healing for me if you had a baby," my dying mother said not once but several times. (Can you believe she went there? Nor could I.)

I was in my early thirties and yearning to become a mother. But it wasn't just an instinctual, cosmic, biological feeling that now was the right moment. Like everything else, it was driven by my mom. I wanted her to see me as a mother. I needed to know that she thought I was a good mother. I needed to know she was proud of my child. And each month, when I learned I wasn't pregnant, I got angrier and more depressed.

One day I had a breakdown smack dab in midtown Manhattan. I was running errands at lunchtime and found myself at Bloomingdale's. Everywhere I looked—literally *everywhere*—there could be glimpsed a woman around my age, lazily walking next to a stroller pushed by her mother, gabbing about the cutest thing the baby did last night.

Shopping wasn't necessarily something that Mom and I enjoyed doing together. We hung out together in our own way, taking walks and doing crosswords. But seeing these duos casually enjoying their ritual left me nearly undone.

From the third floor, I called Lizzie, sobbing—just hysterically crying amid the racks, like a toddler lost in the aisles of a supermarket. "All these horrible people are so casual about their moms being healthy [*gasp*] and they're throwing it [*sob*] in my fucking face, the goddamn [*heaving, gasping sob*] whores!" Lizzie knew there was little she could say to console me. Instead, she protected my soul: "Don't forget to say, 'Those goddamn whores, *may they live to be a thousand*.'"

Joe had to deal with my mania in a much more hands-on way. By May 2005, we decided that I would go to Tucson alone as little as possible to increase our chances of conceiving. While there helping with my mom, I did my usual pee-on-a-stick ovulation test one morning and was alerted that the moment was now. Joe was on the golf course with Bob, trying to help my stepdad to take a break from the heavy drama that now engulfed his life. I texted Joe: "Get back here NOW! time 4 sex."

He knew I was on the verge of psychotic meltdown, so he left the course in the middle of the round and drove back to Mom's. He walked in the door, and I said to him the words every man dreams of hearing: "I have zero interest in doing it, but I guess I have no choice."

I insisted that we keep my bedroom door open so that I could hear Mom call if she needed something. It was not exactly a Romeo-and-Juliet moment.

IN THE LAST six months of Mom's life, she had a lot of visitors to her house, including the midwestern women she was still close to: Nanci, Maxine, Carol, and Linda. She had longed to show off her house to her Detroit friends, but this was never what she had in mind. When Linda came to Tucson, it was the last months of Mom's life. She dropped her bags at the front door, walked directly into Mom's room, climbed into bed with her, and said, "I came all this way; let's talk about people." Mom loved it.

By that time, Mom was barely leaving the house. She slowly shuffled between the kitchen, den, and her bedroom with the aid of a walker that was necessitated by the hip surgery that was necessitated by the bone tumors. Sitting in the dining room, next to the long, rustic wood table around which we often sat for holidays and big family dinners, was a gray metal box. It sat low to the ground, squat and hulking. It was an oxygen machine that heaved indiscreetly twenty-four hours a day as it pumped air through a tube that looped under Mom's nose. She couldn't be without the supplemental oxygen, so we got an extra-long tube—fifty feet long, maybe—that let her roam about. The metaphor was achingly obvious. She was chained. When you're sick, your palace very quickly becomes your prison.

She locked everything inside. That was increasingly tough for me. I so wanted her to share things with me so that I could be there for her emotionally, of course, but my motives were also selfish: I was desperate to understand how she was intellectually digesting what was happening. I wanted to know if, subconsciously, she had any peace. I was tortured by how tortured she was. I was desperate for her to find some spirituality, if not for herself then on my behalf. I needed her just once to say to me, "Sweetheart, this is terrible, but dying is part of life," to be the strong maternal figure. Even before she died, I knew how my grieving would be made more difficult due to the memories of her mental and emotional turmoil.

I needed to talk things out with the person I almost always talked things out with: my mom. But since I couldn't make a comment ("I'm scared") or ask a question that presupposed Mom's death ("Do you think I'll be capable of being a good mother even if you're not there to show me what to do?"), I was rendered mute. I had lost my mother even before I lost her.

It wasn't just the broad philosophical talks about spirituality and the afterlife that I longed for. I wanted to talk about all the little fuck-yous of dying. How did she feel when she looked around? The beautiful vases, for so long empty of flowers. The kitchen free of bubbling pots and spiced aromas. The quiet dance studio. The unused Pilates equipment. Were they all just painful reminders of what she could no longer do? Or was it comforting to be in a place where she had lived so happily?

Since her death, I've come to terms with much of what the world means, in the Post-Mom Era. But that house. That house. My feelings about it are tied up in messy, sometimes contradictory knots that are still hard for me to disentangle.

For example, though I think of it as "Mom's House," it's no longer that. It's Bob's. Then Bob is going to pass it to his children (two of whom hadn't come to visit Tucson when Mom was alive)—and even before that happens, another woman (Bob's girlfriend, Sheila, of whom I am truly fond) could try to make Mom's House her home. Sometimes when I walk into Mom's house, I feel her presence so strongly that I literally feel sick about the idea of it being in the care of anyone who is not acting as her proxy. But just as often, I climb the front stairs, cross the threshold, and think of nothing but the fact that Mom died there and that I want to be far away from that place, physically and emotionally. Touring the house with Bil made me feel more connected to it as a nest that my mother lovingly built. But it didn't come close to erasing the memories of what those walls and I had seen.

Lizzie and I have grieved differently, finding comfort with various aspects of Mom's life and death in our own ways and at our own paces. Lizzie has shown herself to be spiritually centered in ways that surprise me, frankly, and inspire me to believe that maybe I can get there too. In particular, Lizzie has let go of the house because she believes Mom has—that Mom is in heaven and has discovered that materialism is a frivolity of the living.

"Mom is so far beyond 'things,' " she has told me.

She asserts this with absolute certainty, and I am close to believing it myself. I can almost hear Mom saying, "I have let go of all that, and so should you."

IN THE EARLY afternoon, after having spent a couple hours with Bil, talking about and touring the house, I ventured down the driveway and to the end of the street, where the mailbox is. You can't re-create moments in life; they happen, and then they're gone. But I was trying to conjure at least a sensory connection to a memory.

When Mom was maybe five months from dying, we took a

walk down that driveway, Lizzie, Mom, and me. It was afternoon, and Mom had been lying in her usual spot on the couch, her torso sort of upright atop a few pillows. Warm light was coming through the den's rectangular window, which is long and thin like a horizon. Her attention was lost in eBay land; she was using one hand to peck at the iBook resting on the little folding table we had put next to the couch. "Help me walk to the mailbox," she said. It came out of nowhere.

We eased her up from the couch. I stood on her right; Lizzie was on her left. Mom looped her arms through ours like a bride walking down the aisle. We took slow steps, small steps, across the den, to the hallway, out the door, down the steps, through the courtyard, down the driveway, and up the street about thirty yards to the mailbox. Lizzie pulled down the door of the box and grabbed the bills and catalogs. We turned around and began the walk back.

Just as we were about to reach the driveway, Mom stopped. She didn't say a word at first. She just tipped her head back, jutted her chin skyward, puffed her chest outward, and with her entire body, absorbed a cool desert breeze.

It wasn't a huge breeze, and had Mom not gotten so still and so quiet, I might not have noticed it at all. But she somehow sensed that it was coming, and she gave herself to it. "Isn't that delicious?" she said. It felt as though she was talking to God as much as to Lizzie and me.

What I most take from that memory is this: what moved her was what surrounded the house—the mountains, the wildflowers, the desert breeze. Never have I seen anyone so joyful in her environment.

Chapter Eleven

The Golf Caddie
Carries a Legacy

I first e-mailed Mary Bitkowski Petrovich on June 19, 2005. Her name came to mind unexpectedly, and when it did, I acted swiftly. I hadn't thought of her in decades. But once I did, connecting with her took on urgency.

The significance of finding Mary registered with me instantly, even as little else did. We were once again in full crisis mode, and I lacked perspective. Sleep slurred into wakefulness. Tuesday was suddenly Saturday. I was at the office. I was at home. I was in Tucson. I didn't know where I was. I didn't know when or how it would all end.

But I knew that it would. When I left my mom's bedside in Tucson a few days earlier, she had been worse than dead. Down to about seventy pounds, her body was slouched in an awkward configuration: the left side of her pressed against the headboard, seven pillows woven between the twiglike limbs pushing her onto her side, a massive diaper that swallowed her, bedsores devouring the flesh off her back. The lung cancer was killing her, but the tumors attached to her hips, sacrum, and spine were torturing her. The pain, at times, was mitigated by the oxycodone, but the fear was not. When she was awake, and when she could draw the requisite energy, she cried. She didn't want to die. But when I sat on the plane headed back to New York a few days prior, I had prayed that she would, soon.

A few days after returning home, I slumped on the couch next to Joe as he watched a golf tournament on television.

It was a gorgeous weekend in New York City, and he and I had spent most of it in our living room, in front of the television. He was at the outset of what quickly developed into a full-blown obsession with golf. And I was at my nadir, happy to let my brain melt into the pixilated nothingness of white-ball-on-kelly-green.

On a good day, which this wasn't, I care to watch sports only when there is a good backstory to draw me in. When Tiger Woods won his first major title after the death of his father, for instance, you couldn't peel me away from the TV. I love narratives, the orderly way they can place random events into a compelling context.

This tournament was being played at Pinehurst No. 2, a course in North Carolina that is among the world's most famous. Michael Campbell, a longtime also-ran from New Zealand, was battling Tiger Woods to become the first of his countrymen to win the U.S. Open. It had all the trappings of an underdog-gets-his-day story. But not even that interested me.

Instead, I zoomed in on Campbell and his caddie, Michael Waite: the rhythmic way they passed the club, the impression that the win mattered as much to Waite as to Campbell, the sense that their fates were intertwined.

Amid all the strain, it hadn't occurred to me that a televised golf tournament could bring on a fresh wave of anxiety, but it did. Playing sports has never been a big interest of mine. But that wasn't the case for my mom. And as she was about to die, I suddenly realized that I didn't know what she was like as a competitor—how she approached a game and how she measured her success as an athlete.

I didn't know my mom in this way, but Mary did. Thus the urgency.

Though we had been out of touch for twenty-three years, I found Mary's e-mail address on Google within three minutes. "I wish I was reaching out to you under different circumstances," I wrote to her. "My mom is really sick."

At 9:10 the next morning, Mary wrote me back, initiating a daylong back-and-forth—and a relationship with a deeper reach than I could have imagined as I sat on the couch that summer evening.

MARY BITKOWSKI WAS my mom's caddie from about 1975 to 1982. When they met at Franklin Hills Country Club in suburban Detroit, Mary was twelve years old, and my mom was thirty-one.

Mom had picked up the sport, in earnest, a year before Mary started caddying. Within a few years Mom had a 7 handicap, making her one of the club's best female players. She had natural talent. But she was a disciplined student of the game, too. She practiced a lot. From late April through October, she played eighteen holes at least twice a week. When Lizzie and I were off at sleepaway camp from mid-June to mid-August, Mom played twice as much, if not more. And Mary was on the course with her a lot of the time.

My summer memories, from my school days, don't much involve my mom or dad or anyone in Michigan, really. Lizzie and I spent our summers at Camp Thunderbird for Girls in Bemidji, Minnesota. We were only at home the last weeks of summer before school started again. Those late-summer days were defined by being on the boat and hanging out at the club. Mary is present in many of those memories.

Which is not to say Mary and I were close; we weren't. Lizzie and I were totally extroverted, and I think our dynamic was intimidating and overpowering. Mary was shy—sweet and polite, but uncomfortable with eye contact.

On the golf course, though, Mary had presence. That was evident the few times each summer that I would watch my mom play. She and Mary would walk the course with Mom's blue-and-red leather Burton golf bag slung over Mary's shoulder. Both their gaits and their body language seemed comfortably in sync. There was an obvious politic to their relationship, and each seemed comfortable in her role: Mom was leader; Mary was her trusted advisor. Even then it was clear to me that Mom solicited and took Mary's counsel.

MARY WAS BORN on February 10, 1963, in Ferndale, Michigan, a working-class suburb just north of the Detroit city border. Arnold and Eunice Bitkowski had eight children in nine years. Mary came second, the oldest girl.

Mary's parents, both hairdressers, met while working together at a hair salon. After marrying, they opened Mr. Arnold's Beauty College, which was situated across the street from the family's nine-hundred-square-foot brick house. They lived in tight quarters. Eunice and Arnold slept in one room. The three boys (Ron, Paul, and Jason) took another. Mary and her four sisters (Suzanne, Sheri, Lori, and Angela) shared the third.

On October 1, 1971, when Mary was in the first grade, Arnold came home from work early. He was doubled over and groaning. He was a tough man—sturdy and thick—and it scared the kids to see him stricken. Eunice gathered them and explained that she was going to take their dad to the hospital. The kids stayed cloistered for the night, with the older siblings trying to pretend they weren't afraid.

The next day, Mary's parents returned home. The doctors had told them Arnold was suffering from nothing more than a bad stomachache. Still in agony twenty-four hours later, though, Arnold returned to the emergency room. By then, his appendix had ruptured completely. He died a month later, on Halloween, at age forty-four.

Suddenly widowed at thirty-two with eight kids, Eunice took to her financial responsibilities with sad determination. Six days a week, she left the house for work at seven thirty in the morning and returned at nine thirty at night. She would tell the kids that she owed it to their late father to keep the business running.

By the time of Arnold's death, the Bitkowskis had moved into a slightly bigger three-bedroom house in a better neighborhood and had opened up two more beauty schools. The schools were about twenty miles away from one another—and about twenty miles from the family's new house. The distance between the various beauty schools and home left Eunice wasting a couple of hours of her workday in the car. Neither she nor Arnold had gone to college, and they opened up the shops without any sort of business plan or budget. As she fought to preserve her husband's memory and provide for her kids, Eunice fell further and further behind.

They lived frugally. There weren't many toys or books. At the start of the school year, each child was allowed to buy two outfits at Kmart—and they had to last until the next fall. When Mary was playing sports, she often ripped holes in her pants. She'd patch them up herself so she didn't have to go to school in raggedy clothes. As the oldest daughter, she tended to a lot of childrearing and housekeeping, and she tried not to complain. She was very aware of the poverty. Even as a little girl, she thought the family should receive welfare. But Eunice refused to apply.

HOW POOR THE Bitkowskis were came into sharp relief when Eunice moved the brood again, this time into a house on the outskirts of Franklin Village, Michigan. Like the homes before it, this one had three bedrooms and one and a half bathrooms for nine people.

Franklin Village is a 2.7-square-mile swath of sophisticated suburban affluence. About a thousand (mostly white) people live in Franklin, a designated historic district marked by rolling hills and beautiful homes with winding driveways. Not surprisingly, the area's public schools are among the best in the nation.

Eunice was determined to see her children get a good education. That's why she chose a small house off Northwestern Highway—a highly trafficked artery connecting many of Detroit's upper-middle-class suburbs. The house had a Franklin mailing address and sat just inside the boundary of the well-funded, reputable Birmingham Public School District.

Walking the school halls, Mary would point her glance at the ground, petrified of calling attention to herself. Amid classmates representing some of the wealthiest families in Detroit, Mary lived a different reality. She was self-conscious about being the poorest kid in the class.

Bright and curious, she was an excellent student who earned mostly As. And she was physically strong—about five foot three, thick with muscles, gifted with speed and coordination. She excelled at pretty much any sport she tried, but her great loves growing up were baseball, softball, and basketball. On the field and on the court, she was outgoing, confident, even aggressive.

By the time she was twelve, Mary had focused on softball. She loved playing, and was a talented shortstop. During the school year, she borrowed a mitt from the athletic department, but with the summer approaching, she'd have to make other arrangements.

She knew better than to ask her mom to buy her a mitt. She needed to look for a job. Her fourteen-year-old brother had started the year before working as a golf caddie at Franklin Hills Country Club, so she decided to see if she could get a job there too. It was about a mile and a half from their home—close enough to get there by foot, which was a necessity. She walked along Inkster Road, a quiet street dotted by expensive, tasteful houses.

Stone gates—simultaneously discreet and blaring symbols of

wealth—mark the entrance of Franklin Hills. There is a long, sloped driveway, which sweeps past a driving and putting range, and a parking lot filled with sleek imported cars. At the top, the drive circles into a cul-de-sac, at the far end of which sits the elegant Tudor-style clubhouse.

Mary was a little intimidated as she walked through those gates for the first time and climbed tentatively toward the golf pro shop, situated near the putting green and first tee. She took a nervous step across the threshold and let her eyes do a sweep: shiny new clubs, collared T-shirts with embroidered FHCC crests, tasseled cleats, the smell of money. Mary approached the man who ran the caddie program.

"I'm Ronnie's little sister, Mary," she said. "And I want to be a caddie too."

"We don't hire girl caddies," he said.

Mary cleared her throat: "Well, maybe you could just give me a chance?"

Gumption and persistence paid off. "We're doing this as a courtesy to your brother," the caddie master said, putting her on notice.

THE REDFORD COUNTRY Club was founded in 1920 by 250 Jewish business and philanthropic leaders who could afford the country-club lifestyle—but whose religion prevented them from gaining admission to most of Detroit's existing clubs. By 1926 the membership had purchased a nearly four-hundred acre parcel of land on which the modern-day club—renamed Franklin Hills—is still located. Albert Kahn, a German Jewish immigrant who established himself as one of the Industrial Age's most important architects, designed the Tudor clubhouse with fieldstone turrets. It opened in 1928. Donald Ross, who is remembered among the great American golf course architects, was retained to create the course.

Historically, Franklin's membership was made of Detroit's Jewish elite. Over the decades, it collected members like A. Alfred Taubman, who amassed a tremendous fortune by developing shopping centers. (He's perhaps best known as the owner of Sotheby's who was fined $7.5 million and served nine months in prison as a result of a price-fixing scandal.) Another well-known member was the late Max Fisher, the gas station and real estate baron and major backer of Jewish philanthropies and Republican politicians. There are others, too, like Bill Davidson, the late billionaire owner of the Detroit Pistons and NHL's Tampa Bay Lightning. Throughout most of the twentieth century, the club was very exclusive, with the most sophisticated and affluent membership of the area's Jewish clubs.

There, on the tenth tee, Mary met my mom.

I WASN'T SURPRISED to learn from Mary that the caddies at the club—guys in the throes of teenage boyhood—were hot for my mom. In 1975, when Mary first met her, Mom was a thirty-one-year-old blue-eyed blonde with a gorgeous figure, always carefully turned out in slim Bermuda shorts with fitted collared golf shirts. She had an adorable outfit for cold weather or windy days. It was two-piece—nylon pants and a long-sleeved V-necked pullover with white racing stripes. She had two such outfits: one in red, one in pink. She looked fashionable, but never like someone willing to sacrifice athletic comfort for style. She almost always wore a visor.

The hundred and fifty or so caddies had coined a number of nicknames to describe players, and had implemented an informal rating system based on tipping largesse, skill, and speed in play. Mary told me that my late paternal grandfather—longtime Franklin member Carl Rosman—was nicknamed by the caddies "Quick Carl." (On the golf course, that's a compliment.) With women golfers, looks earned a player a lot of points. As a good-looking, well-tipping, skilled player who didn't endlessly linger over her shots, Mom cleaned up. "She got a four-star rating in every category," Mary says.

During Mary's first summer as a caddie, she was hazed constantly. The caddie shack, a little hut behind the pro shop, had one bathroom for the 150 caddies. That is, there was one filthy toilet to be shared by 149 guys and Mary. There was no lock on the door.

When Mary could hold it no longer, she would attempt to enter the caddie shack on the sly, hoping to relieve herself without incident. As the sole girl, though, she almost never went unnoticed. She would squat over the toilet—what girl is going to sit on the seat of a toilet used by all those teenage boys?—and extend her arms to try to hold the door shut. The guys reminded her every day of the futility of her efforts. In groups of eight or ten, they would rush the door, ramming it open amid their adolescent laughter. But Mary didn't let it get to her. Having seven siblings inured her to such indignities.

That first summer, she was routinely assigned to the least desirable "loops," which is caddie-speak for a round of eighteen holes. Invariably, she was accompanying older ladies who teed off in the middle of the day, played slowly, and tipped scantily.

Ambitious, Mary wanted to reposition herself. She decided that she would walk to work at about five thirty in the morning so she could be the first to sign up for the coveted loops. Those efforts were derailed too when one of her tormentors would simply cross her name off the list.

But the guys couldn't prevent my mom from introducing herself to Mary, which is how the two of them initially came together. As it did on all Thursday mornings in the summer, the club was hosting a "ladies' tournament," with each foursome starting simultaneously from different tees. Mary was standing on the tenth tee, a 425-yard, par-5 hole. With her were three other caddies, all waiting for the group they had been assigned to caddie for.

My mom's group was starting on the eleventh tee. To get there, you needed to cut through the fairways of the tenth hole, but to walk directly by the tenth tee prolongs the distance. However as my mom made her way, a young girl standing on the tenth tee box caught her eye. Mom diverted course and headed for Mary.

"Hi, Mary! You must be Ronnie's sister."

Shy and completely without social confidence, Mary remained silent. She waved awkwardly.

Behind her, the other caddies were whispering to one another: "Why is she talking to *her*?" Mary stood frozen, saying nothing. With a casual wave, my mom turned away. "It's really nice to meet you," she called out.

To this day, Mary calls it a critical moment in her life. Members rarely greeted caddies in a friendly manner that disregarded the club's hierarchies. But what affected Mary even more deeply was that my mom considered her someone worth meeting. No adult had ever walked out of the way to say hello to her. No adult had ever told her that they were happy to meet her. "That still sticks with me today," Mary told me.

About ten days later, she was assigned to go on a loop with my mom, who, apparently, had requested her. And for the next seven summers, Mary caddied regularly for Mom.

As a well-matched golfer and caddie do, Mom and Mary developed a rhythm. Sometimes they talked about golf, with Mary advising Mom on what club she should next use. Or Mom would teach Mary a bit about strategy. There was plenty of silence between them, too, with Mary toting my mom's bag as they walked in the shade. There was an instant and easy comfort between them.

Mom knew about Mary's situation—about her dad's death, about her mother's struggles to stay afloat while raising eight kids. But she never asked Mary about it, which allowed Mary a genuine escape amid the towering trees. And she didn't preach about rising above one's circumstances. She kept it light. "She never probed me," Mary said. "She wanted it to be a happy time together. She was just a very positive person to be around." Mom didn't try to push herself as a mentor, and that's how she became one.

She did frequently ask Mary about school—what classes she enjoyed, what she found challenging. Once, when Mary was sixteen, she told Mom she wanted to go to college at the University of Michigan. Mary knew that Mom had grown up in Ann Arbor and that, like Mom, half of the Franklin membership had graduated from U of M. But she had no idea if it was within reach.

Mom stopped walking and turned to Mary. "You are *perfect* Michigan material," she said. Mom's reaction lit a fire under

Mary, provoking her to get serious about looking for scholarship opportunities. "When no one in your family has ever gone to college and then someone you respect says, 'Of course you're going to go there,' I can't tell you what a boost that is," Mary said.

They spent time together off the course too. A couple of times each summer, Mom would invite Mary to come to the house on her day off. She would make a picnic and take Mary boating on Pine Lake, along whose shore we lived. At the annual end-of-summer softball game pitting the country club's pros against the caddies, Mom always coached the caddies' team. And Mom and Bob also hosted backyard barbeques for the caddies after they played in interclub leagues.

Mom and Mary didn't see each other much during the winter, though Mom occasionally checked in on Mary, calling her to babysit even though that required Bob to drive fifteen miles in each direction to pick her up and take her home.

My mom talked to Lizzie and me about Mary frequently. How brilliant she was. How sweet she was. What a tremendous athlete! A champion golfer if she set her mind to it. A tough girl, with every reason to be angry, but instead a total ray of sunshine. You just watch, my mom would say, there is nothing she can't do with her life.

For her part, Mary worshipped my mom. When she walked to work—climbing the long, twisting driveway past the member parking lot—she'd instinctively do a quick search for my mom's car (a powder blue T-top Cutlass and, later, a white Cadillac the length of Long Island). Back at home, her siblings teased her for gushing on and on about Mrs. Rosin.

Yet, for all their mutual adoration, they never expressed it to each other. Instead, they went to lengths to be together without explicitly acknowledging their efforts to one another.

Mary always caddied for my mom during the club championship. But in August of 1980, a few days before the tournament's start, the caddie master (who seemed to be no fan of Mary's) approached her with an autocratic message: "You're not caddying for Suzy Rosin this year. I'm in charge here, not you."

Dejected but not defeated, Mary walked over to the driving range where my mom was hitting balls. "I'm sorry, I'm not going to be able to caddie for you this year, Mrs. Rosin," she said.

"What are you talking about?" my mom asked, her brow furrowed. Mary explained what the caddie master had told her. Mom listened, seemingly impassive, and then returned her focus to her long game.

The next day, Stuart Schwartz, who was then the president of the club, approached Mary outside the pro shop. "What's going on with you and Suzy Rosin?" he asked. Mary told him that for seven years she had caddied for my mom during the club championship—but that this year, the caddie master was prohibiting her from doing so.

"Long story short," Mary told me, "I caddied for your mom during the tournament. She didn't say anything to me, or allow herself to seem pissed off in front of me. She was way too classy for that. But she wasn't going to waste her time working her way through the chain of command. She went straight to the top. She knew how to get things done."

While I was interviewing Mary, it seemed to me that the most important thing Mom had done for Mary was to show interest in her: to ask her questions, to solicit her opinions. But Mary explained that Mom's impact went beyond that.

"She symbolized for me at a very young age everything I wanted to be," Mary said. "I was from a very undereducated background, and here I was crossing the gates of Franklin Hills every day into the world of very successful, very wealthy people. Your mom was extremely well educated. She was nice to everyone. She was a positive person. She was so classy. And by the way, she was a darn good golfer. It was almost secondary, but it wasn't. It was an example of, 'You should be really good at everything you do.' She didn't wear her accomplishments or wealth on her sleeve. But when she walked into a room, people could just tell, 'Man, she's *got* it.' "

MY MOM HAD taken up golf as a casual pursuit about four years before meeting Mary. But she became much more serious after she married my stepdad in 1974. Bob was then at the top of his game and had won the club championship a few years earlier.

Early on, golf played a central role in their marriage. Just after marrying, Mom and Bob first took four of their collective five kids to Disney World in Florida—and then headed to Pebble Beach for a golf honeymoon. Together they spent a lot of time on the course at Franklin, playing every Wednesday and Saturday during the fall and spring, and much more than that during the summer.

Mom picked up the game relatively late—she was twenty-six when she started—but she was determined to excel. She lacked patience and could be an unforgiving critic of her own play. When playing with Bob, and playing poorly, she wouldn't spare him her crankiness. She'd purse her lips in an angry pout and refuse to respond to his suggestions or encouragements.

In some ways, Mom didn't fit the stereotype of an athlete. She was slight, sometimes quiet and demure. But her size belied her strength. By the time she started playing with Mary in 1975, "she could bust the ball over two hundred yards and only weighed about a hundred pounds," Mary said.

My clearest memories of my mom on the golf course center around the women's club championships. Year after year, she fought her way through the ranks, inevitably reaching the finals. And year after year, she was pitted against a woman nine years her junior named Julie Dale (whose married name, at the time, was Korotkin). In our family, their rivalry took on mythic proportions. They were Chris Evert and Martina Navratilova, with my mom playing the role of Chris Evert: perpetual underdog. Mary said these weren't just the overblown imaginings of a little girl. "The whole club knew it was a huge rivalry," she said.

The differences in personal style and approach to athletics between my mom and Julie were stark. Julie was tall with a big build that dwarfed Mom's litheness. Once when playing in the finals, Julie wore jeans. She almost always rode in a golf cart. Between shots, a cigarette dangled from her mouth.

With a visor keeping her blond wavy hair out of her eyes and the sun off her face, my mom was always well primped. But fashion didn't come first. She considered golf a sport, not a pastime. She wouldn't consider traversing the course by cart. She always walked.

Julie started playing golf in 1959, when she was six years old. A skilled golfer by the time she was a teenager, she met her future husband on the golf course. They got married when Julie was twenty-one and they joined Franklin Hills. Her husband pushed her to improve her game. Julie started taking lessons from the pro at Franklin. He helped propel her from good to great. "A lot of male teachers don't know how to talk to a woman," Julie told me. "They talk about planes and these geometric things." But the pro would tell her she could get into proper position by making sure her hands covered the crease of her shorts. He also emphasized the importance of confidence in play, of not overthinking; of being deliberate in selecting a club and making a shot.

My mom was a different kind of player. "She was very calculated," Julie said. "She would check her swing, and recheck it a lot. She watched the club go back. I remember her taking the club back in a very mechanical way. Your mom was always working."

But it wasn't enough: in the finals, my mom *always* lost to Julie Korotkin.

In late August 1982, Mom and Julie teed off for the nineteenth hole of the ladies club championship finals. It was sudden-death play in which the winner of the one hole would win the entire tournament. After falling behind in the middle of the round, my mom had won the last few holes of regular play to finish the eighteen-hole round tied with Julie. Momentum was on her side.

It was a sunny day, and several dozen club members watched from the gallery. Any time my mom and Julie played in the finals, they attracted a cluster of spectators. But as word spread that their match had gone into sudden death—that this might be the year that Suzy finally beat Julie—the crowd thickened. Even my dad and his second wife came out to watch.

Mom took the first shot. She hit the ball straight down the center of the fairway, about thirty yards ahead of where Julie's ball ultimately landed. Julie's second shot was mediocre. "I thought, 'Oh God, I'm going to lose this one,' " she remembered. Then Mom lined up to hit her second shot. Her jaw was clenched. As soon as she struck the ball, everyone could tell it wasn't going to be good. She choked and double-bogeyed. Julie eked out bogey and won the hole—which meant she won the match and the tournament too.

Lizzie and I rushed to Mom's side and hugged her tight around her waist. She shrugged her shoulders and said, "It's okay, girls." But I had a sinking feeling. I had prayed for her to win. It would have been fun to point to Mom's name on the wall near the club dining room highlighting all the tournament winners. But more than longing for bragging rights, I wanted her to win because I could tell how much she wanted it. She wore her desire to win, and then her discouragement too. I was ten, but I distinctly remember feeling nervous and unsure how to approach my mom's failure, and her obvious disappointment in herself.

Mary stood back as Lizzie and I clung to Mom in her moment of defeat. It was a devastating moment for her too. "It didn't matter that she had the talent," Mary said of Mom. "She never could get over the hump." As a young girl, Mary spent hours ruminating over Mom's record. "It drove me to paranoia," she said. "To this day, I am certain to overdo everything to make sure I win."

Uncle Eddie had come into town to watch Mom play in the finals. After the match, the whole family sat around the dinner table lamenting the loss. My mom got drunk—the only time in my life I ever remember seeing her like that.

"I'm never playing golf again," she said. We all considered it a drunken promise. But she never picked up a club again.

Mary went off to college, and that chapter of Mom's life ended—completely and abruptly.

Mom said she quit because she was concerned about the potential effects to her health of constant exposure to the pesticides and fertilizers used to maintain the course. And she said she was bored spending so much time doing the same thing, again and again. She didn't seem to wring her hands over the decision. There were no second thoughts, no apparent anger or angst. She was just done.

When I called Julie, I was hoping to find some clarity as to why Mom always lost and why she quit so suddenly. Julie was generous with her time, spending several hours on the phone with the daughter of someone she played golf with more than twenty years ago. As a reporter, I was trying to cultivate a comfortable tone because I wanted Julie to speak freely about her impressions of Mom. But as a daughter, I was fighting feelings of defensiveness. I could tell Julie was aware of the strange position she had been put in: asked to outline the abilities of a competitor she had always been able to beat—by the daughter of that competitor.

At first, Julie stuck to general niceties, telling me that she remembered my mom laughing a lot and telling stories about growing up on college campuses, an astronomer's daughter.

But I pushed her to speak openly, and she did. She said Mom could seem really nervous at times—both on and off the course. "Your mom was easy to beat, mentally," Julie says. "I remember her hands shaking a lot." She knew all about the pesticides and fertilizers, and my mom's fear of their effects. "I don't want to be mean," she finally said, "but your mom was a little neurotic."

There was another layer to their rivalry because it played out against the backdrop of a country-club membership—the sort of group that is prone to social cliques and exclusionary behavior. My mom may have been the underdog on the golf course. Off it, she was not.

My mom was blond, fit, upbeat, and very good at golf. At a country club, that makes you pretty popular. Julie, by her own admission, struggled. "I was way out of my league in terms of the social stuff," she said. Among the lady golfers, Julie explained, she was excluded from the girly chitchat and recreational play. Many of the club's members could be nasty, she said.

I was nervous to ask if my mom was among those who were unkind. I was nervous because—in that way that you don't like someone who beats you all the time—my mom didn't like Julie.

"Was my mom mean to you?" I asked her.

"We weren't close friends, but she was always nice to me," Julie told me. "She was a good sport. She was never nasty to me. She never excluded me."

I think that Julie's ability to outplay my mom in tournaments had everything to do with Mom's quitting, but not entirely in the way that those who followed their rivalry assumed. I truly believe that Julie's cigarette habit had a lot to do with it. Mom hated losing to someone who smoked and felt that if someone who smoked could outplay her, then golf was not sufficiently athletic to capture so much of her time and attention.

Mom put a ton of pressure on herself to excel in all sorts of physical pursuits. She was mentally determined, physically strong, and competitive. I think she derived most of her self-confidence from athletic achievement and found the ultimate challenge in starting from scratch at a given pursuit—mastering it and moving on. But she heaped a lot of self-loathing upon herself all the while.

After interviewing Mary and Julie—and reflecting on Mom's demeanor throughout her illness—I am convinced that she approached cancer in much the same way she approached golf. In golf, she believed that if she practiced enough, she would beat Julie. Later, when facing off against lung cancer, she believed that if she had enough operations, if she were willing to try every last experimental form of treatment, if she lay under the radiation machine enough times—if she wanted enough to live—she'd live. In this competition with cancer, she could be excruciatingly hard on herself. When test results pointed to the intensification of the disease, her response didn't just reflect sadness, fear, or anxiety. She seemed to take it as an indictment of her character. It was as if someone were telling her she hadn't shown sufficient determination, prayed enough, subjected her body to enough poison.

When Julie called Mom "neurotic," it didn't upset me at all. I always assumed that many Franklin members of that era had made the same assessment. They thought my mom was crazy for quitting a game at which she excelled, a game that was central to her social life. That she cited "environmental" concerns—some twenty-five years ago—was enough to convince them that my mom was unconventional, if not downright bat-shit crazy.

Which, of course, she was. But she was really intuitive too.

I have to give proper respect to my mom's concerns about the environmental hazards of golf. In today's enviro-PC age, the chemicals used to maintain courses are a liability for the sport.

And after years spent on courses treated with potentially poisonous fertilizers and pesticides, my mom developed a type of lung cancer that is most often found in those who didn't smoke. It can't automatically be assumed that she got cancer from the cigarettes she smoked as a young woman.

Sometimes I wonder if—in giving up a pastime she loved—she was subconsciously making a desperate, preemptive strike against fate.

IN JANUARY 2005, a few weeks after her sixtieth birthday, the pain in Mom's hip became unbearable. Mom insisted that if she could drag herself and her oxygen tank out to the Pilates studio, she could heal her hip. Yet she couldn't find the energy, and she'd curse herself for laziness.

In fact, a massive growth of cancer cells had decimated her hip joint. Mom had to lean on a walker as she hobbled even the smallest distances in her house.

As the radiation and chemo failed to adequately shrink the bone tumors, Mom's oncologist referred her to an orthopedic surgeon. Mom and Bob went to see him, a young, handsome hotshot. He recommended "palliative" hip replacement surgery. "This will ease the pain in the hip, but won't prolong your life," he told her.

"But I'm not going to die, am I?" Mom asked.

With incredulity, the doctor stared at her—a woman with a relentless sprawl of tumors colonizing her organs and bones, and a complete unwillingness to acknowledge it. "Well, yes," he responded. "This cancer is going to kill you. But maybe I can do something about the hip pain in the meantime."

My mom was devastated by his comment—*devastated*.

"I'm not letting that butcher operate on me," she told us. "How dare he speak to me like that!"

She had decided that this guy had it in for her, that he didn't believe she was tough, that he saw her as a lost cause. Anyone who didn't embrace the view that Mom had the power to will herself to wellness was a force as dangerous as the cancer itself. "With that kind of negativity, he might just end up killing me," she said—and she said it as if this was a fact so obvious that anyone who didn't immediately agree was moronic, if not sinister.

Mom put her own need to ignore the inevitabilities of cancer before our need for help in caring for her. That was her right, I suppose, as the person who was dying. But her children paid a high price.

Even after the palliative hip replacement, Mom had less and less mobility—and a greater reliance on oxygen tanks, catheters, and dozens of prescription drugs. She willfully held on to every detail of her existence that she could control. Always a methodical and particular woman, she wouldn't accept anything less than perfection, even when she could no longer care for herself. For instance, she was as unyielding as ever when it came to the way the linens on her bed were matched with one another, and how the top sheet was tucked. It didn't matter to her that we were often making the bed while she lay in it, a skill Lizzie and I picked up while Mom was in the hospital for those many months. Even when we were exhausted from catering to her all day long, she took her time tending to her end-of-day rituals— all of which she did while in bed with Lizzie, me, Dorothy (our family's longtime housekeeper, who would fly in from Detroit to Arizona to help Mom for two-week stretches), and various home health aides ran back and forth to her bathroom with Tupperware bins and toiletries. She was a manic toothbrusher and flosser. And then there were her face creams—antiwrinkle/pro-collagen, Retin-A, eye cream, and the like. Don't get me started on the refusal to miss an application of antiaging eye cream when you are dying from late-stage lung cancer. She had so lost control of her body that she needed to maintain despotic reign over what she could.

Toward the very end, when Mom was so sick that even she couldn't deny what was going on, she gave me the exquisite, painful honesty I had longed for throughout her illness. She confided in me twice about being afraid to die.

"Will I suffocate?" she asked me.

"I don't know, Mom. Should we ask Dr. Brooks?"

"No," she said. "No, I don't want to ask him that."

The real moments of closeness came when her mental control slackened—when she was drugged up, dangling just above unconsciousness. Sometimes she seemed to be hallucinating, but during those moments, she gave off an aura of mysticism and spirituality.

Once, at the very end, I flew to Tucson, walked in the front door, dropped my bags, and headed straight for my mom's room. With the heavy curtains drawn against the sun and the airless stench of stale urine, the room felt darker than usual.

A receding, wispy figure swallowed up by the king-size bed, Mom was slouched over in her usual position, pillows propping her in an almost mangled pose of partial recline. Without making a sound, I approached the foot of her bed. Her lids flapped open suddenly, startling me.

"Katie!" she cried out. "My angel has come!"

Then she closed her eyes again, returning to drugged unconsciousness.

Her declaration elevated me, however temporarily. For a few weeks, I had been on the brink of some sort of breakdown, unsure how long I could maintain the pace of flying into Tucson once every ten days while working full-time. Emotionally, I didn't know how I could continue to stomach the suffering my mom was experiencing. The feeling of being so powerless in the face of her physical and emotional suffering was destroying me.

And then here I was being greeted as my Mom's savior, an angel whom she received as a source of deliverance.

Of course, that feeling of relief didn't last. The realities of stage-four cancer only allowed my mom a certain type of denial, and similarly, they withheld from me any lasting moments of satisfaction. I could give her pain medication, but I lacked the expertise to anticipate the pain's ever-shifting patterns. And I lacked the grace to ease her turmoil.

One afternoon in June 2005, I sat on a chair next to her bed, holding her hand as she slept. I looked at her, and I thought—as a parent might think when looking at her sad or feverish child—I would do anything, anything at all, to bring her comfort. At about two, she awoke, and I gingerly lifted a cup of water to her lips. The drizzle of moisture in her mouth brought on an approximation of lucidity. Mom focused her sunken blue eyes—with the left lid drooping ominously, a sign that the cancer might have spread to her brain—and fixed them intensely upon mine.

"Please, Katie," she said, literally begging. "Please don't let me die. Give me some of your strength, *please*. Promise me that you won't let me die. *Promise me.*"

"Mom, I can't promise that," I said, in a voice full of ache. Mom squeezed my hand and grimaced. She was too weak to cry. I was too weak not to.

A few days later, I flew back to New York to make an appearance at work and spend a few days with my husband. On Sunday, Joe tried to get me to talk about what I was feeling. But I was exhausted and traumatized. I couldn't focus on conversation; I couldn't articulate a linear thought. So he asked if he could flip on the TV. He tuned into the U.S. Open.

And then at 7:12 in the evening, I e-mailed Mary.

THE CHICK EVANS Caddie Scholarship is named for golf champion Charles "Chick" Evans Jr., who earmarked most of his golf winnings to help caddies. He created a trust in 1928, and more than eighty years later, the foundation that grew out of that trust feeds one of the nation's largest privately funded college scholarship programs. To date, nearly nine thousand young men and women have benefited from his generosity. There are Evans Scholarship Houses at fourteen universities nationwide, including the University of Michigan, Northwestern University, and the University of Colorado at Boulder.

Evans Scholars—there are about 850 in total each year—must have a "superior caddie record" for two or more years at a country club that nominates them. Potential Scholars must "rank in the top 25% of their high school class, show financial need and have outstanding personal character."

In 1980, armed with her stellar high school transcripts and a letter of recommendation from my mom, Mary applied for an Evans Scholarship. The Western Golf Association, which administers the scholarship foundation, agreed to cover Mary's tuition to the University of Michigan.

Unlike many college students who spend much of their time drinking, smoking pot, and taking for granted that their tuition will be parentally covered—why are you all looking at me?—Mary set out on a methodically and strategically designed course of action. She was drawn to engineering and law. What she needed was an undergraduate degree that promised immediate employment. She chose engineering because a career in law would mandate that she go for a graduate degree after finishing college.

She majored in industrial engineering. A program heavily dominated by men, engineering school reminded her of being Franklin's first female caddy. She found camaraderie on the University of Michigan's varsity softball team, which she joined as a walk-on. By her senior year, she was in the starting lineup and the team's captain. Despite being an engineering school student and an NCAA Division I athlete, Mary had a well-rounded college experience, she said, replete with "drinking and partying and kissing boys."

After graduation Mary landed a good job right away with General Motors. The job was technical, and she learned a lot. But she was oppressed by the lethargy of a bureaucracy filled with fifty-year-olds whom she felt discouraged innovation and enthusiasm.

After two years, she decided to pursue an MBA. She applied to and was accepted by the University of Michigan. Her supervisors at GM told her that the company was willing to pay for her education if she attended U of M's business school. When she was mulling over GM's offer, a friend at work said to her, "Why don't you apply to Harvard?"

It hadn't occurred to her. She had always thought of Harvard as a school for the rich. Still, she decided she had nothing to lose: she applied there as well as to the business school at the University of Chicago. She was accepted at both.

As she did when deciding between law and engineering, she mapped out the facts and ran the numbers. She knew that if she went anywhere but Michigan, she'd incur debt. To forgo a scholarship, she told me, felt "frivolous in terms of the luxury." But she found herself filling out Harvard's enrollment forms. "You only get a chance once in your lifetime to go to Harvard Business School," she said.

AFTER GRADUATING FROM Harvard, Mary returned to Detroit and embarked on a climb, assuming ever more responsibility in the automotive industry at companies like Chrysler, AlliedSignal, and Dura Automotive Systems. In 2001, she was offered a job that presented something of a paradigm shift: she was asked to become a consultant for a private equity firm, Wynnchurch Capital, creating a new structure for AxleTech, an automotive component manufacturer that Wynnchurch was planning to buy for $28 million. This would require her leaving a job where she was managing a $1 billion division of a huge manufacturing company. But if Wynnchurch succeeded in its purchase, she would become the company's CEO.

She longed for the opportunity to have autonomy over an

entire operation. Yet she worried that moving to a smaller business was a step back. When she was offered substantial equity in the company, though, she was convinced.

When she took over AxleTech, with its international operations in France, Brazil, and the United States, the company had $140 million in revenue and $4 million in profits. "It was broken," Mary said.

Under her leadership, the company has turned around. In 2005, Wynnchurch sold AxleTech—the company it had bought four years earlier for $28 million—to another private equity outfit, the Carlyle Group, for $345 million. Mary continued to steer the company toward greater profitability. In 2008, it had $500 million in revenue and more than $70 million in profit. That year, Carlyle sold AxleTech to General Dynamics for $750 million. As a result of both sales, Mary netted about $70 million in cash

In November 2007, *BusinessWeek* profiled Mary in a cover story about CEOs of private equity-owned companies. It quotes her former boss Wynnchurch president John A. Hatherly: "She is probably the most disciplined, focused person I've ever met. She's very demanding. You can't hide from Mary. If you're not performing, she'll find you." When I spoke to Mr. Hatherly, he said, "Mary is the best CEO I've ever encountered, and that includes Jack Welch."

When Mary is not ruling the business universe, she's driving her two sons—Kyle was born in 1997, Kevin in 1998—to swim practice or soccer games. She and her husband, Scott Petrovich, built a beautiful house on a lake just a few miles from the Pine Lake Country Club in Orchard Lake, Michigan, where the Petrovichs are members. A 5-handicap golfer, Mary has won the club championship every year since 1998. They recently also joined Oakland Hills Country Club, in Bloomfield Township. The club's South Course has been the site of thirty-seven major tournaments, including the 2008 PGA Championship.

On summer days, Mary and Scott race home after work, grab their boys, and jump on their speedboat. On inner tubes and water skis, Kyle and Kevin circle Pine Lake—the very same lake my mom used to take Mary out on all those summers ago.

ON JUNE 21, 2005, I flew to Tucson to oversee Mom's care for a few days. With his wife near death in Tucson, my stepdad had to go back to Detroit to address a lawsuit filed against him by his niece and nephew. The plan was for me to spend two days alone with Mom (and her aide) as Bob sought to attend quickly to his affairs.

The day before leaving—on the night I first e-mailed Mary—I took a pregnancy test. It was a whim. I had a ton of them in the cabinet beneath the bathroom sink, next to the pile of ovulation tests. But by mid-June, the stress was acute, and there was no room in my brain to focus on pregnancy. I couldn't keep track of the day of the week, much less the days of the month. All of which is to say, I didn't even know if I was late. But there it was, a big old plus sign. I was almost confused to see it.

I HARDLY REMEMBER telling Joe that morning; I just remember that we hugged and that I cried. I remember walking out of the *Journal*'s office as soon as it was a decent hour in Los Angeles, and calling Lizzie as I crossed the footbridge over the pit of the World Trade Center. I was in a trance, and I don't really remember how I told her or how she reacted to the news. But I do remember, very well, that when I told Lizzie I was going to wait to tell Mom about the baby until Joe joined me in Tucson the following weekend, she cut me off.

"You have to tell Mom when you go there tomorrow," she said. "You can't be stingy with good news right now."

The second I landed in Tucson, I couldn't believe that I had even considered withholding. I couldn't get to Mom's house soon enough, and the urgency wasn't just because of how on the brink Mom was. It was because I was entering a phase of life that connects a woman to her mother as few other things do. I couldn't wait to tell my mom her baby was going to have a baby.

Immediately upon entering the house, I headed straight back into her bedroom. As had become the norm, the heavy drapes were pulled. Dead air hung over her bed. Unless you've seen someone after a long battle with a terrible disease like cancer, you couldn't imagine how Mom looked; I don't think I can even describe it.

Because even the slightest shift in the positioning of her mattress and pillows could cause Mom pain, I very carefully climbed into bed next to her. She seemed relatively alert as I settled in beside her.

I didn't waste a second.

"I'm pregnant," I said.

She let her eyes widen with a look of surprised delight. But then her face quickly twisted into a grimace, the visual memory of which I have tried but can't forget.

With the sides of her mouth turned downward and her chin tensed, Mom was acknowledging something that she had fought for so long to deny: she would never meet her daughter's child. She closed her eyes and scrunched them in a pained look. Then she stopped herself. Using all the energy she could muster, she lifted up her hand and set it on my belly. In my mind, I willed my child—an embryo at the beginning of a long journey—to connect with my mom, who was so near the end of hers. It was the most powerful and profoundly sad moment of my life.

THE NEXT DAY, an express-mailed package arrived at my mom's. It was from Mary. There was a framed portrait of her, her husband, and their boys, and a letter written in longhand.

By this day, Wednesday, June 22, Mom was no longer able to speak. So I hovered over the hospital bed we had rented for her, looking for a sign of lucidity. Around noon, her eyes connected with mine, and she blinked at me in a way that felt like *I love you*. I then read to Mom the letter Mary had written.

Dear Suzy:

God certainly works in mysterious ways. I often wonder how and why my life has been so blessed with joy and success. Every day, I am more convinced that it is the people one meets and the experiences they have together. There are few people in my life who have had such a lasting impact and made such an indelible impression on my life as Suzy Rosin.

From the day I met you (30 yrs ago!) as a shy, underconfident 12-year-old girl, you melted me with your warmth and kindness. Our relationship was very special, as you were the best of a big sister and mother to me for seven years. As I reflect back, I realize by observing you and your best qualities, I had a role model who taught me to smile, that there was always hope, and life had so much more to offer than where I came from. I learned a steely determination from you. I admired your class and beauty. I loved your competitive spirit. And more than anything, I enjoyed our togetherness and special closeness.

Please know that I have thought of you with love, appreciation, and affection for many, many years. You helped give me the motivation to make something of my life. Even today, I am not sure what pulled you to me with such warmth and kindness. Perhaps we share a common spirit and you saw an opportunity to make a difference in a young, impressionable life. You developed and nurtured me. You helped make me what I am today in many important ways: driven, passionate and caring.

Suzy, I have a wonderful husband Scott and two beautiful boys, Kyle (8) and Kevin (6). We built a beautiful home on Pine Lake 6 years ago only a few hundreds yards from where you lived. I think of you often.

Please know that my prayers and thoughts have been, and will always be, with you.

Much love, Mary

Mom raised her eyebrows. I took it as "Wow."

THAT NIGHT, ONE of Mom's favorite aides, Almah, came upstairs to wake me. Mom was sick, really sick, and Almah couldn't handle it alone. It was a terrible night.

*   *   *

AT ABOUT THREE in the morning—six a.m. Detroit time—I called Bob and told him to get on the next plane. A few hours later, I called Lizzie in Los Angeles.

"Mom's about to die," I told her. She was by my side in Tucson four hours later.

Bob got back at around two in the afternoon. Uncle Eddie, Aunt Teresa, and Grandma Charlotte were already there. Grandma, then ninety-one, was afraid of getting too close to Mom. We set a chair at the foot of the hospital bed we had rented, and Grandma sat there silently.

Mom seemed to wake up around three p.m. Lizzie, Bob, and I fanned around her. The hospice nurse told us we needed to give her permission to die. Lizzie took the lead: "Mom, it's okay for you to let go," she said. "Katie, Bob, and I are going to take care of each other, and we're going to help Eddie and Teresa and David and Margaret take care of Grandma. We're going to be okay. You don't have to fight anymore."

I tried to join in, repeating Lizzie's refrain—"It's okay, Mom, you can let go." Bob just said, "Suzy, sweetheart, I love you so much," over and over again.

Mom listened for a second—and then decided she was having none of it. She pursed her lips and shook her head no in a way that was both nearly imperceptible and forceful.

Trapped in a broken-down body—deprived of the ability to speak or move—she made it clear, as she had throughout the long road to the end, that she did not want to hear how it was okay to die. It wasn't okay, she told us with the faintest and most powerful of gestures. I'm not at peace, and I'm not going to pretend that I am. *There is nothing about this that is okay, so cut it out.*

I started crying hysterically. The hospice nurse quickly led me out of the room. In the hall, she said that I was going to add to Mom's psychic distress.

Dr. Brooks, Mom's oncologist, came to see Mom in the late afternoon. He held Mom's hand and said, "Suzy, I've never seen anyone fight harder." Being told that mattered a lot to Mom. I knew this, and so did Dr. Brooks.

Several hours later, the house had turned into a gathering place for mourners. We ordered pizza and spaghetti. Mom's close friends and favorite Pilates students came over. We allowed people to go back into Mom's room, one at a time. From ten p.m. to midnight, Bob, Lizzie, and I hovered around Mom's bed. Even when she opened her eyes, it was difficult to tell if she was compos mentis. At midnight, we told Mom we were going to lie down for a few hours. Bob climbed into his bed—which until recently had been her bed, too, and now abutted Mom's hospital bed. Lizzie and I went upstairs into my room. We slid into bed together and held each other like we did when we were little girls.

An hour later, an overnight aide came to wake us. Mom was dead.

THE FUNERAL WAS in Detroit two days later. We sat shivah at the home of Mom's friend Nanci Rands. Mary spent most of the afternoon there with us. The shy girl with the brunette braids and tentative glance was gone. In her place was an outgoing, confident woman wearing a refined St. John's suit. All the Franklin Hills members who had known her as a caddie so many years before—

and had since learned of her success—mobbed her. I felt like my mom's funeral and shivah were something of a coming-out party for Mary. I hope my mom was watching, because I know she would have been very proud—both of Mary and of herself, for what she had done for a young girl who needed a little attention.

OVER THE COURSE of this year, I talked to a lot of people, and put together, these conversations accomplished what I never imagined they might: they reconnected me to my healthy, vibrant mother—to the person Suzy Rosin was, for better or worse, before the cancer.

They also gave me a legacy. Mary is evidence of just that, as are so many others—those written about here and not. When my mom wasn't being Lizzie's and my mother, and when she wasn't being Bob's wife, she was identifying potential in young people. She said things like, "I like your energy," to let them know that she connected with something special in them. And in her understated way, she then helped them connect to it too. It's a great thing she did, and I am proud to be her daughter.

MARY AND I have remained in close contact. Whenever we're in Michigan, Joe and I spend time with the Petrovichs. One evening, a few summers ago, we went to their house for a barbeque. We took a spin around Pine Lake in their blinged-out yellow speedboat. Then we grilled hot dogs and hamburgers—drinking wine and telling stories. That's when Mary told me that she used to scan the parking lot for Mom's car. I so loved hearing that story. When she reminded me that Mom drove a powder blue Cutlass with T-tops, I laughed so hard I almost wet my pants.

I think Mary set out to repay my mom's kindness by being so open to my overtures. But a sense of obligation has turned to love. My sauciness cracks her up, and I think she is proud of my career success. And in many ways, I admire Mary in the same way she admired my mom.

Mindful of the opportunities provided to her through her caddying associations, Mary is a dedicated supporter of the Evans Scholar program. In fact, she's now a national director for the Western Golf Association, the body that oversees the Evans foundation. Soon after Mom died, Mary came to me, Bob, and Lizzie with a proposal: to honor Mom, she was going to make a $25,000 donation to help support the brand-new Evans Scholar House at the University of Michigan in Ann Arbor. Bob decided to match Mary's offer.

At a ceremony in August 2005, the Suzy Rosin Room was dedicated. Mary was there.

Chapter Twelve

Ariella

When Mom was fifty-eight years old, she was renamed.
It was the night before her first surgery. She just had been diagnosed, and as the news trickled out to her friends in Tucson and Detroit, many of them called asking for Mom's Hebrew name. They told her they wanted to ask their rabbis to include Mom at the upcoming Shabbat service in the Mishaberach, the prayer for the sick.

These inquiries made Mom panic. She couldn't remember what Hebrew name her parents had given to her when she was a baby. She called Grandma Charlotte, but she didn't remember either. Suddenly, my mom got it in her head that God wasn't going to protect someone who didn't even know her own Hebrew name.

Her friend Nanci suggested she call the rabbi at Temple Beth El back in suburban Detroit. Beth El was where we belonged as a family—where Lizzie and I went to religious school, where I was bat mitzvahed, where we all attended holiday services. Even after relocating to Tucson, Mom and Bob remained members, though they hadn't been a part of the congregation in fifteen years, and they hardly knew the senior rabbi, Daniel Syme. But Mom still called him. He became the first of the virtual strangers she would confide in. I saw her as she sat on the couch in the den, speaking on the phone to the rabbi. She looked so vulnerable.

As Mom told us later that night, she had explained to Rabbi Syme that though she was raised Jewish, she felt disconnected from conventional Judaism. "I'm not religious," she told him. "I'm spiritual."

Did she have any knowledge of Jewish spiritual literature? he asked her.

She had read a little bit, she told him. What she knew of it resonated with her.

Rabbi Syme told Mom about a teaching found in such writings that says someone who is in danger can assume a new Hebrew name in an effort to trick, and perhaps evade, the angel of death.

"You are now Ariella Chaya," Rabbi Syme told Mom, anointing her with a name that in English roughly translates to "lioness of life." The next day, as nurses rolled her from the admitting area to the pre-op room, Bob, Lizzie, and I walked along side of her. "Roar, Ariella, roar!" we called out.

Ariella was more than a name. It became an alter ego and a nom de guerre. Mom printed out pictures of lions from the Internet, and they were scattered randomly all around the house. She even took the steps to legally change the name of her Pilates studio from Suzy's Pilates to Studio Ariella. It was a name she passed down before she died to one of her most adored students,

Cate Noble Morales. Cate has hung up her own shingle in Tucson with the name Ariella: A Pilates Studio.

Like Cate, people who were close to Mom knew about Ariella. A year before she died, Mom received an e-mail from Dr. Bruce Lowenstein, the psychologist at Helen Hayes Hospital, where she had been rehabilitated after the coma. She had left the hospital seven months earlier, but Dr. Lowenstein was still checking on her. He wrote to Mom: "Was thinking about you and hoping that sending Ariella hunting, along with the protocol you'd begun, had you feeling well and strong. I can imagine her relentless pursuit of the intruders into her domain and her fierce, yet effortless eradication of them—banished by a flick of her strong tail or a lazy chomp of her jaws." Mom began meditating to this image. But she added one element that she felt was absent from the picture. "Ariella is always protecting her cubs," she told me.

I THOUGHT ABOUT that frequently in the months after Mom died.

Had I not been pregnant, I would have been drinking a lot and not eating much. But I had my very own cub growing inside of me, and I was mindful of the responsibility.

Throughout the fall and winter after Mom's death, I would wake up early in the mornings and I would walk. Stuffed in maternity workout pants and a comfy college sweatshirt, I'd grab a bottle of water, cue up on my iPod Indigo Girls, Dixie Chicks, and Christina Aguilera, and head out. Joe would beg me to let him download a few mixes onto my iPod for me to listen to. "You're going to destroy the baby's taste in music before it's even born!" he would say. But the songs those women sang were an important part of the ritual. As I walked, I would listen to the melodies and think about Mom's funeral. I'd follow a stretch through Riverside Park, south from 103rd Street, heading back north again by circling the Eleanor Roosevelt Monument at Seventy-second Street. In both directions I would stop in the public toilets at Hippo Playground near Ninety-first to relieve my pregnant woman's bladder. The round-trip time was about an hour. Throughout these daily loops, I again and again would recite aloud the eulogy that I wrote against Mom's wishes, my own personal Kaddish.

I WAS DUE to give birth on February 23, 2006. I didn't. Nor did I on the next day, nor the next day, nor the next. I was huge. I was miserable.

Lizzie was as antsy for this baby to come as Joe and I. The plan was for Lizzie to head for New York City the first second I felt any signs of labor. But she finally just got on a plane February 27. When she arrived, I had been in my apartment for ninety consecutive hours, watching a marathon of *The Price Is Right* reruns. She forklifted me off the couch. "If you don't get moving, this baby is never going to come," she said. We went for breakfast at Nice Matin on West Seventy-ninth Street, and then she bought me pillow covers (not to be confused with pillow cases, because they're very different, she assured me) because she was horrified (literally) to learn that I owned none. "Seriously," she said. "Promise me that you'll use these."

That night, Lizzie sat on the closed lid of the toilet seat as I soaked my massiveness in the bathtub. We had both spoken to a lot of people on the phone in the few prior days, friends of Mom calling to ask the status of the baby. "People keep saying, 'Your mom is with you girls in spirit,' " Lizzie said. "But I just feel her absence." I felt exactly the same way.

We went for breakfast the next morning and spent the rest of the day relaxing and getting the apartment organized. When Joe got home from work, we all ordered dinner from the diner. Then Lizzie headed back to Long Island, to her sister-in-law's house, where she was staying. Joe and I went to sleep.

At two a.m., I woke up. It was happening. "Joe," I said, "I'm scared." I started to cry.

"I don't think you need to be scared," he said. And then he added something that was a bit out of character, coming from him. He said, "You shouldn't be scared, because I think your Mom is here."

"Why would you say that?" I snapped at him, almost angry that he would dare make me hopeful in such a way.

"It's two in the morning," Joe said, "which means it's tomorrow. It's March first. And as the saying goes, 'March comes in like a lion.' "

WE CALLED LIZZIE at her sister-in-law's a few hours later, and she set the world record for fastest trip from Long Island to the Upper West Side.

We then called the doctor, who told us that we really needn't rush to the hospital until my contractions started to come more often and at a regular pace. I was having none of it. Joe, Lizzie, and I were at the hospital by seven in the morning.

A young resident checked my progress. Not only did she not look old enough to be a doctor, she hardly appeared to be of childbearing age. "You're only two centimeters dilated," the tenderfooted obstetrician said. "We need to get you up and moving around. How do you feel about doing some stairs?"

I remained impassive, restrained by the uncertainty of whether "But Your Honor, I was in labor" is an admissible defense for murder.

The doctor banished us from the hospital and told us not to return for three hours unless my water broke. And she forbade me to return home. It was a cold winter day. I was bundled in the men's extra-large parka that I had bought at Target. It made me look like the Michelin Man, but it kept me and my considerable girth warm. Joe, Lizzie, and I walked the half-dozen blocks toward the Time Warner Center at Columbus Circle.

We passed the mouth of Central Park, swarming, as always, with tourists. "Bikes for rent," a man shouted to us, making him the second person that morning to risk his life by talking to me. "Do I look like I want to ride a bike, you dumb fuck?" I replied. Lizzie and Joe looped their arms through mine and led me away.

We entered the Time Warner Center. I snarled at Lizzie as she insisted on taking a few photos of Joe and me. We rode the escalator up to Borders. (On principle, I refused to take the stairs.) Joe stayed in the front of the store, nervously tapping on his Black-Berry. Lizzie followed me to the nonfiction paperback section.

A contraction came. I leaned against the stacks, upright but with arms and legs spread wide like I was about to be frisked by the police. I was moaning. I might have called out "MOTHER-FUCKER!" oh, a dozen or so times.

Joe stared at me, mouth partially agape, a look of terror on his face. Then he turned back to his BlackBerry and unleashed his anxiety upon it. Lizzie stood helpless for a minute. And then she started chanting, again and again, "What would Mom do? What-wouldMomdo? WhatwouldMomdo? WhatwouldMomdo?"

She then took a big Lamaze breath and found her clarity: "We should buy something," she said. It was as if she had just solved the problem of global warming. A sense of Zen and certainty washed over her. She took one of my hands and led me out of the bookstore and into Sephora, the cosmetics emporium. Joe trailed behind while holding my other hand.

Lizzie walked up to a salesclerk. "Listen," she said. "My sister is in labor. We need eye shadow."

THERE IS A photograph that Joe took that evening. I am lying down in the hospital bed. Lizzie is standing up on the left side of my bed, and she has contorted herself such that we are cheek-to-cheek, smiling. Joe is a skilled cameraman, but this photo isn't tightly focused on Lizzie and me. Instead, the shot takes a wider angle, with me at the center, Lizzie on one side, and a big empty space on my right. That's where Mom would have been. And it is, I believe, where she was.

A few hours after that picture was taken, at 11:57 p.m., with my sister and husband beside me, I gave birth to a son. Joe and I named him Ariel. He is a lion of life.

Epilogue

Mom's curse upon Lizzie—that she should know the intensity of being a mother to a daughter—has befallen us both.

In November 2008, I had a little girl, Eleanor.

Four months later, Lizzie had one, too. We call her Baby Suzy.

Acknowledgments

I am enormously grateful to the friends and acquaintances of my mom who opened their lives to me, generously sharing their time, memories, and personal histories. Dozens and dozens of people—including a number not mentioned by name in the book—spent hours speaking to me, agreeing to multiple interviews and fact-checking sessions. I am indebted to all.

I thank *Wall Street Journal* editors and reporters (past and present) who have been supportive of this project. To name just a few: Peter Lattman, Randy Smith, Jonathan Kaufman, Amy Stevens, Jeffrey Grocott, Mike Miller, Robert Thompson, Paul Steiger, Marcus Brauchli, Eben Shapiro, Emily Nelson, Emily Gitter, Robert J. Hughes, and Paula Szuchman.

A team of women kept my children safe and happy while I reported and wrote. They are Jean Marie Thompson, Sabina Reyes, Maria Baran, Aileen Luksic, Lauren Miscioscia, and Tara Mac-Dowell, and it's no overstatement to say they were the sine qua non of this project. My children love them and we all consider them family.

So many friends read drafts, listened to me think out loud and talked me out of insecurity. Jill Silverman, Rachel Axelrod,

Natalie Tessler, and Elizabeth Victory Anderson have been my friends since I was a girl. They weren't just there for me during the writing of this book but during the unfolding of events that I memorialized. I have also been buoyed by Rachael Combe, Janice Lee, Alanna Fincke, and Katie Pottinger, my first friends in New York City. Gwen Potiker gave me key advice. Alyssa Dragone Wilson, herself a wonderful writer, urged me to overcome my discomfort with the genre of memoir. Anne and Sean Madden have acted as loyal (and boisterous) boosters. Sandy Taylor copy-edited my drafts—and then, as the very best copy editors always do, came up with a fantastic title. Elaina Richardson, a mentor and friend for fifteen years, encouraged me to take time at Yaddo. The progress I made at Yaddo allowed me to give myself maternity leave and still meet my deadline. I also thank the Corporation of Yaddo for the honor of working on this book in the woods of Saratoga Springs. Nicholas Varchaver—who in addition to being one of my closest friends and a godparent to my children is the best journalist I know—pushed me to report further, to track down additional sources, to ask more questions. Then he painstakingly edited every word I wrote. I also appreciate the support at important moments in my early career that came from Steven Brill, Eric Alterman, and Tad Low.

Katherine Beitner, the publicist with the mostess, worked so hard, and she deftly and patiently dealt with my insanity. Jason Sack, Larissa Silver, and Jocelyn Kalmus were responsive and vital liaisons. Jonathan Burnham took time out of a very busy schedule to assure me than *If You Knew Suzy* was on his radar.

Gillian Blake got behind this project from the first moment I told her about it. Her fingerprints, and those of her father, are very much upon it. Gail Winston took me in when I was orphaned and wholeheartedly embraced me and this book. She is a brilliant, tough editor and a woman of warmth, humor, and insight. *IYKS* and I have benefited immeasurably from her involvement. Kate Lee has believed in me from the very moment I told her about a half-baked concept that involved blending memoir and report-age on my mother's life. She was savvy and tireless in translating these still-naissant ideas to publishers. Then she served as a cen-tral sounding board as I reported and wrote. She is an incredible advocate and an even better friend.

I thank my big-tent family—including my steps, my in-laws, my halfs, my twice-removeds. Absolutely everyone cheered me on and helped me juggle motherhood and memoirs. Among the many who carried me: Herb and Fritzi Owens, first my husband's grandparents and now mine, gave me space in Manhattan in which to work, allowing me the quiet I required as a writer and the proximity to home that I needed as a mother of an infant. Robert Owens and Evie Klein gave constant encouragement. My brother-in-law Todd Ehrlich was gracious when I begged him to lend his expertise to the production of my book trailer, and then he refused to accept any payment. My sisters Amanda and Emily Rosman stood by me throughout Mom's ordeal and then again as I struggled to commit it all to paper, as did my stepbrother and -sisters: Jim, Sheryl, and Natalie Rosin. My stepmother, Carolyn Frohman Rosman (aka Nani), flew to New York and stayed for weeks, tending to the kids (and me!) at critical moments in my work. My mom loved Carolyn, and I imagine it gives her great comfort to see how Carolyn nurtures us all. My father, Robert D. Rosman, has been unconditionally and unhesitatingly supportive of a book that marginalizes the significant role he has played in my life. He has been the single biggest (certainly the loudest) cheerleader of my career. His gifts as a communicator fomented my love for words.

My stepfather, Robert Rosin, helped me to recreate scenes, to identify the right people to call, to nail down facts. And he never missed an opportunity to tell me how proud I have made him. My uncle Edward Goldberg spent hours explaining to me family dynamics and connecting me to the girl that became my mother. My grandmother Charlotte Goldberg talked to me about things that were tough for her to talk about. Grandma, Eddie, and Bob all entrusted me with their personal memories and let me use them to draw my portrait, setting their own emotions to the side. This process brought me even closer to all of them and that has been its own reward.

My sister, Elizabeth Rosman Schwartz, put my need to write this book before her own preference for privacy. She considered and reconsidered every single word I wrote, helping me to get my facts right. This is her story too and my telling of it was, at times, painful for her. When the book was completed, Lizzie told me that not only did she love what I had created but that she believed Mom did too. That response was the greatest gift she could give me and for this and so many reasons, I feel incredible gratitude to her. I look up to my big sister more than she knows.

It was my husband, Joseph Ehrlich, who suggested that I could report about my own mother the sort of stories I have been reporting for years about other people, to turn one part of myself upon the other. He knew Mom's death was a life-altering experience for me and he pushed me to take the time I needed—as a writer and a daughter—to examine it fully. Joe has made tremendous sacrifices for me to have the luxury of a writing career. He is the husband I dreamed of and I am a very lucky girl that he sticks with me. (I'm high-maintenance.) I love my sweetie.

My children have brightened my life and made me experience a kind of joy I hadn't known existed. I hope that one day they and all their cousins will read this book and come away feeling like they know Grandma Suzy.

About the Author

A staff reporter for the *Wall Street Journal*, Katherine Rosman writes about popular culture. Her work has also appeared in the *New Yorker*, the *New York Times*, and *Elle* magazine. She lives in New York with her husband and two children.